— JOHN KEITH FALCONER
(Inscribed by Dal Washer
on the flyleaf of his Bible)

One Candle to Burn

The Lives of Dal & Kay Washer

Kay Washer

with Alison Gray

Association of Baptists for World Evangelism
P.O. Box 8585
Harrisburg, PA 17105-8585
(717) 774-7000
abwe@abwe.org

ABWE Canada
980 Adelaide St. South, Suite 34
London, Ontario N6E 1R3
(519) 690-1009
office@abwecanada.org

PUBLISHING®

ONE CANDLE TO BURN
The Lives of Dal & Kay Washer

Harrisburg, Pennsylvania 17105

First printing, June 2007
Second printing, June 2008
Third printing, September 2009

Library of Congress Cataloging-in-Publications Data
(application pending)

One Candle to Burn
Autobiographical, Non-fiction, Missionary
ISBN: 978-1-888796-39-1

Printed in the United States of America

CONTENTS

ACKNOWLEDGMENTS

Whenever we would come home from Africa, we looked forward to visiting our friends and the churches that supported us. We wanted to thank them for helping us carry the gospel light into Africa. As we told them our stories and showed them our pictures, many would say, "Oh! You must write a book." I would thank them and tell them that Dal was the writer in the family, and that we too hoped he would write down all of our experiences. I wanted our children and grandchildren to know how God had blessed us and helped us through many difficult times. I wanted them to know about the African people who received Christ that they will meet someday in heaven.

When God took Dal home to heaven, I knew there was no one that knew the story except me. If I did not try to write it down, it would be forgotten. But I am not a writer or even skilled in English grammar. Because of my polio, I can type with only one hand. Writing a book seemed impossible.

After my fall in Africa in 1996, my home at the Blind Center had to be cleaned out. The mission chose Marla Allston to take care of the clearing out. When she came to my files, instead of throwing them away as "junk," she thought, *Gramma is a pack rat like me. I think I'll pack these letters in cartons and send them home to her.* When, several years later, I was encouraged to write a book, I remembered those boxes that were now in my attic. My family helped me pull them out and we found our prayer letters, going all the way back to 1949. What a miracle!

With this treasure-trove, we started thinking more seriously about the book. From the start, God sent many friends to help and encourage us. My niece, Kim Hibbard, and Doreen Hallford were both sweet friends who wanted to see the book become a reality and a blessing to others. And then God sent Alison to help me. As Alison and I worked together over many months, I came to appreciate her beautiful way with words and her typing and organizational skills. She was a special gift from God, and He sent her at just the right time. My life story and Dal's were a joy to retell. From our old prayer letters, there were many stories I had forgotten about, which I could have never retrieved from my too-full brain.

But when we had finished our writing, we faced a problem we had never anticipated: the book was twice as long as it should be! The Lord knew our needs and sent Alison's husband Will to edit the book down to size. I thank the Lord for Alison and Will and their great part of making this book possible. God gave us everything we needed, and it is my great pleasure to share my story with you—the story God gave to Dal and me.

Kay Washer, 2007

FOREWORD

There are missionaries, and then there are missionaries. By this I mean that there are some missionaries who see missions as something exciting and different, but when the allurement wears off or very little seems to be accomplished, they lose their vision and turn to other areas of service. Then there are those missionaries who live, eat, and sleep missions from the time God calls them to serve Him until He calls them home to Heaven. Dallas and Kay Washer defined this kind of missionary.

While Dal was not well when he and Kay departed for what proved to be his last term on the field, he chose to return to Togo where he hoped to die and be buried. God granted him the desire of his heart, and his body is awaiting the resurrection among the people he loved so dearly.

Although Kay is retired from the field, her heart for missions is as big as it ever has been. You cannot be with her for very long without the subject of missions entering into the conversation.

I consider Dal and Kay Washer as one of the premier missionary couples of the last part of the twentieth century. Of course, they have always been quick to give God the glory for anything that was accomplished through their efforts.

Dal was like a brother to me. We first met in the late 1960s, and our relationship was one of great blessing to both of us. I was privileged to go to Togo to preach his funeral message, and in all my years of preaching I was never more aware of the Holy Spirit's presence than I was on that occasion. Though there was sadness, there was also great rejoicing in knowing that Dal, like the Apostle Paul, had fought a good fight, finished the course, and kept the faith.

Kay has done a magnificent job in putting the story of their lives together, and I appreciate the opportunity of writing the foreword.

Dr. David Yearick
Pastor Emeritus
Hampton Park Baptist Church
Greenville, S.C.

A F R I C A

TUNISIA
MOROCCO
ALGERIA
LYBIA
EGYPT
WESTERN SAHARA
MAURITANIA
MALI
NIGER
CHAD
SUDAN
ERITREA
DJIBOUTI
SOMALIA
ETHIOPIA
THE GAMBIA
SENEGAL
GUINEA-BISSAU
GUINEA
BURKINA FASO
BENIN
NIGERIA
SIERRA LEONE
CÔTE D'IVOIRE
GHANA
TOGO
LIBERIA
CENTRAL AFRICAN REPUBLIC
CAMEROON
EQUATORIAL GUINEA
GABON
CONGO
DEM. REP. OF CONGO
RWANDA
BURUNDI
UGANDA
KENYA
TANZANIA
ANGOLA
ZAMBIA
MALAWI
MOZAMBIQUE
MADAGASCAR
ZIMBABWE
NAMIBIA
BOTSWANA
SWAZILAND
LESOTHO
SOUTH AFRICA

Dal Washer, 1967

DAL'S CALL

Faithful is He that calleth you, who will also do it.

— I THESSALONIANS 5:24

Sometimes it is difficult to say exactly where a story starts. Especially with the story of a life, which is influenced by many people, who have been influenced by people who came before them, and so on. But perhaps we could say that my husband's story started with his mother, Lillian Washer Weber, since she was the first missionary in her family, and since her interest in African missions shaped Dal's life.

Lillian became a Christian at the age of twelve in a revival meeting in Tennessee. Shortly after her conversion, she read a missionary book called *Mackey—The White Man of Work*, which described missionary work in Uganda. Soon after, Lillian told her parents of her desire to be a missionary to Africa. Unfortunately, they were not at all pleased. So Lillian spoke little of her desire, continuing to pray and trust that some day she would reach the foreign field.

About a year later, a pastor visited Lillian's church, calling for volunteers to go to foreign fields. Lillian wrote later, "I was the very first young girl to walk down the aisle . . . my heart fairly bursting with such joy as I had never known before in all my young life." Lillian's joy was dampened, however, when she saw her parents' faces. They would not soon give up their little girl to go to such a dark and dangerous continent.

According to her parents' wishes, Lillian went to college and then worked as a secretary for a lawyer named Mr. DeMontegue. He became interested in missions while working with Lillian. Their friendship grew, their interest in church work developed and, after a few years, convinced she could never gain her parents' consent to go to a foreign field, she married her employer.

With her marriage, Lillian seemingly forfeited any hope of going to Africa, especially after her husband contracted tuberculosis and his chances of being accepted for service were negligible. Then he died after they had been married only six months. A lovely but sickly baby boy named Larry was born four months later, never to know the tenderness of his father's love and care.

Heartbroken, Lillian plunged into work again as soon as Larry was old enough to be left with his grandmother. But three years later, Larry developed tuberculosis like his father. Lillian quit her job and took her son to Colorado, where she hoped the climate would improve his health.

During this time, Lillian grew discouraged and admitted that she was "off the path of duty according to God's standard; on the path of duty according to man's standard."

> When I would pick up [Larry] and hold him close to my heart, I used to wonder what I might have done to ease the aching heart of an African mother as she picked up a little son and pressed him to her aching heart. When they buried their husbands they had no "blessed hope" such as I cherished of a glad reunion, and I was doing nothing about it.

When she and Larry visited Ohio a few years later, Lillian took a secretarial job with an executive visiting from New York. This man, Mr. Ephraim Washer, was an accountant who had owned a successful electric vacuum business and then a sugar refinery. Mr. Washer fell in love with Lillian almost immediately, and they were married by the time Larry was five years old.

In her second marriage Lillian experienced a life that most women would love to lead: furs and fine jewelry, extensive travel, a large elegant home, social prestige, many friends, the devotion of a good husband, and—best of all—increasing health for Larry. As if all that weren't enough, God blessed the Washers with a healthy baby boy. Edgar Dallas Washer (Dal for short) was born on December 29, 1921, while the Washers were living in Cleveland. Soon after, the Washers moved to Chicago, where Dal spent most of his childhood.

Lillian should have been happy. But she wasn't. She wrote later,

> I felt like a fugitive from justice. God was burning His command into my soul with the words: "Lillian, what doest thou here? Here, amidst wealth, ease and luxury, with maids to serve you, and time on your hands to enable you to think of what your life was meant to be in God's service? Leisure to make you soft and miserable? What are you doing with it while ever-dying souls are holding out to you their helpless hands from Africa?"

Lillian's husband was unaware of his wife's spiritual struggle. But one day Lillian spoke frankly with him, telling him the whole story. She said she would of course be happy in her situation if it were not for the fact that she was disobeying God. Mr. Washer understood completely. They decided together to dedicate their little son to God. Lillian prayed that God would allow Dal to be a missionary and promised she would do her best to lead him down that pathway.

Then 1929 came. People were suddenly losing everything they had in the wake of the stock market crash. The Washers were no exception. Their possessions, money, investments, luxuries, and home vanished. What they had accumulated and enjoyed was suddenly gone. Before they could recover from the shock, another loss came. A heart attack took Ephraim Washer's life so swiftly that there was no time for even a word. Soon Lillian and her two sons had nothing material left to count on. Even Lillian's health had evaporated with the shock and grief, leaving her in no condition to look for work.

But, amazingly, the losses drew her closer to God than she had been in years, and Lillian actually experienced joy as she heard again that "still, small voice" that she had avoided for so long. Every night, Lillian knelt before God, asking him to chasten her no further. She promised that nothing would ever stop her from going to Africa. At that point a great indescribable peace descended on her heart. She knew there would be obstacles, but she also knew that God could lead her. All she had to do was follow Him.

As soon as she could, Lillian began pursuing missionary training, enrolling in evening classes at Moody Bible Institute in Chicago and working during the day to support her children. Her full schedule was tiring, but she found that the hours of study helped to ease the ache in her heart. After two years, Lillian completed a course in nursing.

Toward the end of these years of spiritual growth, Lillian's elderly mother, in a beautiful answer to prayer, urged her daughter to go to Africa so she would be able to share in Lillian's joy before she died. However, other obstacles lay in Lillian's way. Regardless of education, desire, or money, it was virtually unheard of for single women to go to the mission field. It was equally rare for an older woman to be accepted by any mission board. But in the impassioned, eloquent speech for which she became well known, Lillian convinced the Baptist Mid-Missions Board to take her on as a widowed missionary to Africa. She was soon making plans to travel. Lillian's older son, Larry, was now married and working as a fisherman off the coast of California. But Lillian took fourteen-year-old Dallas with her. Seven years after her second husband had died, the two sailed to French Equatorial Africa on April 10, 1937.

While in Africa, Lillian worked as a nurse while Dal took correspondence classes and helped at the mission. At the age of 17, Dal wrote an article on his work in Africa, describing the class of boys he helped to teach:

> Please pray for the boys in my class, [who are] daily reading the Gospel of John in their native tongue, Sango. These boys may be the coming evangelists of this area. . . . It's not only a joy but a privilege to be permitted to do this little bit for the Lord on this busy station. . . . You should just hear the boys' class—just think of it—113 black boys in one class, lustily singing with all their might, "Are you washed in the Blood of the Lamb?" . . . For the young people who read this paper, I just want to say that the life yielded to Jesus is the only happy life—and what joy it will be to say at its close, that most of it has been in the service of the King.

Unfortunately, Lillian became ill not long after they arrived in Africa, and after a few years her health demanded that they return to the States. However, those years were long enough to inflame Dal's passion to evangelize the African people. Once he had seen the need, he knew he had to go back.

For Lillian, prayer and God's answering were as normal as the rising sun each day. Dal used to say that his mother prayed and God worked accordingly. There is no question that Dal's desire to minister to the people of Africa began with the prayers of his mother, asking God to make her son into a missionary. She prayed, *Wherever you choose, Lord;* but Africa was her life, and her enthusiasm for missionary work in Africa spread to Dal as well.

In a small pamphlet, "His Pattern for Me," Lillian expressed some of the wisdom she had learned along the way, wisdom she certainly passed on to Dal.

> Talk to your Father over your opened Bible, with His precious promises staring you in the face. . . . God cannot work out a design intended for someone else in you, nor your design in them, but each can find the plan intended for his or her individual life before the pattern is spoiled, and can enjoy an ever increasing revelation of exquisite workmanship in designing—looking beyond the design to the Designer.

Once Lillian had reached Africa, she had no doubt that she was in the center of God's will. She had found the specific plan and pattern that God had planned for her to carry out in her life. With these words she defined her life, and Dal's, and the lives of all who carry Christ's name abroad:

> To hear orisons of praise ascending to the vaulted skies . . . supplanting all the vileness of former generations; to realize the satanic yells and weird notes of obeisance to the evil spirits have been conquered by the All-powerful Name of Jesus; to be endued with that power from on high, and to be sent out . . . with His strength, is sufficient. . . . Christ never asks of any one more than their best, but He does ask that much.

Have you ever wondered?

Have you ever wondered how heaven will be
When all of God's children are there?
The yellow, the black, the red, brown and white
The glories of heaven to share?

Regardless of color they'll come the same way,
Through simple belief in the Son,
They'll sing the same song, "giving praise to the King.
God's Lamb, yea, the crucified One."

Have you ever wondered how heaven will be
When trophies are laid at His feet?
As His searching eyes lovingly ask of you,
"Was your life for the Master made meet?"

Why be undecided should God call to you
Salvation's glad message to share
With people whose color is different from yours
For whose hearts the Saviour doth care.

To gather our cloak all about us and say,
"I'll go any place except there."
To close up our hearts to the heathen's last cry
Will leave them in Satan's tight snare.

Away with our wills, seek His only and say,
"Just anywhere Lord will I go,"
Bond Servant to be where Thy will calleth me,
Then the lost Thy salvation will know.

—DALLAS WASHER

KAY'S CHILDHOOD

Teach us delight in simple things,
And Mirth that has no bitter springs;
Forgiveness free of evil done,
And Love to all men 'neath the sun.

— RUDYARD KIPLING

Despite all that happened during the fifty years and more since my childhood, I still remember clearly the excitement that pervaded those years. How could my childhood not be exciting, with eight children in the family? Some of my favorite memories are the wonderful stories my mother and father told around the dinner table. My father, Harold Hettema, described his childhood in Holland and how he came to assurance of his salvation later in life. My mother, Jennie, told captivating missionary stories from books she had read and from missionaries she had known. Our parents used stories to teach us to look at what God was doing in the world, not just at our own difficulties.

My father told us how, as a young boy of ten, he sailed with his mother and four sisters across the Atlantic from his native Friesland in Holland. They landed in New York City and made their way down to Paterson, New Jersey, at that time the fabric capital of America, where they had relatives to receive them.

He went to school while at the Christian Reformed Church there, but when he turned fifteen, he determined to help with the family finances. Though he was still quite young, he had great mathematic abilities. His brain worked like an adding machine and he could easily add columns of two- and three-digit numbers with no pencil or paper. Despite his youth, and despite a hole in the knee of his knickers that he hid with his hat during the interview, he got a job at the bank. When we children realized the amazing gift our father had, we relished making lists of three-digit numbers which he would total in his head faster than we could on paper.

As children, we were enthralled to hear our father tell how all the men in Holland used to smoke cigars, even the young boys. In Holland, if a man's cigar wasn't finished by the time he got to church, he put it out and laid it in the windowsill. When church was over, he would go take up his cigar again. Of course, my father told us, the first one out got the longest cigar.

My father had been raised in the Calvinistic Dutch Reformed Church in Holland. When he came to America, he continued to attend the Dutch Reformed Church, where he played the trumpet and trombone. One day, my father was walking home from work when he noticed an evangelist holding a meeting on a downtown street corner. This evangelist was Peter Stamm, father of the John Stamm who was later martyred while serving as a missionary to China. When Peter Stamm interspersed his street preaching with trumpet or trombone solos of gospel hymns, my father's attention was fixed. Eventually, the two became better acquainted, especially after Peter learned that my father played instruments too. Peter convinced him to help out with the music at some gospel meetings.

Through these meetings my father experienced the world's distaste for the Word of God, as passersby more than once threw eggs or tomatoes at them. But the meetings also introduced him to the virtues of bold evangelism that longed to reach the lost with the gospel. Due to his training in the Dutch Reformed Church, my father regarded religion as personal, something he should not bother others with. However, under the influence of the Holy Spirit and through the friendship of Peter Stamm, he began to recognize the necessity of evangelism.

Even more important to my father was Peter Stamm's preaching on the assurance of salvation. This teaching was foreign to my father. He had received a good foundation in the Bible from the Dutch Reformed Church, but had also been taught that no one but God could know if a person were saved, not even the person himself. My father was surprised and moved to learn that God graciously desired him to know and openly talk about his sure salvation in Christ. Perhaps it was at this time that "Redeemed" became my father's favorite song, when he could sing with certainty that he was a child of God:

> Redeemed—how I love to proclaim it!
> Redeemed by the blood of the Lamb;
> Redeemed thro' his infinite mercy,
> His child, and forever, I am.

While he was still a young man, my father moved with his sisters to Denver, Colorado, where the high altitude and clear air supported good sanatoriums. Each of my father's sisters had by that time contracted tuberculosis, so the move was important to them. One, Martha, had already died. The other three benefited from the good care they received at Bethesda Sanatorium.

While in Colorado, my father met Jennie Van Wyk, whose ancestors had also immigrated from Holland. Jennie had also yearned for assurance of salvation, so she and my father understood each other right away. On January 1, 1919, they were married in the Christian Reformed Church in Denver. It was so cold that the roses in my mother's bouquet froze during the short ride to church in their open Model T.

For several years my mother and father lived in the upstairs of her family's house at 1711 Washington Street in Denver. My older brothers, Harold, Clarence, and David, were born in that house, with the help of a Christian midwife. Heart problems forced my mother to go to the Denver hospital for the birth of my older sister, Cornelia. While my mother tended to her growing family, my father worked as a bank teller during the day and attended the Denver Bible Institute at night. He continually studied the Bible, learning to teach it better.

I was born on July 10, 1926, on the south side of Denver. As soon as my mother saw me in the arms of the midwife, she said, "Oh, look! She has dimples!" My full name is Katherine Jo-ann Hettema, but from the very beginning I was called Kay, except when I was disobedient. Then I was called Katherine *Jo-ann!*

Three years later, my parents, we children, and my mother's parents all piled into one big car to drive out West. We were heading for California because the warm weather would be better for my grandparents' health.

The first house I remember was 2184 Glen Avenue in Altadena. I loved that house. The lots on Glen Avenue were deep and had enough space for a house in front and another in the back for our grandparents. There was also room for a big vegetable garden and space to grow olives, figs, citrus fruits, and apricots, my favorite. I loved to perch like a bird in the limbs of the big apricot tree growing in our backyard, eating apricots for hours.

Our home in Altadena was the perfect place for children to grow up. And, wonderfully, three more boys, Joseph, George, and Bobby, were added to the Hettema family there. When there were seven children, one of our neighbors dubbed us "the seven little devils," a name well earned by all the ruckus we made in the streets or on the sidewalks during the warm California evenings.

But the noisy play on Glen Avenue did not involve the Hettema tribe alone: all the kids who lived on our street wanted to join in our daring games, and we never lacked for players. Roller-skating games were probably our favorites. On one side of Glen Avenue the roots of pepper trees had fragmented the cement. But, on the other side, the sidewalk was smooth all the way down the block. At the top of the street stretched a large patch of cement where children gathered to invent all sorts of roller-skating stunts. My brothers made up funny rules and, though there were more than twenty kids, there was little fighting.

The good skaters would get in a chain, each holding on to the next person's belt or shirt. The leader of the chain would say, "Crouch down!" or "Lift a leg!" and everyone would follow in suit. We all became pros on the old-fashioned metal skates that came in two pieces, one for the heel, one for the toe, each with two wheels, and connected by a strap around the ankle and a clamp over the toes. The clamp was tightened by means of a skate key, which kids wore proudly on a shoestring or on a nice cord around their necks.

At night, when it was too dangerous to skate, we would resort to games more suitable for the dark, like "hide the flag," "kick the can," or "hide and seek." A streetlight shone down on an electrical wire running across the street and it drew us a perfect line for all our games. I never remember any arguing about who would be on whose team: we were so eager to play that we all knew how to keep the game going smoothly. After dark was also the time that the big boys managed to steal kisses from the big girls, or so I heard. At that time I was a full-fledged tomboy who cared about boys only as athletic competitors.

I regret to say that my mother visited the emergency room with me just as often as with any of my six brothers. My older sister, Cornelia, who had more common sense and restraint than I did, knew where to draw the line in our wild games. I, on the other hand, thrived on excitement. I was always a ring-leader in our neighborhood sports and I was proud that I could do everything my brothers did, even when we played wild, rough games. Once my brothers and I decided that normal tag was just too ordinary, so we came up with a brilliant new twist: we put flour sacks over our heads and played "blindman's bluff tag." That did not work too well, since none of us could see through the flour sacks to tag anyone. So we modified the game slightly. My brothers cut eye holes in my flour sack and put it back on my head, pronouncing me the "ghost" who was supposed to chase everyone else. Everything went well until I tripped over the low fence my father had made across the driveway to keep us from going into the street. I fell headlong over the fence and landed on my face in the driveway, breaking one of my front teeth. I was not happy to have to go to the dentist, but I was thankful that he was able to repair my broken tooth so that it looked as good as new.

A few years later, my brothers taught me to ride my bike standing up, one foot on the seat and one foot on the handlebars. I loved to skim down the smooth, slightly sloping street with my arms outstretched and the wind blowing my hair straight out behind me. My brothers were impressed at my bravery. But one day I went a little too fast and hit a bump, sprawling face down on the road. When I stood up to brush myself off and see whether any bones were broken, I noticed that my two front teeth, including the one that had been repaired, were extremely loose. A shudder went through my body as I realized I had just wrecked my permanent teeth, not baby teeth that would fall out and grow back.

Sheepishly, I returned to the emergency room. This time the dentist had to pull out both front teeth because I had ruined the roots. I know the whole episode upset my mother very much because she thought I was going to have to live forever with broken teeth. Instead, the dentist fitted me with a little plate with two false teeth. I was embarrassed to wear false teeth and also ashamed that I had forced my family, who had very little money, to spend a great deal on me for dentures. However, my brothers thought my false teeth were the cat's meow, so I tried to be a good sport. But inside I was convinced I would never marry. I thought, *Who would ever want to kiss a girl with false teeth?*

Since she was the oldest daughter, Cornelia (or "Corny") became the second mother to the younger children. Mother gave her permission to oversee chores, which meant that she could tell us all what to do in Mother's absence. She was also the one allowed to hold each new baby when Father brought Mother home from the hospital. We, as siblings, always complained about how bossy she was, but I'm sure this sort of pecking order occurs in many families. But I was always amazed by how she managed to corral our little brothers on Sunday mornings so she could dress them beautifully for church. As I grew up, I admired Corny more and more. I was sure she would get married right away. And I, the accident-prone tomboy with false teeth, would be a spinster.

I had another handicap that convinced me I would never marry. At age one, after I had suffered from flu-like symptoms for a long time, my mother noticed I did not use my left hand and dragged my left foot. Because polio was so common at the time, she realized early that I had contracted the feared disease. We were thankful for President Franklin Roosevelt, another polio victim, who had started the March of Dimes to provide money for children with polio. As a result, my parents didn't pay anything for my polio treatments. Mother took me to clinics where I received therapy to help me keep the use of my muscles. I remember sitting in crowded waiting rooms to see the doctor, smelling the sweetness of my mother's lavender perfume. She would put her arm around me, hugging me to herself and communicating in unspoken words that she knew this disease would change my life.

When I was older, doctors performed surgery on my left hand at least three times, trying to graft tendons into my hand that would enable my thumb to touch my fingers, allowing me to hold things. But none of the surgeries succeeded, except to keep my hand from hanging limp. Even now, my left hand is smaller and weaker than my right.

My father also contracted polio during the nationwide epidemic. When they learned he had the disease, the city health department came out and put a quarantine sign on our house, informing us that we could not go anywhere, nor could we have visitors. Most people were so frightened that they would not want to visit us anyway. But some from our church were concerned and tried to bring us food, though they would not come too near to deliver it. The brave ones brought a big kettle of soup, set it on our porch, and rang the bell so we could come to the door and bring the kettle inside.

It was also difficult during those days because of the Great Depression, as it came to be known, which overshadowed my first ten years. As a child, I did not especially notice that things were harder to get, that money was more scarce, that people were losing homes, investments, and hope. It was normal for me to see my mother and father praying over the monthly bills. I was used to Mother economizing in every way she could, making the hamburger last longer by adding oatmeal or breadcrumbs, or going without new clothes so that her children could have what they needed.

During one of my parents' financial sessions, I climbed up on a chair and waited for a lull, wanting to tell them that I was going to be in a special program at school. My trouble was that I hadn't any nice shoes to wear. My father took great interest in what I had to say and told me he was proud of me. He asked Mother to find me some nice shoes *and* a new dress. Somewhere she found me a beautiful polka-dot dress with a sash and shoes I could only have dreamed of.

One of my most pleasant memories from childhood was our dinnertime ritual. We ate around a long table: eight children, Mother and Father, and Grampa and Gramma. On weekdays Mother spread a red-checkered oilcloth over the table so she could easily wipe up any messes her children left, but on Sunday we had a real tablecloth. For each meal Mother fixed a huge casserole or a big platter of *balletjes* (Dutch meatballs), along with a large bowl of macaroni, rice, or potatoes. We were not allowed to touch anything, fix our plates, taste our food, or even take a piece of bread from the basket until prayer was done. Either Dad or Grampa would pray, and then we would all chime in together, "Lord, bless this food and drink for Jesus' sake, Amen." Whenever we had *balletjes*, my brother Clarence would count them during prayer, after which he would announce how many meatballs each of us could have, whether it was one or one and seven-sixteenths. Dad was so proud of Clarence's mathematic skills that he usually did not scold him for counting the meatballs during prayer.

After dinner, Mother had a schedule all planned out, and each child knew his job. One was in charge of cleanup, another had to put the food away, and another one or two did the dishes. When cleanup was over the family sometimes got together for a game, or we kids spread out around the big table to write, color, or work on school projects. Other nights the family gathered around the radio in the living room. We loved to listen to the radio stories and we had our favorites, one of which was "The Green Hornet," whose introduction had an eerie insect buzz that terrified us. Another program, "Inner Sanctum," kept us in suspense as a squeaking door let in a different strange visitor each night.

There was never a dull moment in our family and, though in reality we experienced many deprivations both during the Depression and also during World War II in the next decade, my parents made sure their children had a happy, innocent childhood. I am still amazed that they brought such a large family through such difficult years. But then again, I am not surprised, because they put their trust in God.

KAY'S CALL

Being confident of this very thing, that he which hath begun a good work in you will perform it until the day of Jesus Christ.

— PHILIPPIANS 1:6

When we moved to California in 1929, my family made the switch from the Dutch Reformed Church to a more evangelistic church. My father felt the Lord leading us to worship elsewhere, so we began visiting Lincoln Avenue Presbyterian Church, pastored by Dr. J. Vernon McGee.

Going to church as a family was quite an event for us. My father and grandfather shared the cost of a huge used Cadillac—practically as big as a limousine. The Cadillac had spacious, upholstered seats with enough room for all twelve members of the family. When we arrived at church, we extracted ourselves one by one, a veritable carful of circus clowns. Collecting the clowns after church was an even larger feat. At least once we drove away, leaving a young Hettema child sweetly sleeping in a church pew.

Even as a small child, the necessity of faith in prayer and God's provision for His children was evident to me. One year, as Christmas was approaching, there was no money for a tree or gifts. My father was out of work due to the Depression, but he often earned money by donating his type O blood when a transfusion was needed at the hospital. So I decided to pray that someone would need a blood transfusion. Sure enough, the Lord answered just at the right time. A transfusion was required, my father provided it, and gifts for Christmas became a reality. A friend heard of our miracle, and added to our blessings by giving us a fully decorated Christmas tree! That Christmas had even more meaning than usual because we saw God work miracles in front of our eyes.

My father, a godly man, loved to point out to his children the providence and grace of God. He was so steeped in the Word of God, it is no wonder that he viewed life with a spiritual perspective. I remember him sitting in his big chair in the living room, studying the Bible. We children took great interest in our father's Bible study time, though not for spiritual reasons. As he got older, my father's hair began to thin, and he developed a theory that head massages would keep his hair from falling out. So he told us that we would be paid a penny a minute for massaging his head. We would all fight over the chance to make such a great fortune. When it was my turn, I sat on the back of our overstuffed chair and with all my strength I massaged my father's head, hoping to be able to endure for 10 whole minutes. With a dime I could go to the corner grocery and, for a nickel, buy a fat dill pickle out of the big jar on top of the meat counter, then move on to the candy counter, pressing my nose against the glass as I chose my five favorite penny candies.

My grandfather, Klaas Van Wyk, was also a strong Christian influence in my life. Once, when I was still a little girl, I remember some friends from church visiting our home. When they saw our Grampa smoking cigars they thought he was a worldly man who did not know Christ. My grandfather had been smoking cigars for years, and that fact did not mar his reputation in my mind at all. Grampa, a businessman and a teacher, had always been very active in the Dutch Reformed Church and had started several Christian schools. I had come to associate him with great solemnity and spiritual excellence. So I was not surprised that when Grampa heard that his smoking bothered other Christians, he said, "If my smoking is a stumbling block, or harms the name of Christ, then I will

Dal's father and mother,
Edgar Dallas and Lillian Washer.

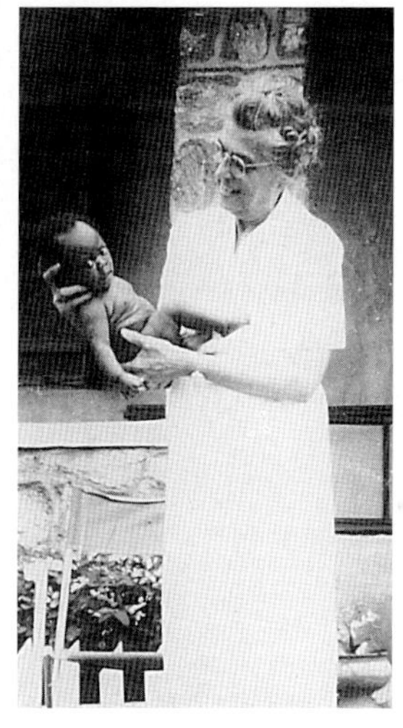

Above and right:
Dal's mother, Lillian Washer,
worked as a nurse.

Far right:
Dal in Africa.

Dal telling of God's love in the Central African Republic.

Kay's Childhood

Right:
Grandparents Klaas Van Wyk and Tryntje Borduin. Kay's mother, Jennie Van Wyk, is wearing a white blouse

Below:
The Hettema family. Kay is in the bottom row, third from right.

The Van Wyk house in California.

Kay and friends roller-skating.

Kay's Call

Left:
Harold Hettema with his two daughters, Cornelia and Kay.

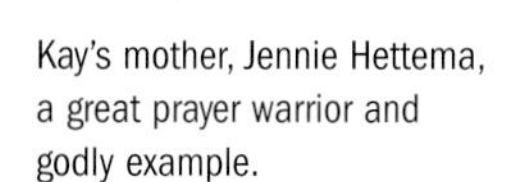

Kay's mother, Jennie Hettema, a great prayer warrior and godly example.

Above:
Ann Berg, missionary to Africa, inspired Kay to serve.

Ann (right) and Kay in their retirement years.

Dal the welder (center) built Victory ships during World War II.

Above: Cornelia on the painting crew.

Right: Kay's family, all in war work, with friends.

Three brothers in the military.

Clarence: Merchant Marines

David: Air Force

Harold: Air Force

stop smoking." And he did. God gave him the willpower to do without that pleasure because he did not want to misrepresent Christ.

With godly people surrounding me as I grew up, I took it for granted that I was a Christian. My parents were good people and we all went to church on Sundays. Not only that, but we had family devotions and Bible reading every night after dinner. For a while I thought that being a Christian depended on whether I knew my Bible, paid attention in family devotions, and behaved in front of my elders.

I also thought it meant going to Vacation Bible School in the summertime. VBS was just one of the many activities our church provided for young people. There was also Sunday School, a big choir, and all sorts of social opportunities. It didn't matter that the church was quite a walk from where we lived. My brothers and sister and I always looked forward to the church activities at Lincoln Avenue Presbyterian, especially VBS.

The summer I turned nine I remember going to VBS and hearing that people should open their hearts to God and let Him come into their lives. The teacher quoted a verse from the Bible that even I, as a little child, could understand. Jesus said, "Behold, I stand at the door and knock: If any man hear my voice, and open the door, I will come in to him, and will sup with him, and he with me" (Revelations 3:20). I realized that if I wanted Jesus in my heart I had to ask Him to wash away my sins. I realized that reading the Bible and praying as a family and going to church would not save my soul. So I invited Jesus to enter my heart and life and become my own personal Redeemer and Savior.

I didn't let on about my newfound salvation for several days for the simple reason that I was ashamed for people to know I was a sinner. It is always hard to admit that you have done wrong. But toward the end of the week, I got up the courage to declare in public that I had been saved and was now a child of God. I wish that I could say I was a perfect little angel from that day forward, but I was not. Salvation is just the beginning of a long journey that ends in heaven.

My family was not wealthy by any means, but the table that already seated twelve always had room for a pastor or missionary too. My mother felt that hospitality was of the utmost importance, and she also wanted her children to hear godly men and women tell about the need to take the gospel to all the world. I loved getting to know these missionaries, though I didn't talk very much. With so many people to keep the conversation going, I just sat back and listened.

My mother had a great love for missions and was determined to pass on her burden for missions to her children. She especially loved to tell stories about Africa. Every night when she came to our beds to pray with us before we went to sleep, she told us fascinating stories and then prayed with each of us. When we were too little to understand, she would hold our hands to pray. As we grew older and had problems, whether at school or with a friend, Mother refused to let it be swept under the carpet. She urged us to tell her about it, and then we would tell God together as we prayed. Then she would kiss us goodnight, and as I drifted off to sleep her words would echo in my head, words describing the plight of lepers in Africa, or how so many mothers died from the disease, leaving behind babies who were often orphans. Those little babies needed someone to care for them, my mother said, and my heart yearned to help them.

As a teenager, my interest in missions grew. My mother had a dear friend, Miss Ann Berg, who was a missionary in

Africa. When Miss Berg spoke at a neighboring church on her furloughs, our family always attended to hear her tell of her work with needy children in Africa. A radiantly beautiful smile beamed from her face as she described her orphanages in the Congo. After I heard Miss Berg's presentation, I began to think a lot about the children who were accustomed to worshiping idols and who were sometimes cut or burned to get the "evil spirits" out of them when they were sick. I began to think I might like to be just like Ann Berg.

Around that same time, I was growing very tall and very skinny, and because of my awkward height, my false teeth, and the polio in my left hand, I took it for granted that I would never marry. But I knew God wanted me to be a missionary and I felt I wouldn't miss having a husband if I had orphan children to love. I never heard a voice in my head telling me where to go, nor did a verse from the Bible jump off the page at me, but I knew very definitely as a teenager that God wanted me to be a missionary to Africa.

As my brothers and sisters and I grew older, we started to visit Lake Avenue Church in Pasadena, which had a strong missions focus and many activities for young people. Through this church we got to know a young couple named Bill and Edith Crouch who, along with their children, were planning to go to Africa as missionaries. I was in junior high at the time, and Mr. Crouch was serving as the church's youth leader. His excitement for missionary work infected the youth group and, as a consequence, a "gang" was formed of about a dozen young people. We were all between the ages of ten and fifteen, and each of us sincerely desired to go to the mission field. We called ourselves "Our Gang" after a popular radio program at that time.

"Our Gang" got together for all sorts of fellowships, including Bible classes, camps, and clubs. In 1938, a young pastor named Dawson Trotman was just starting a program to reach unsaved boys in Southern California by starting "Dunamis" clubs, named after the Greek word for "power" in Romans 1:16: "For I am not ashamed of the Gospel of Christ: for it is the power of God unto salvation to everyone that believeth." Through Trotman's visits to Lake Avenue Church, "Our Gang" heard about his Dunamis clubs and the new Martures clubs for girls, named after the Greek word for "witness." These camps and clubs had indescribable influence on my life. They helped me desire to study the Bible and have quiet time in prayer. I also saw the need to memorize scripture and to witness to those who did not know Christ.

These were important steps in my life if I were to serve the Lord in Africa. At the time I was convinced that I would end up in Africa as a single missionary, running an orphanage for motherless children. But I did not hold my future in my own hands, thankfully, and my path to Africa took a few twists and turns before I reached my goal.

SHIPS AND RELATIONSHIPS

The greatest happiness of life is the conviction that we are loved—loved for ourselves, or rather, loved in spite of ourselves.

— VICTOR HUGO

During my later teenage years, our family moved slightly north to San Rafael, California, so my father could help the war effort by working as a painter in the shipyards. By December of 1941, when the Japanese attacked Pearl Harbor, almost every American was in some way contributing to the war effort. No one minded helping because the whole country was bursting with patriotic spirit: it was considered an honor to help win the war and save the country. So, with our older brothers in the military, the younger Hettema kids spent our summers in the shipyards where my father worked, helping to build "Victory ships." Even Mother and my sister, Corny, painted there occasionally. I admired them for putting on their white overalls, tying their hair in bandanas and going to work.

During the war we had three blue stars in our window, representing the three Hettema boys in uniform. The first to join was Harold, who flew planes in the Air Force and received many honors. Clarence stayed in high school as long as he could to play football, but then he joined the merchant marines, going all over the world to take supplies to the servicemen. My brother David also joined the Air Force and was sent to the European field. Harold would regale us with his dramatic war stories, but David seldom wanted to talk about what had happened to him during the war.

Our family was blessed to have all our boys return to us safe and sound after the war was over. The three blue stars on our window never turned to gold, as they did for families whose boys were lost overseas. It was serious and sad to look at a window and see that a mother had lost a son, or two or three.

Many high school kids in San Rafael helped to build ships in the summer, both out of patriotism and also because the shipbuilding companies paid well. Most of us worked for Marinship, a company which assembled deep tankers from the bottom up. For many weeks the ships were open until the inside was divided into cargo sections and until upper decks were added. When the hulls were finished, there was great excitement in the air and many people came to see the ship they helped to build launched down its ramp into Richardson Bay.

The first year I worked on the Marinship tankers, I was only fifteen years old. For those of us who were so young, the only available work was sweeping welding slag off the scaffolding that hung like shelves inside the ship. The welders would perch on the scaffolding and weld large seams together deep inside the hull. Sweepers would follow the welders, sweep up the slag, and push it off the scaffolding down into the bottom of the ship where it would be picked up. In retrospect, when I think about working in those ships, I cannot believe my fearlessness in scaling the scaffolds like a monkey. The ships were extremely deep and the unstable scaffolding was held together by taut cables. We all knew that if someone fell, he would tumble to his death at the bottom of the tanker. It was extremely dangerous work.

As I grew older, I was eligible to be a sheet welder, responsible for welding the thousands of light, galvanized metal vents that carried air and heat throughout the ship. We sheet welders wore flame-proof leather jackets and pants to protect us from sparks. We also sported the typical welder's hood, a big black squarish mask with a glass screen that we could flip down over our eyes with a jerk of the head. If we did our job well, we could make a beautiful seam and brush it smooth with a steel brush so our work could be inspected. But sometimes we got into a thin spot or an awkward place and we would accidentally burn away the sheet metal, leaving a big blotchy mess that had to be filled in with another bead of metal. I dreaded making mistakes because it was so hard to fix them. But I enjoyed welding for the most part, and I tried to be just as cheerful and industrious as Rosie the Riveter.

When I was sixteen years old, a new family showed up at the church we attended in San Rafael, just a young man and his mother. My mother made it her business to befriend them. She found out that the mother, Mrs. Lillian Washer, was a widow. After the death of her husband several years previously, she had traveled to the Central African Republic as a missionary nurse, taking her young son Dallas with her. Now they were back in the States because of Mrs. Washer's illness. Dallas, or Dal, had graduated from high school and was doing war work. He was allowed to stay in the States to take care of his mother.

Since Mrs. Washer had recently returned from Africa, she had a lot of letters to write. But her illness, probably malaria, prevented her from writing as much as she liked. So my mother volunteered me to help her. I didn't mind at all. I was eager to hear more about Africa, and Mrs. Washer was a friendly, lovable woman, even when she was feeling ill. Every time I visited her house, she smiled and showed me her big basket of letters, and I sat down at her little writing table to write her replies as she dictated. Sometimes she was so ill that I also helped make supper. She and Dal always invited me to eat with them, but I was shy at first and didn't like to stay.

As I got to know Mrs. Washer better, she began to tell me about Dal, who was several years older than I. Although he had lived in Africa only a few years, he had developed a great burden for the African people. At first I thought Dal was very mature and intimidating because he had already graduated from high school and was taking courses at a local junior college after his work at Marinship. But I soon found out that he was as friendly as he was good looking. As I got to know him, I became impressed with his burden for missions. He reminded me of my older sister, Cornelia, who was away at Biola, a Bible school in Southern California, preparing for the mission field. So I got the idea to play matchmaker. She and Dal were perfect for each other, I was sure. I began to cultivate a friendship with Dal, just so I could introduce him to Cornelia when she came home.

That summer Dal and I became even better acquainted. Dal was a welder for Marinship like I was, but while I worked on the small vents, he was a leaderman, an experienced welder doing big metal seams. Sometimes he would come up to help us sheet welders fix our blotches when we burned holes in the metal. He was my guardian angel in the sheet metal department. He always seemed to know when I needed his expertise to repair a hole. He would patiently show me how to fill in my mistake with a bead of hot metal slowly flowing to fill up the gap. I was thankful that he would come and help me, but I also noticed that he seemed to help me much more than any of the other girls I worked with.

Soon it seemed that I couldn't do anything without Dal

being close by. Everywhere I went it seemed he was there, too. I saw him at shipyard work and when I worked with his mother, but since he went to the same church, I saw him plenty there, also. We both sang in the youth choir and went on youth activities with our church youth group. In fact, Dal once took another girl to a church skating party and left with me instead. He seemed to enjoy my company very much, and I considered him a good friend. Soon we started playing tennis together, which all the kids in California did.

Sometimes, after a game of tennis, Dal would urge me to sit down beside him and talk. I would sit with him, but I constantly turned the conversation to my wonderful sister, Cornelia. I told him how she had dark hair and large dark eyes. I told him how she did so well in school and had so many friends because of her personality—a perfect mix of grace and fun. I told Dal how she made all her own clothes and wore such smart outfits. But somehow he did not seem to be quite as impressed as I was.

If you had told me then that I would someday marry this tall, brown-eyed boy who wanted to return to Africa as a missionary, I would have laughed. I really did feel that Cornelia was the perfect match for Dal. However, Dal had his own ideas concerning the woman he wanted to marry, and though he liked my sister, he made it clear he was setting his cap for me.

It took many tennis dates for Dal to convince me that I was the one he really wanted. When he tried to talk about our future, I would get a little nervous and say, "But Cornelia's so good at everything, Dal. She is going to make the best missionary ever! You just wait and see." Dal would smile and listen politely, and then he would go on talking about how I would love it in Africa. And, of course, I paid close attention, because my heart's desire was to go to Africa as a missionary.

Looking back, I'm sure Dal went through considerable

frustration throughout our romance, which grew, not gracefully like a flower unfurling its smooth petals, but in fits and starts, like an inventor trying to perfect a flawed creation. At first, I just wasn't interested in boys yet. Since Cornelia was older than I was, I thought she should marry first. What business did I have going steady with a boy when she wasn't married yet? Later I realized I was trying to be like my old friend Ann Berg, who seemed so happy and fulfilled as a single missionary. Dal had to remind me that God had never declared, *Thou shalt be a single missionary!*

It took a long time, but Dal finally persuaded me that it wasn't my sister he was interested in—it was me, despite my physical flaws. And it was perfect if my desire was to go to Africa, because he wanted to go to Africa, too.

WAR WEDDING

I have many reasons to make me love thee,
whereof I will name two, first because thou lovest God,
and secondly because that thou lovest me.

— MARGARET WINTHROP (Letter to John Winthrop)

I graduated from San Rafael High School early because in our move from Southern to Northern California I skipped a grade, having completed the required courses. So I decided to go to school at the Bible Institute of Los Angeles (Biola). In our family, my father had made a rule of sorts that none of us could get married or start a vocation until we had spent a year at Bible school. He wanted us to be able to take some Bible classes that would challenge us spiritually and mentally. I was looking forward to Biola, and I had already saved $300 for my school bill from summers in the shipyards. And Cornelia had secured a place for me to work with her in the school cafeteria, so I had no financial worries.

Before I left for school, Dal asked if he could write to me. Calmly, I said, "Of course. That would be fine." I didn't realize just how much I would love getting his letters. Our cafeteria uniforms were white aprons with a little fold in the skirt, and I would tuck my letter up front where everyone could see I had a letter from my boyfriend. Taking after his mother, Dal wrote long, affectionate letters which I read over and over again, marveling at his neat handwriting and his eloquent words. I wrote him back as soon as I could find a moment in my busy schedule. Through our letters, we were able to express our love to each other for the first time. It was also through these letters that Dal convinced me that we should get married and prepare for the mission field together. When I finally realized that God was calling me to become the wife of Dallas Washer, missionary-to-be, I felt like the happiest girl in the world.

While I was at Biola, gas was rationed because of the war, and it became impossible for me to travel home. As a result, we kept ourselves busy in other ways: Dal welding for the war effort and taking classes at a community college, while I went to Bible school and worked in the school dining room.

Throughout my first year at Biola, I continued to follow in my sister's footsteps. It was Cornelia who got me on the basketball team. We used to laugh about the red bloomers with elastic at the knees that we had to wear for the games. And, in spite of the polio in my hand, I came alive when I stepped onto the basketball court. I was tall and skinny and my brothers had taught me a lot about the game.

During this time, almost everyone at Biola attended The Church of the Open Door for chapel every day and for church. The church was an integral part of the Biola campus, located between the men's and women's dormitories. We felt honored to go there since it was such a large, imposing building seating hundreds of people, but also because it was theologically sound and visited by many famous pastors from all over the world.

On some weekends, I joined a college ministry to the Long Beach area that helped at a community house in Victory Park, one of the housing projects the government built quickly during the war for workers from Midwestern states. These were kind people who loved to host us, and I especially enjoyed working with the children in Sunday School, where I could put to good use the Bible story flannelgraphs I had made for class projects.

Even when I was at home in my dormitory room, I could not escape excitement. Our dormitory building rose thirteen stories tall on the corner of Hope and Sixth streets right in the middle of downtown Los Angeles, and I lived on the top floor. One day, while I was in my room doing some homework, the building started to shake. When we looked out the window, we could see an earthquake hit Los Angeles, causing the city to vibrate visibly. As I lay in my bed on the top bunk, I watched our light, hanging from the ceiling by a cord, sway gently back and forth. In Southern California, earthquakes were a part of life.

By the time summer came, Dal was ready to give me an engagement ring. He had been making payments on it back in San Rafael. Since I knew he couldn't wait to propose, and I couldn't wait to wear my ring, I had a feeling we would get engaged sometime that summer.

I came home when classes ended and joined in the summer youth activities that were already in full swing at our church. Sometimes Dal and I took off to the beach in his '39 light yellow Ford, which had a black top and a rumble seat in the back, and which my younger brothers thought was the "cat's pajamas." We especially savored the two-hour drives to the beach. We would pack all our towels and a picnic in the rumble seat and start down the road, only to find that two of my brothers, Bob and George, had hidden in the rumble seat so they could go to the beach too! Up they would pop after about an hour—as long as they could stand it in the stuffy rumble seat—and by that time, we were too far along to take them back home.

One night, later in the summer, the entire youth group went down to the beach for a bonfire and picnic. There must have been poison oak in the firewood, because the next day, a rash broke out all over my body. My doctor had to give me injections, but my face swelled noticeably, and someone had the audacity to take a picture of me in that state. The reaction was so severe that my doctor said I had to stay in bed. I felt ugly and messy, like one big, oozing itch.

Dal chose that particular time to ask me to marry him. He had been saving up for the ring all year, and he just couldn't wait any longer, I suppose. But I couldn't even fit the ring on my swollen finger. I just lay in bed and gazed at it sitting on my bedside table. It was a terrible time for me. But since all terrible things come to an end, my finger soon slimmed back down so I could wear my beloved ring. It was, and still is, a beautiful ring, all of white gold, with small diamond chips around a larger diamond in the middle. I was so thrilled to finally be engaged. It was easy to resign myself to lying flat on my back in bed, since it gave me time to plan my wedding.

A few weeks after we were engaged, and after I had time to heal, we planned to surprise our friends at church with the good news. However, they surprised us instead by throwing a wedding shower and giving us many gifts. We were moved by such a loving gesture of friendship and kindness.

Since we were married near the end of World War II, our wedding had to be simple. Fortunately, I was able to borrow a wedding dress from my sister-in-law Norma, whose parents had bought her a lovely, traditional white satin gown with a long train. It was generous of her to lend it to me. We were both quite tall, but the dress had to be altered slightly. Later, Cornelia borrowed the dress too. We were thrilled to wear such a beautiful, stylish dress.

Because of the war, factories weren't making the wonderful decorating items and household goods we expect to find in stores nowadays. The rules were strict. All raw materials had to go towards uniforms, parachutes, and other items for the war effort. Our friends at church gave us wedding gifts, but they were an odd assortment of whatever was left on store shelves after years of war. We received such gifts as a brown tray for fruit, a glass centerpiece, and eight vases of various sizes and shapes.

But everyone gave generously, and I had all I needed to start a little home. It didn't matter that I lacked extra towels or sheets or cookware because we were going to be missionaries, and we would be traveling around a lot. If there is one thing I have learned from being on the mission field, it is that active missionaries cannot be collectors of pretty, unnecessary things. They can take with them only what is necessary on the field.

Dal and I were married at 8:00 p.m. on May 4, 1945, in the San Rafael Congregational Church. The local paper titled our wedding column "Under an Arch of Roses" and called it "one of San Rafael's most beautiful weddings." I remember bits and pieces about my wedding, but I was nervous, especially because I had never been the center of so much attention. Dal was nervous, too, but he had already spoken in churches, so to be in front of the public was nothing new.

The altar was decorated with Calla lilies and there was an archway of latticework covered with baby roses. All the flowers, including the gardenias and orchids in my bouquet, came from personal gardens around town, since florist shops were not very active during the war. My sister, Cornelia, was my maid of honor, and Dal's good friend Reuel Reitzel served as best man. Both Rev. Robert Kay, the pastor of our church, and my father performed the wedding ceremony. We said the traditional vows while kneeling on a white satin pillow and exchanged rings under an arch of roses.

Following the wedding ceremony, everyone gathered in the church parlor for a beautiful reception. Someone in the church had made our cake, even though sugar and flour were strictly rationed. Apparently, people had donated their rations for our cake. We were aware of the sacrifice, and grateful, as were those who ate the delicious four-tiered cake!

Finally, it grew late, and we left on a brief honeymoon to a hotel by the ocean. My brothers did not pass up the opportunity to decorate our getaway car, our old faithful Ford. Fortunately, there were no little boys in our rumble seat, and we drove off to our hotel in peace.

After our wedding, we lived in Kentfield, a suburb of San Rafael, while Dal continued working as a welder for the war effort. Our little furnished cottage had a view of the small Mount Tamalpais, and near us was an old Catholic church called Mission San Rafael Arcangel. We could look out our back window and see monks walking the mountain paths in brown robes with cords tied at their waists, moving solemnly, stopping to pray by each station of the cross. The mystical atmosphere bothered me and I didn't love our little house on the mountain, despite the beautiful redwoods and oak woodlands that would have made for wonderful hiking.

My little brother Bobby was one of our first guests at Kentfield. He had to hitchhike up the hill to visit. I was proud to have a dinner guest, but though I worked all day to make a fancy dinner, the carrots had thick hearts in them that stayed as hard as rocks no matter how long I cooked them and my cake fell apart when I tried to serve it. Bobby says I burst into tears, but Dal put his arm around me and told me I had done a wonderful job.

Finally, V-J day came on August 15, 1945, and released us from war work. This was the moment we had all been waiting for, but San Rafael was too small to contain our excitement so everyone headed to San Francisco. We had gone there several times for ballgames, but we had never seen the city so joyful as when the military men came home. We celebrated with thousands of sailors and soldiers and friends and family, all mingling and laughing and crying in the streets. San Francisco was already known for its sailors who kissed girls, but with the streets swarming with servicemen, there were sailors picking up girls and kissing them on every street corner.

Once the war was over, we knew just what to do. We packed all our wedding gifts in the rumble seat of our little yellow Ford and started our drive down to Los Angeles, where we both planned to take classes at Biola. That trip down to Los Angeles was really our honeymoon trip. We traveled along Highway 1, one of the most beautiful highways in America. On one side of the road, huge black cliffs hold the ocean prisoner, and the waves break into feathers of foam over the rocks below. Sometimes we caught glimpses of seals sunning themselves on the wet rocks, flipping in and out of the water to keep cool. The other side of the highway is bordered by a forest, old and thick and green. It was exhilarating to finally be on the road to Bible school.

When we arrived in Los Angeles we set off immediately in search of a place to live. We chose a semi-basement apartment, the lower floor in a big Los Angeles apartment building, right downtown. We had a funny, eccentric landlady and a lot of strange neighbors. I am ashamed to admit that we did not make friends with most of them because we were a little afraid of them. It wasn't the best apartment in the city; we didn't live there for the joy of it. But we were at school all day, and the rooms were within our price range. Best of all, it was close enough to Biola that we could walk to school instead of fighting for parking on the busy city streets.

Shortly after we arrived, I started getting sick every morning and realized, to my astonishment, that I was pregnant. I had already signed up for classes so I decided to defy my morning sickness and go to class anyway. When second semester came, I didn't register for another semester, though I did keep working in the school dining room since we needed the money. I stopped working in the last two months of my pregnancy to reserve my strength for the delivery.

Through the school we found a wonderful, old Christian doctor who gave me good care and advice, and who delivered babies at Hollywood Presbyterian Hospital. Our only problem was that we knew the hospital stay would cost a lot of money. In those days there was no school insurance, and definitely no work insurance. We knew we had to make a hard decision. The only way to get enough money for the hospital was to sell our cherished Ford. We loved that car and it had played a big part in our lives. But when we thought of the wonderful gift from God we were about to receive, we knew it was well worth it.

One day after a check-up in Hollywood, we decided to take a walk through Forest Lawn, a nearby cemetery well known to movie stars and other wealthy people. We did not make it a habit to walk through cemeteries, but Forest Lawn looked so beautiful and peaceful that we just couldn't resist. Inside the cemetery was a section just for babies, and in the baby section was a gravestone with the name "Luann Linda." We both liked the name instantly and decided on it for our new baby's name, if the baby turned out to be a girl.

Our first child and only daughter took her time in coming,

and the long delivery left me extremely tired. When my baby girl was finally placed in my arms and Dal came into the room, the first thing I said was, "I want to count her fingers." Somehow in my subconscious mind I feared that since I had suffered from polio, perhaps my child's fingers and hands would not be normal. Dal indulged my fear and helped me hold her tiny hands and count her fingers so I could be reassured that my little girl had perfectly formed hands.

SOLDIERS FOR CHRIST

The steps of a good man are ordered by the Lord, and he delighteth in his way.

— PSALM 37:23 (The theme of Biola's 1948 graduating class)

Going to college right after World War II was one of the most invigorating things Dal and I ever did. Our school was full of soldiers returning home from posts all over the world. Many had traveled extensively, to the Hawaiian islands, to Japan, to idyllic archipelagos all across the Pacific. They had seen Europe and Africa and the Middle East up close. A surprising number of them left America vaguely Christian and returned on fire for the Lord. They considered it a precious gift to have witnessed the great need that entire peoples and nations had for a Savior, and they planned to return to these nations not for the Allied Forces, but as soldiers for Christ.

It was a thrilling time and, as I look back on it, a miraculous time. Our country had just survived the most terrible war in history, a war with more casualties, both in and out of battle, than any other single conflict—a war "to end all wars." Secular philosophers would look at our survival and victory as the greatest good that came out of World War II. But God, as He delights to do, graciously intervened in human history in many ways that might be invisible at first glance. For example, God brought couples together in marriage who would otherwise never have met. He increased the value put on human life by at least one generation and changed the perspective of many a soldier who realized that his life on earth could cease at any moment. From the ashes of a war-torn world, God raised up men and women with an insatiable desire to bring the light of Christ into nations that had wandered long in the darkness of ignorance and sin. God matched a record number of war casualties with a record number of lives added to His kingdom.

The students at Biola felt a special bond, having come through the war together, starting families at the same time, and heading to the mission field. Seventy-five percent of Dal's graduating class made their way toward the mission field after graduation. Such a statistic was, and still is, unheard of. I am always excited when I hear about a country on the other side of the world and remember acquaintances who went out from our graduating class to that field. Our preparation for ministry was a sweet time in our lives, and we maintained close relationships with many families we knew from school. They became our friends for life.

A typical day for us in Los Angeles began with a hurried breakfast and coffee, after which we would rush out to class. We usually went to class in the mornings and worked in the afternoons and many evenings. It was a hectic schedule, but somehow we found time for diversion.

One of our favorite amusements was getting together with friends to play sports. Dal and his buddies had organized a touch football team, and though their uniforms were just sweatshirts with numbers on them and they had to go to the park to play, the wives would make the most of it and bring our little children and a picnic lunch. We would dress our children in the colors of the school, as if they were our mascots, and encourage them to cheer for their daddies. Those afternoons of recreation kept us from buckling under the daily burden of work and classes.

We tried to keep classes our highest priority amid the many demands upon our time. I remember we had some very good teachers. Dr. J. Vernon McGee, whose radio broadcasts would later become so popular, was one of my Bible teachers. He was extremely animated, and he amused us by walking briskly back and forth across the teaching platform until we tired of seeing him pace. One day, just for fun, some of my classmates made a barricade of chairs around the platform so he was fenced in next to the podium and could not go anywhere. He was not upset in the least and took the joke well.

I enjoyed my course in child evangelism, for which I had to gather up a file of stories and visual aids so I would be prepared to hold a child's attention. We also cut out figures for flannelgraph stories, a wonderful teaching tool not as often used today in this age of the computer. Biola was not a university, but a Bible institute, and it made us strong in practical work whether we went out to teach or work or to the mission field. The most important aspect of Biola at that time was that it was truly an institution centered on Christ. On top of both thirteen-story dormitories—high buildings at the time—huge neon signs proclaimed "Jesus Saves" to the city of Los Angeles spread out below. Those signs were well known all over the city and were bold proof of Biola's witness for the Lord.

I was able to make good use of my story file and flannelgraphs when we held church services in Victory Park in Long Beach. After Luann was born, I was a little embarrassed to nurse her, so I hid in a ladies' restroom. But I soon relaxed, and the ladies of the church made me feel right at home when they all pitched in and bought us a bassinet for our new baby.

Dal's classes were more challenging than mine, and he took more of them. He studied preaching as well as mission work and dealing with different cultures. Dick Hillis, one of Dal's favorite teachers, became Dal's role model and guide at Biola. Dick Hillis was a respected missionary who had ministered to the Japanese during World War II. The Lord had given him a great burden for Muslims, and he had come to

Biola as a teacher to put out an urgent plea for missionaries to take up the challenge to evangelize Muslims. If someone could show Muslims a God of love, Hillis said, their minds would be freed from the chains of a man-made religion. He believed that Africa especially needed the gospel, and he pleaded earnestly with his students to drench the Muslim nations in the living water that is Christ.

When the war ended, Muslims were not yet so strong in Africa and the Middle East. Colonial rule still covered Africa and no one was rejected from an African country because of religious convictions. Missionaries could have expanded their work with Muslims and abated the great force of this terrorizing religion. But missionaries generally shied away from Muslims because their culture was neither easy to understand nor to work with, and the results of ministry were not very good.

Dal and I had never felt drawn to working with Muslims until we heard Dick Hillis speak. Through the urging of this zealous missionary, God put a heavy burden on Dal's heart to reach Muslims in Africa. The next big decision, then, was to decide which mission board, out of all mission boards that have a work in a Muslim country, we should apply to.

The most promising one seemed to be a board called Evangelical Baptist Missions, or EBM. We had heard about this mission board from Dr. Ken Masteller, a pastor we met while on the East Coast. He told us that EBM had recently started a work in Niger with the Muslims. As soon as Dal graduated, we began EBM's application process, which was a little more than we had bargained for. We had to fill out application papers, write doctrinal statements, list references, and take medical exams. Once we qualified, we were then invited to meet the mission board. The last stop was an interview with Dr. Joseph McCaba, director of EBM. When we went into his office we took two-year-old Luann with us. He asked us many questions about our call and our desire to reach the lost so he could judge our reaction to things that could be difficult on the field. As we approached the time to leave his office, he looked at us and at our beautiful blonde little curly-haired daughter, and asked, "If you knew that your child would catch some terrible disease and would die on the field, would you still be willing to serve the Lord as missionaries in the Niger?" We searched our troubled hearts to answer him, looking at each other with tears in our eyes. Weakly, Dal responded, "We pray God will never ask that of us. But we do know that God has called us to serve Him in Africa." Then dear brother McCaba stood beside us with his arms around us and prayed to the God that knew our future, committing us into the loving care of our Heavenly Father, who would oversee each step of our lives.

We were thrilled to be accepted by the board of EBM, which promptly set us a new task: writing letters to churches to present our program for support, then visiting churches that invited us to speak, a process called "deputation." We had a very easy deputation period, since Dal's mother and my father had many wonderful friends who invited us to their churches and offered us their support. At that time $10 of monthly support per church was normal; $25 was a lot of money. In our first years, the mission estimated our needs at only $130 per month for total support, including insurance, transportation, living expenses, and general ministry supplies. It was less than a year before we raised 100% of our support. We saw the promise of Philippians 4:19 resoundingly fulfilled: "But my God shall supply all your need according to his riches in glory by Christ Jesus."

It was while Dal and I were busy making plans to go to Africa that his mother, Lillian, surprised us by announcing that she was getting married again! While on a speaking tour, Lillian's path had crossed unexpectedly with that of Dr. H. L. Weber, whom she remembered from a brief meeting at a hospital in Cameroon. Dr. Weber had by this time served 42 years in pioneer missionary work in Cameroon, where he founded and superintended the largest hospital on the West African coast. Near the hospital he had also developed a colony for patients with leprosy, some of whom came from hundreds of miles away. His outstanding scientific research and unusual work in surgery and dentistry had earned him a place in the French Legion of Honor, an award seldom conferred on those who are not of French birth. Most importantly, Dr. Weber included in his ministry the planting and cultivating of God's Word in the hearts of the African people.

When Dr. Weber's first wife passed away, Lillian sent him a letter of condolence. Later, they saw each other at missions conferences and speaking engagements. Soon, through the encouragement of mutual friends, their renewed acquaintance developed into an intimate friendship, and they announced their plans to be married in December of 1949.

Their wedding took place in Orlando, Florida, with three-year-old Luann serving as the flower girl. After their wedding, Dr. and Mrs. Weber continued their speaking circuit and eventually returned to Nigeria to serve at a new leprosarium operated by Sudan Interior Missions (SIM). While they traveled, Dal and Luann and I were able to stay at their Orlando home, which served as a base for our missionary deputation work.

ALGIERS

Let us give of our work, our thoughts, our plans, ourselves, our lives, our loved ones, all unto His hands. When you have given all unto God, there will be nothing left for you to be troubled about.

— HUDSON TAYLOR (Inscribed by Dal in his Bible)

Finally the date was set for us to leave. On March 24, 1950, we would sail from New York City to Algiers, North Africa. Joseph McCaba, the mission director at EBM, had advised us to study the French language and Muslim customs for one year before going on to Niger.

But before we could leave, we faced the massive job of packing for our trip. We had to list and label each item in our tall wooden boxes for the benefit of customs in Algiers. This process took us a long time, even though we were allowed very little freight. We also had to secure passports and visas and get typhus shots (two each) and a yellow fever shot.

There was one more unexpected item before we set out to sea. Just weeks before we left for Algiers, I found out that I was pregnant again. By this time, Luann was three years old. I was flustered by my discovery and did not want to tell the mission board because I imagined them gasping, "Oh, my! She's got so many children that she's not going to be doing her duty as a missionary!"

The S.S. *Fernfiord* was late to arrive because of rough seas, so our ship to Algeria sailed at 8:00 in the evening four days late. However, on the day we left, the weather was unusually balmy for March in Brooklyn. We were especially thankful for good weather since we had to wait on the pier for several hours before boarding the ship.

People came from New York, Connecticut, New Jersey, and even Canada to see us off. Dal's mother, Lillian, and her husband, Dr. Weber, came all the way from Florida. At nearly 3:00, about eighteen or twenty of us gathered on the upper deck for a farewell service. We sang hymns, prayed, and shared testimonies. Finally, our friends had to leave the ship, but we could converse with them as they stood on the pier. With the bittersweet farewells came the peace of Christ's personal presence, which Dal's mother once claimed "no one can describe, which cannot be understood by the world, and which no circumstance of life can remove."

As the ship slipped her moorings and the old tugboat pulled her out of the channel, the waters began to widen between us and our friends on the pier, who sang "Take the Name of Jesus With You." Then, as passengers on the boat drew near to listen, we all sang "God Will Take Care of You."

Finally, the handkerchiefs fluttered for the last time, and the lights of the pier were swallowed up in the darkness of the night. We returned to our cabin and found more than 150 letters, cards, wires, parcels, and packages waiting for us. We were moved by the love and good wishes but, even then, we seemed to hear a voice asking, *Lovest thou me more than these?* We were finally launching out, far out into the deep with our Savior, where we looked forward to letting down our nets and filling them with precious souls.

The trip overseas was uneventful, until I got seasick. The ship hit stormy seas and the stern went up and down while huge waves washed over the deck. The whole ship seemed to skim up to the top of a mountainous wave, and then fall down into the next deep valley, upsetting my balance and my stomach. But the Lord stilled the seas for our deckside Easter service, which the Captain had asked Dal to lead since he was the only pastor on board. This service allowed us good chances to witness for the rest of the trip. As far as we knew, we were the only Christians on board.

It took twenty long days at sea to reach our destination, since our ship was not a cruise ship, only a freighter that just happened to carry passengers. We were relieved to sail through the Strait of Gibraltar and into the Mediterranean Sea because we knew we would soon be on dry ground again. Within a few hours, we caught a glimpse of Algiers, an impressive sight. It truly is a city set on a hill, whose white buildings are all topped with red tile roofs. The city seemed to glow mysteriously in the morning sunlight. Its pristinely white architecture had earned Algiers the French nickname *Ville Blanche*, or the White City.

Our ship arrived in Algiers ahead of schedule, and no one was at the dock to meet us. We decided it was best to wait on the ship until someone arrived. The French pastor there was the first to greet us, and he informed the others of our arrival. Soon the missionaries from the few Protestant works in Algiers had assembled. From the pier below, they all shouted French greetings to us up on deck. We were plunged into the French language in a hurry!

The country of Algiers was, and still is, inhabited chiefly by Arab Muslims, with a few scattered Europeans, most of whom are French. I was especially curious to see the Muslim women, who wore long dark robes and big, heavy veils, even in such hot weather. Dal described Algeria for our supporting churches back home. The country, he said, was quite similar to Palestine, even to the wild thorns like those used in the crown placed on Christ's brow. Ox-driven carts and shepherds tending their sheep completed the picturesque scene.

The little village where we lived was about twenty miles from Algiers, in the Atlas Mountains that run through North Africa. Souma was about two city blocks long, boasting one Arabic store. Dal joked in a letter that this store was a good place to purchase "general commodities like beans with boll weevils in them." Mud-plastered, whitewashed houses lined the road. The village square was a meeting place where local Arabs converged to discuss everything from Ramadan to the easiest way to make money. We lived in the foothills, so we were not bothered with the flies that infested the markets during summer months.

Most people who lived in the mountains were poor. However, the family that housed us was more well-to-do than the average villager. The Seltzers were of French descent, though they had lived in many countries over the years. They were Christians and owned a large plantation covered with the olive groves common to North Africa. On their land was a mill where they harvested the olives, and on the back of the mill Monsieur Seltzer had built a little apartment for his workers. This was our home while in Algeria.

Monsieur Seltzer and his wife had one son, and Madame Seltzer's sister, Madame Tavelle, also lived with them. Madame Tavelle was certified in education and had offered to be our French teacher. She came to our apartment twice a week for lessons and assigned us a massive amount of homework. It helped that the Seltzers spoke French all the time. When we visited their home, we would practice all the vocabulary we could think of. Madame Tavelle knew English, but she wouldn't use it around us. She wanted us to hear French all the time.

Dal did well with the language, partly because he had taken French in high school, but mostly because he was good with languages. I did fairly well, but not as well as I would have liked. Language study demands perspiration and determination, but my brain didn't seem to work. I thought only of the new life developing inside me.

While Dal and I studied, Luann did her own schoolwork. I had brought a kindergarten course in the Calvert curriculum for her to start in Algiers. She was excited to have her own school supplies, and she still remembers how she loved her paints, crayons, and writing materials. We were not surprised that she grew up to be a first grade teacher.

By September of 1950, a second Washer child was about to appear on the Algerian scene. We were eager to receive such a welcome blessing. Mrs. Seltzer assured us that it would be perfectly fine for me to deliver my second child in nearby Blida at the French *Maternité*, where Catholic midwives delivered all the Arab babies. So I had all my checkups at the *Maternité*, and the Lord gave me a calmness about giving birth in a foreign country.

As the due date drew closer and closer and then passed, Dal and I started to get nervous. Mesdames Seltzer and Tavelle clucked over me like sweet aunties, making sure everything was all right with the baby. They told me I should take castor oil. I did, but nothing happened. Then they told me I must take walks. So Dal and I walked and walked, past the Seltzers' house and up the road that winds into the foothills. I felt rather silly hiking all over the place when I was so large. We certainly went to a lot of effort convincing our first son to make his appearance!

The night after our long hike, I started to experience labor pains. Monsieur Seltzer had a funny open French car with awnings, but no doors. They called it an open coupe. It was in the back of this little coupe that I was taken to the *Maternité* in Blida to give birth. Dal said goodbye to me, and Madame Seltzer took me to the clinic. I felt lonely, but I understood it was the Arabic custom for the husband to be out of the way. I prayed that there would not be an emergency, since I did not trust my French enough to do any explaining. In fact, I had a hard time explaining that I wanted a drink of water.

When the Catholic midwives took me in to deliver, they put me on a rolling cart which functioned as a delivery table. I delivered my little boy with no trouble, really, considering I had nothing to take away the pain and nothing to speed the delivery. It was after the birth that I felt most uncomfortable, as I had to lie on the rolling cart all night. They would not let me walk and they would not carry me, so I was not allowed to move from the cart until the next morning, when they considered me strong enough to walk to my room. I was glad to escape that cart.

So Dennis, or Denny, as he came to be known, was finally born on September 27, 1950, the only blonde child among an array of dark, olive-skinned babies with lots of dark curly hair.

In spite of Dal's impatience to learn whether he had a new little boy or girl, he stopped in the market that morning to buy me a bright bouquet of chrysanthemums before racing to the *Maternité*. When he arrived, one of the midwives came and told him I had given birth to a *fils*. His excitement drove all his French out of his head and he could not remember whether *fils* meant a boy or a girl. Just then, the midwife noticed the flowers in his hand and stood in front of him to bar his way. She was in great shock and told him the flowers he had bought were only to be used to decorate graves of the dead. She snatched the flowers away from him and put them beneath a statue of Mary. When I told Dal he had a son, his eyes filled with happy tears. After that, we didn't mind the confiscation of my flowers.

Kay and Dal's wedding.

Kay's engagement picture.

Kay with poison oak.

Above:
BIOLA (Bible Institute of Los Angeles).

Above:
Men's choir. Dal is third from right.

Sisters Kay and Corny worked in the Biola kitchen.

Taking Luann to nursery on the way to class at Biola.

The Washers sailed to Algeria on the S.S. *Fernfiord.*

Friends came from many states to say goodbye.

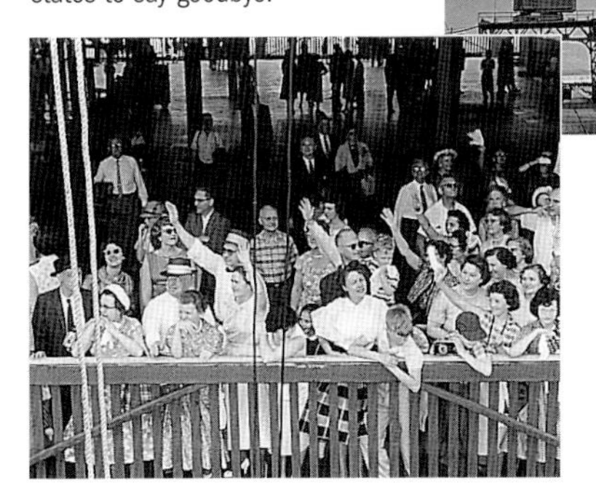

Dal studying French with Madame Tavel.

Baby Denny arrived at the French Maternité in Blitta, Algeria.

Dal preaches to Arabs in Algeria.

Mosquito nets for sleeping outdoors.

Lee House, the residence for new missionaries in Niamey.

Baby Ronald Washer, born February 7, 1953, Niamey, Niger.

Above:
EBM missionaries, 1950–1956, Baptist Chapel, Yantela, Niger. Dr. Joseph MaCaba, founder of the mission, stands at far left rear.

Left:
Missionaries at Yantela, Niger, 1951.

Our quaint French cottage behind the mill included an old iron bed with a big feather mattress. The bed had no soft pillows, just a hard bolster. The combination of the iron bed, feather mattress, and hard bolster is very French, but not very comfortable. At night we would hear rats roaming the mill: "Skch, Skch, Skch!" But even the rats, the bed, and a bathtub in the middle of the kitchen did not dampen my excitement. I loved being a real missionary and living under such "hard" conditions.

On market day, Dal would ride four and one-half miles on his $48 bicycle to Boufarik, the nearest market. In the city, the long road would be filled with Arabs and many beggars, some blind, some lame, all chanting in their unusual melancholy Arabic manner. One beggar beat his head in a pan of ground glass, the blood streaming down his face, just to earn a few francs. When Dal looked across the sea of faces, he thought, *How many know the Lord?* Such disturbing sights strengthened his desire to learn the language so some of these souls might be won to the Lord.

Dal always had to bargain for the fly-covered fruits and vegetables, since prices are always quoted higher to a white man. There was ample opportunity at the marketplace to put our French language lessons to use, but we always found the hands a most helpful part of our conversation. After making his purchases, Dal would begin the long uphill ride home. Luann, Denny, and I would greet Daddy at the door, anxious to know what he had in his *panier* (basket). No matter what else he had brought, he always had a piece of candy for Luann.

Luann usually played inside the apartment or outside close to the mill. She did a good job of amusing herself and was always very healthy. But her one brush with death came when she was playing alone in the yard. We had built a wonderful swing outside on a big tree, and Luann was putting it to good use one morning. Suddenly, a wild cat ran out of the mountain bushes and bounded toward her, scratching her violently. She screamed and howled, making just as much noise as the cat. Dal and I rushed outside in a hurry. We ran towards Luann, and I saw the cat sprint back into the mountains. It looked harmless enough, but when we saw the damage that had been done to our daughter, we were anxious. The Seltzers knew just what to do. They rubbed all of Luann's scratches with lemon juice, and soon she was as good as new.

There was no such thing as a Christian church in Souma, but we would often go into Algiers and meet with the Arab and European Christians there. The times we spent there were blessed. We would go on Sunday mornings and spend the whole day with our friends. We especially loved their French food at lunchtime. The missionaries would share what God was doing in their lives and how He was blessing their efforts. They were aware that political trouble was brewing, but they never talked about leaving.

But the Seltzers were careful, and with good reason. In the foothills of the Atlas Mountains, there was only a small dirt road that led past the Seltzer farm; travel was primitive out there. Arab Muslims would walk up that road and, many times, they would stand in a group and stare at the Seltzers' house. "Some day our people are going to chase away all you white people and this is going to be our house!" they would call out. But this was after we had left. While we were there, Mr. Seltzer was hiring Arabs and using them to be his workers.

Sadly, after we left Algeria, we heard news that gunmen had come in and killed Mr. Seltzer and his young son. The rest of the family could not run the farm by themselves so they had to return to France. Our hearts grieved with the hearts of our generous friends as they experienced unexplainable losses of family and land just as Job did.

Realizing that few people in the towns around Blida and Souma knew the Lord, Dal passed out tracts in his spare time between language lessons. He also came up with other ingenious ways of reaching the Muslim people with the gospel. I remember one day Dal and I and a group of missionaries loaded donkeys with used clothing and little bags of school supplies for the children. We visited native villages in the mountains. It wasn't long before word got around that we were going to distribute clothing, and we soon had quite a procession following us. As we began our little service in the center of a village, we noticed the eagerness of the children who gathered at our feet, but also the skepticism of the men and the fear in the eyes of women who listened at a distance. As Dal preached the Word, the Arab interpreter perspired heavily, for the words he interpreted were directly opposed to Muslim teaching. One man brushed his hands in Dal's face, indicating his discomfort with the message. But the gospel went out that day, along with school supplies and used clothing, for which the people were extremely eager.

STARS AND SAND

How sweet the name of Jesus sounds
In a believer's ear:
It soothes his sorrow, heals his wounds,
And drives away his fears.

— JOHN NEWTON

By the end of 1950 we had completed our language study in Algiers. Our next step was getting to Niger. We were privileged to reserve seats on a cargo plane that would fly across the Atlas Mountains and the Sahara Desert into Niger. Had we arrived in North Africa only a few years earlier, we would have had to travel on primitive trucks that laboriously crossed the Sahara.

Torrential rains made our scheduled flight to Niamey for December 29th impossible, and we learned we would fly New Year's Eve instead. When we arrived at the airport, we happened to see our crew at a bar celebrating the end of the year and welcoming in the new. We hoped that our flight would not be the worse for their celebration.

Dal had never flown before. When he had gone to Africa years earlier, he had traveled by boat and bus, not airplane. Somehow Dal's fear of airplanes leaked out to the other missionaries, and at our farewell party, they gave him gag gifts like an envelope with a rubber band—in case the propeller fell off.

Our hearts were gladdened by the little group of missionaries who came to the airport to see us off. They sang the same song that rang in our ears as our ship left New York, "Take The Name of Jesus With You." We boarded the airplane and tried to get settled in the small space with cargo hanging above us in big nets. We were strapped in our seats, even baby Denny and Luann. Dal's head was down and I heard his muffled voice, "You tell me, Honey, when we take off." As the pilot revved up the engines Dal asked, "Are we in the air yet?" I said, "Honey, we haven't even taken off yet!" I have to admit I laughed at Dal's fears, but anyone would have been tense in such a small, overloaded plane.

As we flew over the mountains and down across the desert, we underwent a terrific change in temperature, as it was cold in Algeria and hot in Niger. In fact, shortly after our arrival in Niger the temperature was documented at 153° F, which was not abnormal. We began peeling off clothes when we neared our landing at Gao, where our mission was planning to start a new work that year. We had to stop to refuel and drop off cargo for that area. The plane taxied to a stop on the tarred dunes, and then the crew directed us into an Arab tent where they served us extremely strong coffee. This was the extent of our beverage service on our flight to Niger. There was no way they could serve us iced drinks, of course. I gathered my courage and asked where I could go to the restroom. The Arabs gestured over the sand dunes and said, "Go wherever you want."

Soon we took off again. It was midday, and from the windows of the airplane we could see sand dunes stretching out forever in every direction. We saw very few signs of life, with the exception of a few antelope and, every once in a while, palm trees crowding around a small pool of water.

After many miles we arrived in Niamey, the capital of Niger. We landed safely, gathered our belongings together and burst out of the plane, only to discover that nobody was waiting for us. So we trudged into the tiny waiting room and sat there to wait for the missionaries to rescue us.

We were in that hot little waiting room until nightfall, and still no one had come for us. Finally, a Frenchman who had come to pick up someone else took pity on us and asked where we were going. We told him we needed to get to the mission station but we didn't know where it was. He was kind and offered to take us in his truck. At last we arrived at our long-sought-after destination and asked the missionaries why they hadn't come for us. They were very apologetic and explained they had not received our telegram informing them when we would arrive. It was probably in the mail sack carried by our own airplane. We thanked God that we had arrived safely, because with no one awaiting our arrival, we could have crashed in the desert and no one would have known. We decided afterwards to make a habit of asking our pilot to fly in a circle over the mission compound so our friends could come pick us up.

Niamey is a busy, buzzing city, the site of the presidential palace and the only good hospital for miles around. After our brief introduction there, our next step was to go to Yantala, a smaller village down the road and by the river. Years earlier, the president of Niger had given Joseph McCaba, the first EBM missionary there, a piece of land in Yantala so he could start a mission station. The president thought he was doing well to put the Protestants far out on one fringe of the capital city and the Catholics on the other side. Nowadays, Niamey has swallowed up both Protestant and Catholic stations, but back then, it seemed like we were in the middle of nowhere.

At first, Dal and I were surprised by women nursing their babies openly and kids running around naked. But it wasn't long before we didn't even see the differences between our cultures and learned to love the people of Niger. The people were pleasant and friendly, laughing at our language mistakes, bringing milk and eggs to sell, and always stopping to listen to the gospel message, though few seemed to receive it.

Baby Denny was terrified when he first looked up into a black face, but soon he had nothing but smiles for Isaka, our native helper. Luann cried the first few days, wanting to go back to Souma where she had been so happy, but she soon grew to love her new life. She had no trouble making friends of all the little children she met in Niger. Dal wrote in 1951,

> Peering through our window as I write this are about seven or eight charcoal black faces eagerly watching every movement of the *anasara* (white man). Luann appears to be the drawing card as all the native children like to color in her color book and ride her bicycle.

Our best friends these first few months were Otto and Helen Bechtel. Otto was a builder who directed building projects on bush stations, where missionaries in primitive areas constructed houses, churches, and other necessary buildings. He was proficient in Zerma, the native language of Niger, and spoke with an almost perfect accent, having learned the language from interacting with his African workers. Helen welcomed newcomers to the field, and she taught missionaries and Africans to read and write in Zerma.

Helen spent many hours teaching Dal and me how to communicate in Zerma. It is not a tremendously hard language to learn because it is not tonal, nor does it have a great many odd sounds. One of the first words we learned in Zerma was *anasara* (white man). It could be said respectfully or contemptuously. We could tell by the way a person said the word how he or she felt about us. Most of the time, the people's tone revealed that they loved and respected us, mainly because we had made an effort to learn their language.

When the people got to know us, they gave us animal

names. The *anasara* are not always privileged to know their animal names, especially if the name is not very nice. But our animal names were laughable. My name, for example, was *eyau* (giraffe), a name applied to me because I was tall and was thought to have a long neck. Dal escaped without an animal name, as far as I know. Because he was a man of God, the Africans respected him and called him *malam* (teacher) or *alfaga* (priest).

After I learned to speak Zerma, I was expected to teach others how to read the language. If a person was saved, one of the first steps in the discipleship process was to encourage him to learn to read so he could read the Bible for himself. Teaching others to read benefited me just as much as it did my students!

Helen Bechtel was also a wonderful cook. She knew how to prepare all the African dishes. She taught me how to make papaya and mango jam, how to grind coffee and cereal, and how to make butter and peanut butter. She advised me to start every meal with a soup because liquids are important in such a dry, hot climate. She also told me to put plenty of salt into the soup since we would lose a lot of salt by sweating.

Most importantly, Helen taught me to accept strange foods as part of a missionary's life. African children often roasted rats or grasshoppers over a fire and considered them a great treat. The rats in question, though bigger than American rats, eat only herbs and are considered as clean as any other animal in Africa. I learned from Helen not to be picky, but to prepare the occasional meal of frog legs or crocodile meat along with the usual guinea hens, wild pigs, and gazelles.

Every day I spent some time on Helen's back porch while she operated a little home dispensary. I did whatever she did: mixed up medicine for the tropical ulcers that afflicted a great number of Africans, treated sores with ointment and wrapped them in torn bed sheets, gave medicine to babies who suffered from malaria. If there was a situation that required professional help, we always volunteered to take the person to the hospital.

Helen and Otto were wonderful examples to Dal and me of how missionaries should conduct themselves on the field even while suffering losses. First Helen's best friend, Nina, died of cerebral malaria. Then Otto developed liver problems. After we had been in Yantala almost two years, the Bechtels' young son, Elwin, began to experience heart problems after a bad bout with the flu. His heart grew worse until he was unable to breathe lying down. Then one day, Elwin, who faced his illness cheerfully, took his last breath. His father arranged for a coffin to be delivered. When it arrived, it was too short for Elwin's body. Otto and Helen had no idea what to do. They did not want to bury him without a casket, but there was no other casket to be had. Finally, Otto did the only thing he could think of: he broke his son's legs so he could fit the body into the casket. I'm sure it was one of the hardest things Otto ever did.

The Bechtels continually looked to God for strength as they grieved for their son. Helen wrote, "We thank the Lord for every moment we have had him. . . . The natives keep coming and giving their sympathies and telling us their sorrows; surely now we can better enter into their lives and pray that out of it all many will turn to Him." Two months after Elwin's death, Helen gave birth to a second son, Raymond. Helen wrote, "How good it was of the Lord to send him . . . at this special time. I don't believe anything in this world could have been a greater comfort to us . . . Otto must love him too, by his willingness to wash the diapers."

In Yantala we learned to sleep outdoors on the porch-like enclosure at the back of our house. Aside from the rainy season, we slept outdoors through the year, because inside the house at night the temperature could rise to 115°. Each night we took our rollaway beds out to the porch, where we had hung mosquito nets on posts to guard against malaria-carrying mosquitoes. Those mosquito nets took a lot of work to keep intact, as bats would fall into the nets, or crickets and grasshoppers would chew holes through them. I would get up often to put clothespins on the holes that needed to be mended. I kept dreaming of ways to make a kind of Band-Aid for torn mosquito nets. I was sure I could make a lot of money if I could come up with a quick mosquito net patch.

One night, a determined insect crept through the mosquito net, buzzing straight into Denny's ear. Denny awoke immediately and proceeded to rouse the rest of us with his frantic screaming as he performed a war dance on his bed, trying to get the bug out of his ear. We could hardly get him to tell us what was the matter but, when he did, I tried to pull the bug out. I couldn't. It was buried too deep. Finally, though it was the middle of the night, we took our screaming child to the doctor. We were surprised and relieved when all he did was pour oil into Denny's ear. The bug did not want to be in the oil and it crawled right out.

There were other drawbacks to sleeping outside. As our time in Niger drew to a close, thieves would steal from us while we slept. There were also many nights I got up to check on the children and just missed stepping on a snake.

In general, though, we felt so invigorated by the night air that we would never think of giving it up. I cherished those nights outside when we lay out on the terraces and prayed and talked and looked up at the stars. I believe my children were drawn closer to God during those times because they saw the majesty of God's stars shining as if they were only a hand's breadth away. Once, while we were lying out on the terrace, talking about God's stars, four-year-old Luann turned to me and said, "Mommy, I love Jesus and want Jesus to come and live in my heart." As parents, Dal and I wanted our children to turn to Jesus in God's timing, not ours, so we were thrilled to hear her childlike desire for Christ come so early.

About a year after we arrived in Yantala, I became pregnant with our third child. After my peculiar experience giving birth to Denny in Algeria, I could only imagine what would happen with this new child's birth. My imagination could never have done justice to the real story.

We went to the maternity clinic in Niamey for a checkup and blood tests once we knew I was pregnant. At the clinic they said that when my delivery time came, Dal was to drive me the few miles to Niamey, check me into the maternity section of the French hospital, and then go to pick up a trained African midwife who could help me with the birth.

My pregnancy went smoothly, and it was not long until one evening, several days before my due date, I realized it was time to go to the hospital. Dal loaded me and my suitcase into the mission vehicle and drove into Niamey, where he dropped me off right at the steps to the hospital. I walked up a few steps and then sat down to wait for Dal's return with the midwife. I knew he would be a few minutes, because he had to weave back and forth through Niamey's maze of huts to find the midwife and bring her back. As it turned out, he had some difficulty locating her house, and then locating her. As I continued to sit on the hospital steps, my labor pains grew stronger and stronger. As the minutes marched by, I became increasingly worried. I had horrible visions of delivering my baby right on the filthy hospital steps.

Finally, when I had become desperate enough not to care where I delivered the baby, Dal arrived with the midwife. She took one look at me, ran into the hospital and found a tiny room with a simple bed. The room and the bed were not pristinely clean, but I didn't mind. I put on a hospital gown and got into bed as quickly as I could, while the midwife ran off to get some supplies. I must have relaxed a little too much because it was not a minute later that a huge contraction came and out shot the baby like a bullet. The midwife was nowhere to be found.

Dal jumped up, ran out of the room and started calling up and down the halls for help, *"Le bébé est né!* (The baby is born!) *Le bébé est né!"* Fortunately for us, he had a much better command of French than he had had at Denny's birth. He finally got our midwife's attention, but she was unfazed by this turn of events. She had probably planned on moving me to one of their rock-hard delivery tables, but she matter-of-factly returned to the room, cut the umbilical cord, put little Ronnie in a cloth, and helped me with the remainder of the delivery process. By this time, I was already holding our new baby boy who, despite his speedy delivery, was fat and dimpled and darling.

Back in Yantala I was met by many friends, both missionaries and Africans. I carried Ronnie into our house and found on our kitchen table a big brown elongated squash called a *cabouza*. I giggled to myself and laid Ronnie next to the squash, proudly announcing, "Look what I got in the market!" Everyone laughed at the similarity between Ronnie and the *cabouza*. My joke tickled the Africans especially, and from then on Ronnie had to answer to *Cabouza, Cabouza*!

Ronnie was almost a year old when I contracted dengue fever. Within a week of being bitten by an aëdes egypti mosquito that carried the disease, I began to experience high fever and headaches, pain in my joints, and a rash. I came to understand quickly why dengue fever is nicknamed "breakbone fever."

Eventually, after I reached through my mosquito net one night and grabbed a kerosene lamp to throw at some imaginary creature, the others realized I was delirious and forced me to stay in bed under the care of our missionary nurse, Arlene Spurlock. Dal also brought a French doctor to examine me. The doctor confirmed that I had dengue fever and that the fever and pain would probably last a long time. "Of course," he said, "dengue fever is the worst if you are pregnant. The fever can go through the placenta and injure the baby. You aren't pregnant, are you?" he asked. But I was pregnant. I was in my first trimester of my fourth pregnancy.

My illness wore me out so much that we decided it would be best to return to America for the birth of our fourth child. So we returned to California and stayed with my parents until after the birth, renting a little house near them for the rest of our stay. My mother was thrilled to take care of the grandchildren she had not seen in three years.

Our son Terry was born in a women's hospital in Pasadena, California, in August 1954. We were saddened to find that my rough pregnancy had indeed affected his brain, leaving Terry with cerebral palsy which weakened the muscles in his arms and legs. I was thrilled with my new little son, but I knew he would have to deal with physical problems for the rest of his life. When he was young, I used to cry to God, *Why did this have to happen?* But I should have known God had a special plan for Terry.

We remained in the States for more than a year to make sure we had done everything we could for Terry. He received extensive therapy, and the doctors showed us how to do exercises to strengthen his muscles and keep his tendons flexible. Because we were not on official furlough, we went back to Africa as soon as we could. We were excited to return to our work and we looked forward to introducing our missionary friends to our new little son.

Laya

Whoso shall receive one such little child
in my name receiveth me.

— MATTHEW 18:5

Soon after our family—now six—returned to Yantala, we felt right at home doing all the things we had missed while we were in America. I especially enjoyed returning to my work at the dispensary with Helen Bechtel. Our work was often demanding, but it gave us great opportunities to share the good news of Christ with the people of Niger. I was happy to find that my Zerma, such that it was, had not suffered too much from our year away.

One afternoon as I was preparing to leave the dispensary, I looked out of the window and saw a man leading a donkey toward me. On the donkey was a frail little girl, wrapped in a cloth. Her father lifted her off the donkey and brought her through the door of the dispensary. "Here's my little girl," he said. "She has sores on her body and we can't make them get better. Can you give her medicine?"

The daughter's name was Laya, and she was eight years old. Laya seemed frightened of me, as she had probably never seen a white person before, much less such a tall one, and her eyes grew wide when I reached out to pick her up. I set her on a chair so I could examine her body and look at her sores. I could tell they were deep tropical ulcers, and I knew the healing process would be long and hard. The examination was obviously a source of great distress to Laya, so I handed her a pretty yellow mango. Its size and beauty astonished her and kept her busy while I questioned her father.

"Where do you come from?" I asked. He told me his wife and children lived in a tiny village beyond Tondibia, a village of only a few small huts on sandy, dry ground. Laya's family belonged to the Fulani tribe, who live almost entirely off their livestock. Amazingly enough, cattle can thrive in the climate as long as their owners can find a grassy area for them to graze every day. The Fulani have a diet of cow's milk and grain and eat vegetables and fruits. They occasionally kill a goat or sheep but only rarely kill a cow.

I probed a little further: "How did Laya's sores begin?" He told me he did not know. He had taken her to the village "doctor" who, thinking he was doing a good thing, packed the sores full of herbs and leaves. Laya's parents did everything they could, but over a period of time she became much worse.

"This is something I can't heal immediately, so I might need to keep her for awhile," I told her father. We did not usually keep patients, but I knew Dal would not mind if we gave Laya a place to stay so she could receive treatment without having to come such a long distance every day.

After talking it over with Dal, I agreed it would be best for Laya to stay in our storeroom, a mud building connected to the kitchen. I went to get a little cot for her to sleep on, but our little African houseboy shook his head at that. "Oh, no, Madame! She will fall off on the floor! She has never slept up high!" He reminded me that beds were not common to the people of Niger. If they slept on anything, it was a woven grass mat. So instead of a cot, we put a mat down on the floor, and Laya seemed quite at home in her new surroundings. I was glad I could see my tiny new patient from the kitchen.

Every day I walked Laya to the dispensary to go through the painful procedure of washing and dressing her sores. The sores on her arms and legs were the deepest and the most painful and I had to clean out the crusty drainage which had hardened. It took me a long time to get the sores to open and soften. Laya would cry and complain that it was hurting her, and it was. But her sores had to be completely cleaned out before they could absorb the good medicine. After cleaning her sores, I wrapped each one with white bandages made of torn-up sheets. When we had finished, Laya waddled out of the dispensary looking like a little mummy.

We tried to feed her a good diet of fresh fruits and vegetables and even eggs, meat, and other foods she never had eaten before. Sometimes we were surprised at what she liked and didn't like. I did not try to wean Laya completely off African food, because I did not want her to experience stomach problems when she went back to coarse African grains. So I always fed her food she was familiar with, adding other things to complete her diet. In the beginning, Laya preferred to eat out on her mat in the storeroom because she was used to eating with her hands and having her dish on the ground. But it wasn't long until she was eating at the table with the family.

A few months after Laya came to live with us, I decided to make a big three-layer cake for Ronnie's birthday. For our children's birthdays, we let them choose something special to eat for supper and a special kind of cake. I didn't mind making a cake from scratch.

While I was working in the kitchen, Laya sat in her room watching me with big round eyes. I thought to myself, "How funny! She's never seen a birthday cake before in her life! But it probably won't interest her a bit." I laughed to myself to think what a delicious treat she would be missing! By the time I had finished the cake, I thought it was quite a masterpiece. I had even made seven-minute icing and tinted it green and blue. I swirled the last bit of icing onto the cake and left it on the counter, waiting for supper time.

We had a lovely dinner that night. After we had finished, I went to the kitchen to bring out the cake. To my horror, the cake was no longer a beautiful masterpiece. It was dismantled, and blue and green icing now decorated the kitchen counter and floor. "Oh, no!" I cried. "I cannot believe this! What happened?" I called everyone into the kitchen to see the mess.

"Denny, did you get into the cake?" I asked.

"No, Mommy. I was helping Dad."

I looked at Ronnie. "Ron, surely you didn't do this to your own cake."

"No, I didn't do it," he said dejectedly.

Laya, on her mat in the storeroom with her head down, was sneaking a look in our direction now and then. Dal's sharp eye had been watching her. He pointed silently to the little guilty one.

"Laya, did you get into the cake?" I asked. She nodded slowly.

I was upset with her, much more than I should have been. I said, "Laya, we've told you that whenever you want something you should ask for it. You mustn't just take things! That was very naughty!" Then I took her over my knee and I spanked her. When I let her go, she sat down on her mat and couldn't seem to stop crying. Soon I felt horrible for spanking her and making her cry over such a little thing, so I took her in my arms and said, "Oh, Laya, it's okay, sweetheart. It's just that you mustn't ever take things without asking. If you had asked me, I would certainly have given you a big piece of that cake!" I hugged and kissed her until her sobs subsided to intermittent sniffles. Later on that night she said, "Well, now I know you love me, because you spank Ronnie, and you spank Denny, and now you spank me!" I laughed as she gave me a big hug, satisfied that she was now part of the family.

Although Laya was always a sweet girl, she showed little interest in the Bible stories I told the children, perhaps because she knew that her family was Muslim. When we asked if she wanted Jesus to save her, she said, "No. My daddy prays to Allah, and I want to pray to Allah like my daddy does." We prayed constantly that Laya would accept Jesus as her Savior and continued to invite her to participate as we read the Bible at the dinner table and prayed as a family. We believed that God had placed her in our home for a reason, but we did not push her in any way to accept Christ.

One day, four years after Laya had joined our family, I was kneading bread in our hot kitchen when Laya surprised me by asking a very serious question. "Mommy, if my daddy died, would he go to heaven?" I realized that Laya had been thinking deeply about spiritual things and that I needed to take time to talk with her. I stopped kneading the bread, wiped my hands on my apron, and asked Laya to sit down with me at the kitchen table.

"Laya," I said, "Your daddy has never heard about Jesus, and Jesus is the only way to heaven. I hope that someday the missionaries here can go up to your village and tell your daddy about Jesus."

Then I took Laya's hands in mine, though mine were covered with flour, and said, "Laya, how about you? Have you got Jesus in your heart?"

Laya's eyes welled up with tears. "No," she answered softly. And at that moment, God reached down and softened Laya's heart toward the gospel. Laya's salvation was very simple. No one had to force the gospel on her: with childlike faith she asked Jesus to save her from her sins. She was discipled by one of her teachers, Gladys Gilson, who encouraged her to be baptized. So on a June day, the Washer clan traveled to Niamey, where Laya was baptized in the Niger River along with several other new Christians.

Tera

Better to love God and die unknown than to love the world and be a hero; better to be content with poverty than to die a slave to wealth; better to have taken some risks and lost than to have done nothing and succeeded at it.

— ERWIN W. LUTZER

In the beginning, the mission talked about opening an orphanage. Dal and I agreed to be in charge after we finished our language study. We raised money to build a big house in Yantala with living quarters on one side and rooms for children on the other. However, the project came to a standstill because there was disagreement about whether it was a good idea. Muslims don't usually permit adoption, so many wondered why we would start a Christian orphanage for children who might be reclaimed at any time. The field council finally decided to abandon the project.

After this unexpected decision, Dal and I began praying about a new opportunity—opening a new station north of Niamey. We were already caring for African children like Laya, so we didn't feel we were missing out. After much research, prayer, and discussion, we decided to start a new mission station in Tera, a bush village of 5,000 people near the border of Burkina Faso. In order to reach Tera, we had to take a crude ferry across the Niger River and then a four-hour drive along sand roads rippled like washboards.

The mission board was hesitant to send us to Tera and made sure we understood the risks of such a remote, unhealthy place. Tera was the exact opposite of a nurturing environment for a growing family. But Dal responded to them with incredulity. He couldn't understand why anyone would not want to bring the gospel to unreached people. To Dal, the greatest privilege in the world was to be the first to tell someone about Christ. It didn't matter what we went through; if God called us to an area to spread the good news, He would take care of us. I was proud to see the light in Dal's eyes as he told the mission board that the people in Tera might never hear the gospel unless we went. So why shouldn't we?

When we finally arrived in November of 1955, we looked for a piece of land where we could build our house as well as a dispensary, chapel, and a Bible Institute. The man in charge of "real estate" showed us several places. We were especially drawn to a lot on the back side of the village. It was highly undesirable because of a big tree right in the middle. People in Tera claimed that the tree was inhabited by evil spirits whose eyes had been seen shining like fire at night. This land also bordered the cemetery, which did not improve its marketability. But we decided that we wouldn't let these problems stop us. We paid $16 for permission to build on the lot.

However, the process of getting permission to build took almost a year. In the meantime, we rented two little mud houses in the corner of the village. "Hut" would be a better word, since I had to stoop down to go through our five-foot doorways. One house contained our bedrooms and bathroom, and the other housed our kitchen, dining room, and living room. Before moving in, we replastered the walls where they were broken and whitewashed them. A mud floor worked for a while, but our children learned that a little water and a stick made digging holes in the floor quite entertaining. To keep from repairing it all the time, we eventually poured a cement floor. There was no bathroom, so we built walls and a seat where we could pour water down into a septic tank.

Since we were in the village, we could talk over our walls to neighbors. We might lock our gate for privacy during Bible study time, but we usually left it open so people could come in and get acquainted. In retrospect, we saw how wise God was to keep us from setting up our compound until we could make friends with the people of Tera.

During that first year, our family was hit by an onslaught of illness. It was *harmattan* season, the windy time of year when the dust, fine and white, swirls down, filling the air and choking the lungs. This white dust travels all the way from the hot Sahara Desert, but the wind carrying the dust turns cold at night, causing great fear in the minds of the Africans. They shut themselves in their huts and cover their heads with sleeping cloths, afraid to breathe this "bad air" that brings sickness and death. This is the wind that steals their children's lives, grabbing them in the throat, causing a high fever, bending their necks backward, until death comes.

Harmattan was the only time of the year that we shut our windows and slept under a quilt, quite a nice change from the usual hot nights. But to the villagers, that year's *harmattan* turned into a nightmare. On the heels of our arrival, a spinal meningitis epidemic had swept the town. The epidemic was so fierce that for years afterwards villagers refused to talk of it for fear that the evil spirits would repeat the curse.

When the meningitis epidemic worsened and many were dying, the Nigerian government decreed that all the dead must be buried immediately to keep the disease from spreading. All night long we heard the digging and processions carrying the bodies. Mourners carried kerosene lanterns and swayed to a slow drum beat.

Our children had been vaccinated for measles but not

meningitis. Ron was the first to catch the disease, soon running a high fever. At first we thought it was chicken pox, and when he did not improve, we thought it was malaria. So we summoned an African doctor from the nearby dispensary to inject him with medicine for malaria. When the doctor came, he told us he needed to perform a spinal tap on Ronnie to see whether he had meningitis. If there was blood or cloudy fluid in his spinal column, the doctor said, he has meningitis and should be isolated. I held Ronnie on my lap while the doctor poked around in his spine with a needle. I was so afraid the doctor would injure a nerve in Ronnie's spine. "God," I prayed, "don't let my boy become paralyzed." Finally the doctor was able to draw out some fluid. He found traces of blood and cloudy fluid. He told us to take Ronnie to Niamey, but we had no car, so we asked the police to radio the mission station there so a missionary could take us to the hospital. Although they came as quickly as they could, Ron's legs were paralyzed by the disease (not by the spinal tap) by the time he reached the hospital. Dal and I took turns sitting by his bed, first praying that the meningitis would not take our five-year-old son from us, and then that Ron would not be paralyzed for the rest of his life. After a month in the hospital, Ron regained movement and began to learn to walk all over again. We praised God that Ron did not have viral meningitis that can kill its victim within hours, but bacterial meningitis, the slower-working type.

It wasn't long after we got home that Terry, more susceptible to disease because of his cerebral palsy, broke out with chicken pox and developed a soaring fever. We nursed him through the chicken pox, but he was listless for days after the rash disappeared. Soon the fever returned, this time much worse. He vomited again and again. A government medical worker came to give him an injection, but Terry was so sick that he didn't move or even cry. We decided to get him to the hospital, but we knew it would be too hard to go by car because the trip was long and difficult.

By the time we realized we needed to evacuate Terry to the capital, a terrible sandstorm was brewing. We knew the winds were strong enough to take the roof off a house, so we were worried that an airplane would fare no better. There *was* an airplane available: the mission had purchased its own small plane after Otto Bechtel died when he was unable to be evacuated after he was bitten by a viper while hunting guinea fowl along the roadside. Though visibility was almost zero, our pilot, Dave Kepple, radioed us he would try his best to pick us up, despite the storm. The wind that came before the rain swept the sand into blinding curtains of grit, endangering our plane—a small, low-winged French *Jodel*. Dave told us later that he would never have flown in such weather except to save a life.

It seemed like we waited for an eternity for the plane to arrive, and Terry grew weaker and weaker. We couldn't help but think how God had allowed the Bechtels' little boy, Elwin, to die several years earlier. We entreated Him not to take our little boy, too. Finally, through the noise of the blowing storm we heard the drone of a plane's engine. "Thank you, God!" I cried, as Dave Kepple flew in and landed on a makeshift runway behind our house. We bundled Terry up and I carried him into the plane. There was no room for Dal, so he kissed us goodbye and committed us to God's care.

As we lifted off, Terry arched his back, a sure sign of spinal meningitis. He couldn't seem to stop vomiting. It didn't help that the plane kept up a stomach-churning cycle of dropping and gaining altitude. We couldn't get very high in the harsh winds, but Dave flew as best he could. Every other second I thought we were going to crash, as the wind bucked us like an angry bull trying to dislodge a cowboy. Fear squeezed my heart and I felt sure we would never make it. At last, after several traumatic hours, we came in sight of Niamey. Fighting the wind, the plane wobbled as it touched down, but we knew that God Himself had set us down on the ground. The missionaries rushed Terry to the hospital for the medicine he needed.

I will always have a soft spot in my heart for Dave Kepple, who trusted God enough to risk his life in saving us. Dave could have held a high-salaried position in the aviation field, yet he chose the joy of missionary service over money. Through Dave, God kept Terry under His wings, as his service on earth was not yet done.

Having escaped meningitis, Denny experienced his own distress when he contracted bilharzia, also known as "snail fever," since snails ingest parasite eggs from urine or feces that have somehow made it into the river. Denny knew the rules: absolutely no swimming in the river. The organisms were no threat after the fish were cooked, but swallow just one mouthful of river water and you could be swallowing a zillion microbes and parasites. We thought we had communicated the dangers of polluted water, but Denny was not as careful as we had hoped.

Like his brothers, Denny loved to fish in the Niger River with his African friends. He had his own pole and hook on a string, and he and his friends could throw their lines out for hours on end. Sometimes, their strings would get caught on a rock or around a plant, and they would wade out to untangle it and continue fishing. Denny didn't think a quick dip in the river would do any harm. It wasn't *swimming*.

One night, the boys came in for baths and I noticed red bites the size of pinholes all around Denny's waistline. I discovered he had been in the river that day retrieving his hook and string, but at the time I thought he had a simple rash.

Though Denny spent only a few minutes in the water, the parasites causing bilharzia entered his system, and within days he was doubling over in agony.

We couldn't bear to see Denny in such excruciating pain. As soon as we could, we took him to the French hospital in Niamey. They did blood and urine tests and, sure enough, found the eggs produced by the bilharzia parasite. They gave us the diagnosis and admitted that there was no medicine to cure the disease. All they could do was try to help the pain.

We were concerned for Denny, not only because of his suffering, but also because the medicine for pain was known to cause anemia. We thought that doctors in the United States might be able to find a cure. So when we came home on furlough, our doctor sent Denny to Duke University for treatment. When the doctors there found the parasite in his blood, they were actually excited, because the disease is so rare in America. They hunted for an appropriate medicine and found an experimental drug in Switzerland that might do the trick. Denny, the guinea pig, stayed in the hospital for ten days so he could be monitored while receiving injections. Dal stayed with him while I was with the children in Greenville. The drug did kill the parasite, but it also damaged a bundle of nerves in Denny's heart, causing occasional spells of arrhythmia to this day. However, in part due to the work Duke University did with Denny, the medicine for bilharzia is now administered all over Africa in a safe and controlled pill. Our Denny was part of a scientific breakthrough.

People sometimes wonder how we could take our children to a country where they had to fight illnesses and endure accidents that still affect them today. In reply, I like to tell the story of how Ronnie cut off two of his middle toes while operating a lawn mower while we were on furlough in America. Fortunately, he can still walk without much trouble. I'm sure Ronnie would agree that accidents and illnesses can happen anywhere, even in a "safe" country like the United States. God takes care of His children wherever they are.

While her brothers traded one sickness for another, Luann stayed perfectly healthy. I really don't remember her ever getting sick. That's not to say that she stayed at home all day with the doors closed—she was an adventurer. Moving to Tera and living in our mud huts was thrilling to her. She and Laya loved to play with their friends from the village, and Dal and I encouraged them to play at our place. Their favorite pastime was outside cooking. Dal had built a mud oven outside our house like the ones the Africans used to make French bread. Luann and Laya loved to bake, and they took over my Thursday baking with glee, making cakes, bread, and cookies. And though Luann said she didn't appreciate it when her brothers ate up everything before she could get it on the dinner table, I think she was secretly glad to please her hungry herd. The fun of baking helped sugar-coat the pill of assisting me with the laundry and ironing. The girls were less than fond of the flatirons we had to heat up on the stove.

When Luann and Laya weren't helping me with the chores, they spent long hours creating scenarios with their dolls, or making innumerable items of clothing for them. When Luann needed time to herself, she would find a secluded place and curl up with one of her beloved books. Dal and I had signed her up for a club that sent a new book each month, and Dal eventually built her a bookshelf for the ones she read over and over. They were her most precious possessions. No wonder she became a schoolteacher!

Luann also loved animals, mothering a continual cycle of lambs and kids as attentively as if they were her own children. She also kept roosts for pigeons and a "pond-in-a-barrel" for ducks. And both Luann and Laya were very comfortable on horseback, even without saddles. I loved to watch them take off across the dusty plains together, Laya's dark figure bending into the wind, and Luann's high blonde ponytail bouncing in perfect rhythm to the horse's proudly arching tail.

Of course, all the children had pets: there were a number of monkeys, goats, sheep, dogs, and cats on our premises. I didn't mind most animals, but I was never excited to have monkeys since they bite and were dirty. But I couldn't come up with a good enough reason to dismiss them from our zoo. They certainly kept my children happy and entertained—sometimes too entertained, I thought. One day around supper time, little Terry was playing outside and didn't want to come when I called. He was having too much fun with his monkey, Boubou. The way Terry tells the story, I came after him with a great big stick (I think it was more like a twig) to spank his legs for not obeying. When Boubou saw me going after Terry, it sprang on me and bit me all over my face. Things did not go so well for Terry or his monkey when Dal saw what had happened. Dal had never liked Boubou anyway, so he wanted to get rid of it immediately. But we had to admit that there was something watchdog-like in Boubou's determination to protect Terry, so we continued to keep it as a pet, though on a much shorter chain.

After a year of living in our square mud huts, we were finally granted permission to construct our mission station. We started out by building a house from cement blocks and a metal roof, and later we built a mud church. There are no wood buildings or even wood furniture in the desert because there is no wood to be had. Even if there were, termites would destroy it. Thanks to the termites, almost all our furniture was made of metal. We did not have the luxury of an overstuffed sofa or chair which, had they survived the termites, would soon have been permeated with dust and dirt. In our opinion, though, our new house was downright ritzy compared to the mud huts.

Since our house was near the graveyard, we became accustomed to burial parties marching past. Sometimes the coffin was carried by pallbearers, but sometimes there was no coffin, and pallbearers would carry a body wrapped in a cloth and held on a woven grass mat supported by bamboo poles. Drummers and mourners would accompany the body to the cemetery, where it would be placed in a deep hole and covered with dirt and sharp rocks to keep wild dogs from digging up the grave. It was sad to see death so often walking past. In a way, I felt that each departing soul spoke to me as it passed by. *What if that man had never heard the name of Christ,* I would think, or, *What if that woman had heard of Jesus but wouldn't follow Him?* To realize that people were dying before we could reach them with the gospel was a sobering, though compelling, thought.

We built our house with double doors so we could have a breeze blowing through. Our house had no glass windows, since glass wasn't available; the openings were covered instead with metal shutters that Dal could lower when the wind started to blow. The shutters would keep sand from blowing in and settling on everything. Sometimes I regretted not having glass windows, especially when the shutters were closed. We would be in darkness, except for our kerosene lamps, while the sand whipped fiercely around our little house. But I had to remind myself that I would rather the shutters keep all the sand out of my house than to be able to look out the window.

My favorite method of beautifying the house was to set a

vase of fresh flowers on the table. I told Dal that I wanted to grow some flowers, so he built me a flower box all along the terrace in front of our house. I especially enjoyed zinnias and periwinkles, hardy flowers which grow well in Africa even with little water. Sometimes, when African women saw me watering my flowers, they would say, "When are you going to eat those?" They didn't understand why I grew something just to look at.

My other luxury came when Dal somehow acquired forty neem trees, either through the American Embassy, or through a governmental agricultural project. He planted them all over our mission station, and I was thrilled, since neem trees grow quickly and make excellent shade. Though we did have to water them, after seven years their roots stretched deep enough to water themselves.

I did do some productive gardening, managing to grow a few vegetables in my sandy yard that I irrigated with well water. I coaxed plants to grow in spite of the heat and was known to be the only person in Tera who had leaf lettuce. In fact, the Commandant at the military camp near Tera knew. One day he notified me that General Charles De Gaulle would be coming to Tera to inspect the troops, as Niger was still a French colony at that time. De Gaulle would then come into town and dine at the Commandant's house, along with important people from our area. Because the Commandant had no wife to play hostess, he wanted me to come and oversee his African houseboys and cooks as they prepared the meal, set the table, and served dinner. I was chosen since I was the only white lady in the area and, therefore, the only person around who had any idea about French dining. The Commandant also wanted me to donate my lettuce to his meal. I really did not do much of the cooking—I mostly just supervised the Commandant's staff—but I did make sure to wash my lettuce well with water and permanganate so

General De Gaulle would not get a stomachache.

Our "banquet' consisted of a *mishoui* (lamb roasted all day over a fire), rice, canned peas, bread, a lettuce salad, and a pineapple dessert. The menu was actually quite easy to put together since our choices were limited. The hardest part was finding enough nice plates to use for such important company.

Charles De Gaulle was very tall, even taller than I, and he was in the habit of looking down his large nose and labeling people with certain phrases. His name for Dal and me was *"Les Amèricains."* I couldn't tell from his tone whether the name was an insult or a compliment.

In Tera, we were again impressed by the stars. In Niger, there is no light pollution to get in the way, and the stars glitter like so many diamonds on a jeweler's black velvet table. But I never learned my constellations. I could pick out Orion, of course, and the dippers. Or at least I thought I could. Dal said I could make a big dipper out of anything. In the African culture, natural events are very meaningful, and Africans knew the stars better than we did. I felt ashamed that I didn't know more about the stars. After all, they are God's creation.

We had two terraces in Tera, and we slept outside as we had done in Yantala, the children on one terrace and Dal and I on the other. We stretched wires like clotheslines for our mosquito nets and tied them in a special way so we could pull them down in the event of a storm. When one did approach, Dal would wake up first and alert us to fold up our beds, take our nets down, and evacuate into the house. Then he would stay outside, closing all the shutters and doors to protect us from the harsh winds. Those frantic times were like fire drills for us; we always tried to get our children to go faster and faster to avoid getting sand in their clothes and their beds.

Sleeping outside gave us many happy nights, though, as the

Left:
Laya at the Mission with Luann.

Below:
The Washers' new house near the Niger River.

Laya with her adopted family, the Washers.

Laya on the cover of SIM mission magazine.

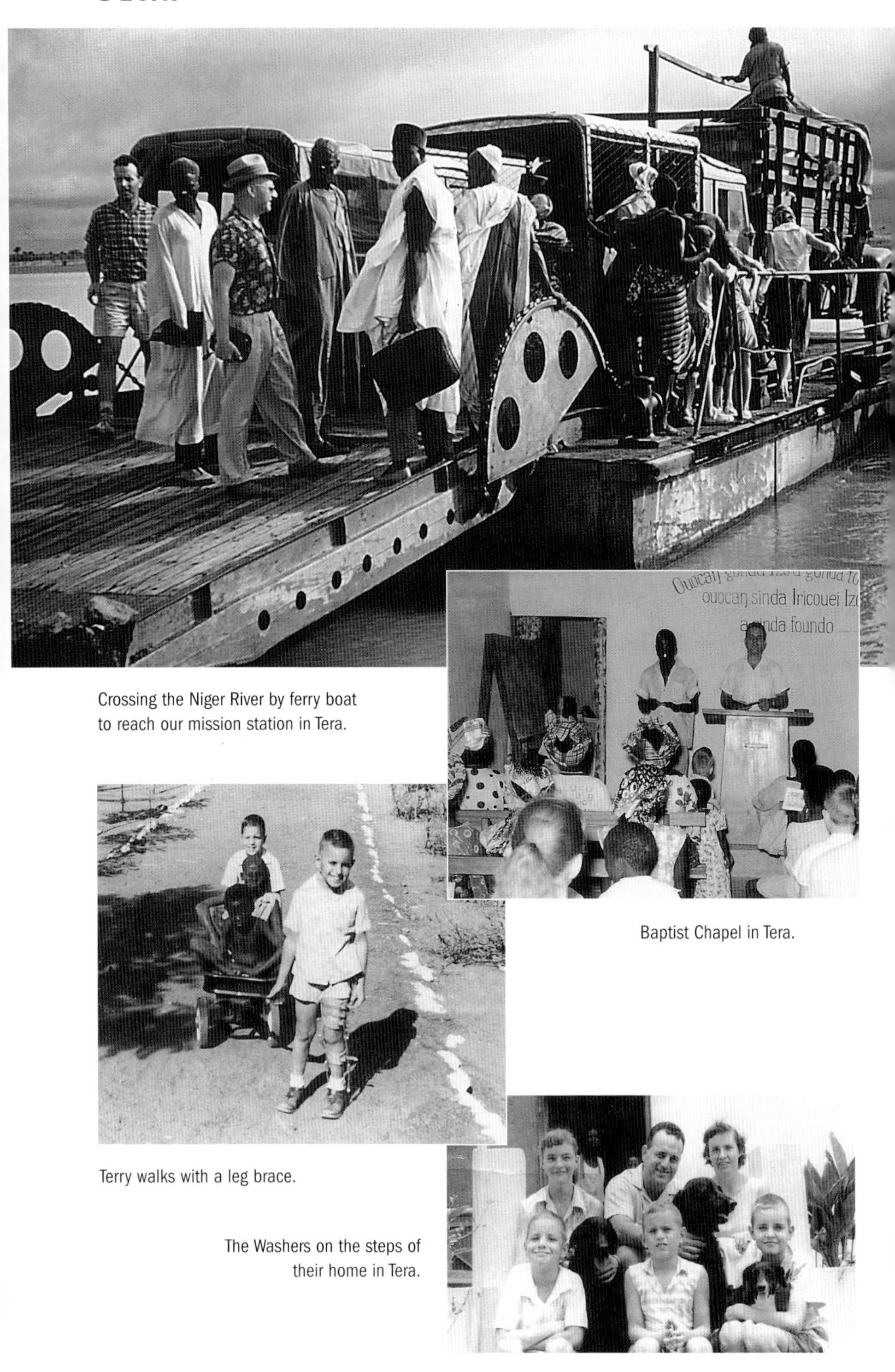

Crossing the Niger River by ferry boat to reach our mission station in Tera.

Baptist Chapel in Tera.

Terry walks with a leg brace.

The Washers on the steps of their home in Tera.

Trekking by horseback.

Dal baptizes Tchétchicouei in the Niger River.

Dal in a Muslim village.

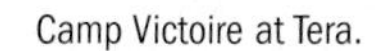
Camp Victoire at Tera.

Left:
Dal presents a diploma to Pastor Moses Oyinwola.

Below:
Three faithful pastors: Pastor Moses, Pastor Tchétchicouei, and Pastor David, Laya's future husband.

The Washer tribe with orphanage children.

Teaching Braille to blind Mousa.

croaking of the frogs mixed with the night bird calls, and sometimes a full moon shone as bright as day. One night as we watched the sky, Dal noticed one of the stars moving quickly across the sky. We saw it for only about an hour, as it flashed and blinked across the constellations. We realized later that we had been watching *Sputnik*, the first satellite to orbit the earth.

I was still benefiting from Helen Bechtel's cooking lessons when we lived in Tera. We would always start our meals with soup and then have another substantial dish like macaroni or meat. We ate a lot of meat—goat, lamb, and sometimes beef. We even had a grinder to make tough meat edible. I also made my own bread, and the children thought nothing was better than bread-making day, when I would serve hot bread with well-salted soup made from whatever I could get at the market. We felt French eating so much soup. In fact, the French word for soup (*soupe*) can also refer to a meal. Even with our deprivations, God answered my prayers, making my children healthy and strong.

Our pioneer-style life was made all the more happy when we did get something nice to eat. Every child on his birthday could choose one special thing from the market at Niamey. It might be a slice of ham or an apple, and this was in addition to his favorite cake. We enjoyed these times; they were pleasant exceptions to our normal diet. On Friday nights, I also tried to make something special to eat, since we set apart Fridays as family nights, when we played games and relaxed.

Though we were excited to live on the mission field, and though we have many pleasant memories of Niger, it was difficult to endure the extreme heat, sandstorms, and dry climate that allowed for little vegetation. There is no such thing as a creature comfort in Niger, and I found it especially hard to raise my family in such a harsh environment. But I would remind myself that Dal and I chose to go to that desolate land because the people there were living and dying in darkness, eternal darkness, and because they did not know that God sent His Son to die for their sins.

The most prevalent tree in Niger is the thorn tree, a short and stumpy tree that is flat on top, as if it had been cut by a landscape artist. Sometimes I would look at the trees and imagine them as symbols for our family. Animals like to eat the hard, oval leaves of the thorn trees and even their thorns. In a country where there are so few trees, it's a great blessing to have a few thorn trees here and there. We also were survivors, by the grace of God, making a home among Niger's people, culture, and climate. We stayed there eighteen years and, though it may not have seemed like we were making a difference, God used us to help those people who were willing to taste what we had to offer. The good news was as undesirable as thorns to many but, by God's grace, some found it to be their spiritual health and life.

Niger

Here is a picture of a bush woman,
her hair shaved far back on her head—
she looks almost as if she is balding.
She wears masses of jewelry—
her ears boast three huge bangles each,
and each bangle has another bangle hanging from it.
Metal bracelets circle her wrists and arms
and necklaces pile up on her chest.
She is working with fiber
and a trio of bowls lies in a sack at her feet.
She looks as if she is trying to say something.
But on the back of the picture is written,
"We have no one that speaks her language.
How will she hear of Christ?"

— ALISON GRAY

SHARING GOOD NEWS

Greater is He that is in you than he that is in the world.

— I JOHN 4:4

It did not take Dal long in Niger before he found his niche. His passion was to reach those who had never heard the gospel, and he was especially excited when he knew he was the first one to take the gospel to a village deep in the bush.

When he arrived in a new village, he would first introduce himself to the chief, greeting him with the proper salutations. Then he would sit down and ask permission to talk with the people. If the chief agreed to let his people hear about Christ, he would call his people to come together in their meeting place, a clearing outside. The women usually remained in their huts until the men sat down on grass mats. Then they would come and stand behind the men, curious to find out why this white man was in their village. It was only then, with the people gathered before him in the shade (if there was any shade), that Dal began to tell the people about Jesus Christ, or *Isa*, the Zerma name for Jesus. Since *Isa* was a common man's name, we used the name "Lord Jesus," or *Isa Almasihou.* We became known as the "Almasihou people."

Sometimes the village meetings went well. After one early visit, Dal described the experience:

> Last night there were five in our little group [who] went to Yantala for a little service. We had an accordion, flute and phonograph with Gospel records in their language. Many eagerly gathered around us with the chief in the center sitting on the ground. . . . It was interesting

> to notice how readily they admit they are sinners, experiencing for the most part no sense of guilt. The chief gave us four duck eggs as we left and thanked us profusely for coming. Now we are earnestly praying, as we continue these visitations to the villages, that the Lord shall bless the Word as it is given forth to the salvation of souls.

Soon after this visit, Dal ventured out alone to Goudel, a nearby village which had heard the gospel many times. He enjoyed himself immensely:

> As we live about one mile from one of the large native villages, I find it quite a joy to go down at night, sit around the fire, and read to them from God's Word. Also, as I am not too far along with the language, I use a phonograph with the Gospel message on it. Last night the men were all cooking one of their favorite dishes around the fire and they were very happy to see me. They ordered one of the boys to run and get a good mat for me to sit on. Then they listened eagerly to the Gospel message on the records. . . . I asked them at the finish if they believed this in their hearts and they all replied they did. Of course the Muslim always agrees, but they seemed more sincere last night than usual. One record was entitled "Why did Christ die?" and they were unusually quiet listening to this.

Often, however, the response was not so enthusiastic. In many villages there was a distinct restlessness and a hard shaking of heads when Dal told them that Jesus was God's Son. Some would start to debate with him and others would begin to leave the meeting, a few even spitting at his feet as they made their exit. With this distasteful gesture the Muslims showed their disgust at the very thought that Jesus was the Son of God. They could not tolerate such words, much less believe them. But Dal wasn't afraid of this hostility, though it bothered me sometimes to think of him in such an unfriendly environment.

Dal learned that he had to unfold the gospel message slowly, so people would not dismiss his words without consideration. The Muslim people cannot understand that Christ is God's Son unless they have learned many other things first. So Dal had to start by teaching the people that the Bible is the Word of God. Once he established the truth of the Bible, it was much easier to prove the doctrines within God's Word. One of the keys that unlocks the door to Muslim hearts is the doctrine of the forgiveness of sin. Muslims desperately want someone to forgive their sins, but in the Muslim religion, only good works can suffice. Many Muslims know that their works are not good enough to outweigh their sins. When God uses the key of forgiveness to unlock their hearts, they realize that a Savior was sacrificed so their sins could be forgiven.

In the area called the Tera Circle were 200 villages which had at least 100 inhabitants and another 200 villages with a population of over 50 people, totaling more than 37,000 people we felt responsible for. Dal believed these people had been imprisoned long enough in spiritual darkness. He was excited to be the first herald of the truth of Christ to them.

His method for spreading the gospel was to preach several times in a village to determine whether the people seemed open. If they were receptive, then he would start a Bible class to teach the Word of God to men and boys on certain evenings. If the Bible class was successful, some souls were saved and a cluster of Christians was formed, then he would begin holding a Sunday service in the village. Of course he couldn't do a Sunday service for every village every Sunday. A national Christian or another missionary would have to conduct some of the services. By using this method, Dal was eventually able to establish tiny churches in a few of the villages.

About once a month, Dal and another missionary or two would plan a long trek deep into the desert. They would usually take along some African workers who helped us operate our mission station in Tera, even if they were not followers of Christ, because the missionaries needed their support and knowledge to successfully make the journey. Preparations for a long trek included making sure each man carried enough food and water for the entire trip. If the travelers stayed overnight in a village, they could eat the villagers' food if it was offered, but it was safer to bring extra food and drink in case they were served such distasteful things as unpasteurized sour milk or beer.

I admired Dal for the determination that led him to the most remote Muslim villages. Even if villagers resisted and opposed him and his message, Dal was glad he could at least try to help them understand the love of God. Dal knew that Niger, though just a tiny dot in the great universe of God's creation, was dear to the Christ, who says, "Him that cometh to me I will in no wise cast out."

Dal found that one of the most powerful ways to reach a Muslim is to talk about the resurrection. He liked to tell the story of a missionary who spoke with a group of women. The missionary "told them how God loves them, and how the Lord Jesus laid down his life for them. Then he told them how the Lord Jesus arose from the dead, and is now a living God." The women replied, "The foreigner's god is better than ours. Ours has no life."

Aside from village ministry, the other important purpose for our time in Tera was to establish a Bible Institute to train young African men to learn the Word of God. It is a difficult task to start a church in Niger, much less see it continue. But when national pastors lead churches and take over the contact with the people, churches have a much better chance of growing and flourishing.

By 1957, our Bible Institute building and rooms for the students to live in were finished, and in May of that year Dal opened the school with four young men who had accepted Christ. Dal, the only teacher at Tera, faced many difficulties in training these young men in the Bible, because the majority of them had had no education. They had to learn to read first, and then advance to studying the Word of God. But, in time, they all finished their courses at our institute and became evangelists and pastors. Though most of them never saw their churches grow very large, they continued preaching the Word of God in order to win people to the Lord one by one.

When he was in Tera, Dal always conducted a Sunday service in our little mud brick chapel whose walls were painted with Bible verses in the Zerma language. Dal most often preached in French, using an interpreter to translate the message into Zerma. Dal knew Zerma and he preached in Zerma sometimes, but if he had someone to translate his French he felt more confident that he was saying exactly what he wanted to say.

We had very good attendance the first time we held a church service at our chapel in Tera. In a letter, Dal explained, "They all call me Priest, a name of high standing in Muslim circles." The Zerma word for priest, *alfaga*, is a name which showed that the Africans greatly respected Dal, though he was not a priest of Allah, but of the Savior, the Lord Jesus Christ.

As the years went by, twenty or thirty people attended the church services regularly. But not all of them were believers. In fact, the majority of them were probably not followers of Christ, though we hoped that the Holy Spirit was working inside them to draw them toward salvation. Children loved to come to the services but were forbidden by their families to come to the *Isa Almasihou* (Lord Jesus) church. If a child disobeyed and came anyway, a parent might come into the service and pull them out. I always felt sad for the children because I was sure they were beaten or punished for their disobedience. But I was also hopeful that the words they did hear ministered to their seeking souls.

Besides our regular attendees, there were some Yoruba traders from Nigeria who frequently came to our church services. Some may have been true Christians, but, for the most part, the Yoruba Christians still embraced traditional African ceremonies and worshiped God the way they wanted to worship Him, not the way He wanted to be worshiped. Nonetheless, we welcomed the Yoruba traders even though their beliefs were different from ours. We were happy for them to hear Dal preach the Word of God.

During the week, Dal often led a Bible study for boys in the area who were interested and able to attend. In hopes that some of them would come to know Christ, Dal spent time teaching the Bible and encouraging them to learn Bible verses. We attracted the boys to the Bible studies by means of "Fun Night," a frequent social occasion when our family played volleyball with the African young people, with a puppet show afterwards. We learned that of all the refreshments we could serve, popcorn would draw children from far and wide. African children like popcorn because it is unlike anything they have ever eaten. The young people would put their pots of kernels and oil on the coals, watching in amazement as the popcorn became hot and started to explode, filling up the whole pot. They never got tired of watching this "miracle."

Eventually, after we had lived in Tera for several years, we began our "Camp de Victoire." The Tera station was transformed into a campground where we prepared sports areas and built large grass huts for sleeping quarters. Missionaries from other stations came to help us with our camp, but even more encouraging was the fact that the African Christians in Tera took such a great part in running the camp.

Our camp soon became very popular with the African young people, especially because of the sports we offered. The kids could choose from football (soccer), volleyball, tetherball, shuffleboard, and boxing. We even taught kite-making in our handcraft classes. Kites amazed the African children, some of whom had never seen them before and called them "airplanes." Of all the camp activities, though, the favorite event which no one wanted to miss was the early morning hike to the top of an old red rock volcano. At the top, all fifty hungry hikers gathered around the cook fire to enjoy fried pancakes rolled in sugar. Our utmost desire in conducting "Camp de Victoire" was to see young people come to know Christ. Each year several decisions for Christ were made. We prayed that the young people would remember the messages on salvation and God's love and carry them back to their own villages.

Whenever Dal got a break between teaching and traveling, he made his way to the Tera market and set up tables under a temporary grass shelter so he could display tracts and sell portions of scripture. He also played Bible records in the

Zerma language. Dal taught all of our children to help him witness for Christ in the market. Through this ministry, hundreds of tracts were dispersed each month. These individual contacts, along with preaching in the villages, began to have a dramatic effect.

In August of 1963, we returned to Africa from a furlough in America. This time, we were not going to Tera, where we had been for eight years, but to Niamey, where Dal had been asked to replace Earl Watson as acting field director for the mission station in the capital.

It was exciting to live in a big city again after our many years in small villages. The country of Niger is shaped like a fish, and Niamey is on the tail of the fish. This big, bustling city is where the action in Niger is. To me, Niamey was like a great big flea market. Every morning hundreds of Africans arrive at the marketplace (a large open field), the women balancing great big bundles on their heads. Everyone is dressed up in colorful clothes for their day at the market, and they set up their wares in rows that stretch across the field as far as the eye can see. If they can afford it, some vendors build little shelters for their wares, while others sit on the ground in full sun with their goods spread out in front of them like offerings.

The market in Niamey was huge, selling anything from roasted rats, fried termites, and chicken, to dried fish, monkey meat, and caterpillars. There were also vegetable stands, though vegetables were expensive because they are so hard to grow in such a hot climate. But if I wanted a vegetable for a meal I could find eggplant, okra, and sometimes green beans. There were also tomatoes, though shriveled up and deformed. Tomatoes would never grow fat and lovely in Niger.

As I shopped, I came to enjoy putting on a dramatic display

of opposition to the Zerma salesmen and their outrageously high prices. *"Albarka!"* I would say. "Give me a good deal!" Africa would not be Africa without its markets. They are one of the biggest parts of African life, whether in a large city or a tiny village far back in the bush.

As field director, Dal's job was to make sure that missionaries had the materials and facilities they needed to carry on their ministries in Niger. He also had to learn how to be the middle man between missionaries and the government, since he was responsible for getting permission for any new programs, whether camps or building projects or schools.

Dal did a good job as field director. He knew how to make wise decisions, and his friendly, sociable personality served him well at all the American, German, and French Embassy receptions to which we were constantly being invited. Although Dal disliked all the political chitchat he had to endure at these social affairs, he knew it was important for him to be there as an ambassador for Christ. He became a good listener and was able to help the Niger missionaries meet many of their needs through friendships he had made with ambassadors and dignitaries.

Even in the midst of a hectic, changeful schedule, Dal encouraged me by his good example of focusing on Christ and God's Word. If I got up early enough in the morning, I would find him in the living room enjoying his early morning time with God. This sweet communion with the Lord was his fountain of strength, and he never missed it. I loved to see him kneeling by the sofa praying, a cup of coffee beside him on the table. For our entire married life together, he was always faithful about reading his Bible. I respected him and felt secure because of his dependence on God.

Dal knew how hard it was for me to get up and have a quiet

time in the Word. But instead of rebuking me or making me feel guilty, he would simply come into my room with a big cup of coffee and set it on the bedside table. Then he would kiss and hug me as if I were a beauty queen instead of bleary-eyed and fuzzy-tongued. He would call me his "Pretty Doll" until I was fully awake, and then he would get me to sit up so I could drink my coffee. He always said he needed five minutes of love in the morning to start his day off right. But another purpose of this routine was to get me awake and alert enough to read my Bible before the day's duties crowded in. I have never been spiritually encouraged in a sweeter way.

HEALING AND HOME

It is by loving and being loved that one can come nearest to the soul of another.

— GEORGE McDONALD

When the EBM board had first interviewed Dal and me, they were not looking for our willingness to obey their orders, but for our desire and determination to obey *God's* orders. We as missionaries were not given a list of things to accomplish in Yantala or in Tera. Instead, the field council in Niger would meet together every so often to discuss the needs that were present on the field. Then individual missionaries would act to meet those needs as the Lord moved them.

My general goal in Yantala, and then in Tera, besides caring for our children, was to contribute to the mission's objective: sharing the gospel and showing the love of Christ to the African people. Especially in Tera, a sense of great responsibility came over me as I realized I was the first white Christian woman there. I would look at the people at the market and feel amazed at the importance of the role I had been awarded by God to bring the gospel to these people.

The Muslim religious leaders, on the other hand, would not only prohibit their followers from believing in Christ, but would also mock and persecute Africans who chose to believe in Jesus Christ. New believers found it hard to continue peacefully in their new way of life. They might experience physical hurt, or lose their possessions or even their job.

For a few years at the beginning of our ministry, Niger was still a French colony, and France declared that Niger should peaceably allow white people to come into their country, with no protests and no fighting. The president of Niger, Hamani Diori, himself a Muslim, was a wise leader who wanted us to come and help the people. During Diori's presidency, the Muslims bowed to colonial command, and people would agree politely with missionaries. But for the most part, the Muslims refused to change their hearts for fear of their religious leaders. I felt somehow that the people wanted to know more about this Jesus but were not allowed to show interest in the white man's religion.

If we as missionaries helped the people in some way, whether by teaching them to read or through medical work, they allowed us to speak to them. As the years passed, I learned not to think of the whole population of Muslims living without Christ, but instead prayed that God would work on one person at a time. Though Islam is Satan's masterpiece in Africa, the strength of the Muslim religion made it that much more thrilling when a follower of Mohammed turned to follow Christ.

There was so much to do in Niger that I prayed God would show me where to start. I hadn't been in Yantala very long before I felt the Lord leading me to make friends with the Muslim women by helping them learn to read. By the 1950s, the government was encouraging and promoting literacy, even for females. Those who went to school were taught to speak and write in French, producing a new generation of French speakers instead of people who only spoke the tribal languages. The girls knew that a command of the French language would allow them to work and earn money.

However, though Zerma women wanted to learn to read, the Muslim culture permitted very few girls to go to school. Men kept the girls in their families from attending school because they felt that the women were needed in the home and in the fields, and to care for the children. They insisted that women did not need to be educated for the jobs they did at home. They believed education would only serve to change their way of life by causing women to be dissatisfied and tempting them to give up their responsibilities.

Once, as I was helping a woman learn to read while sitting in the doorway of her mud hut, our conversation turned to salvation. After I had explained salvation at some length, the woman asked, "Will you pray to your God and ask him to forgive my sins?"

"I do want to pray for you," I answered. "But God wants *you* to ask Him to forgive your sins."

She said, "But I can't follow Jesus."

"Why do you say that?"

"Because I am a woman," she replied humbly.

She did not say it, but I knew the real reason why she felt she could not believe in Jesus: her husband would not have allowed it. In fact, I was surprised that this woman had the courage to ask me to pray to God to forgive her sins. Muslim women rarely disclose what is really going on in their heart for fear of punishment. Everything is hidden. If they feel at risk, which they usually do, they will avoid telling their true feelings.

Unfortunately, this was just one of many instances in which I felt myself powerless against such ingrained beliefs and practices. I hated to drop the conversation, but I could sense it was over for the time being. I did my best to continue to share the love of Christ with my students in hopes that some would come to believe in Christ in their hearts, though they could never speak of it. Our foremost desire and goal in our literacy classes was to teach the people to read God's Word either in French or in Zerma, so they could know of the love that their Creator had for them.

As I used portions of the Bible to teach the women to read, I found that anything concerning a lamb was thought by the Zerma people to be a most beautiful illustration. They are familiar with sheep, as they keep all sorts of animals around them, even in their houses. If I had the chance after a Bible reading session, I would ask, "Will God let sin enter heaven?"

"No!" everyone would exclaim.

"So how do you get rid of your sin?" I responded. "God made a way to take away our sin. He sent a lamb, Jesus, to die for us as a sacrifice to take away our sins." I would have liked to point out that Mohammed could not offer his life as a sacrifice for the sins of the world, but we usually did not mention Mohammed or Allah as it would have caused the people to turn against us for insulting their religion. But even without referring to Mohammed, many times I could tell the women were thinking about Christ's sacrifice of Himself for them, and I could tell that it touched their hearts.

I had always been interested in medicine, even before I took any medical courses. Dal would jokingly accuse me of studying my *Merck Manual* more than my Bible. Every nurse or doctor will know what a *Merck Manual* is: a medical handbook that lists diseases and symptoms to help identify a person's cause of illness. The beautiful thing about a *Merck Manual*, besides the fact that it is readable by laymen with no medical degrees, is that it lists all sorts of exotic, contagious diseases that one might find in a place like Niger. Though medical things did not interest Dal, he was glad I was able to tend to the physical needs of the people and encouraged me to learn as much as I could. The government also encouraged us to do medical work as the need was so great.

Many years after we had come to the mission field, I was privileged to take some courses with Dr. John Dreisbach at

Bob Jones University while we were home on one furlough. But most of my practical training came from Helen Bechtel, who taught me everything she knew at the little dispensary on her back porch in Yantala. I was grateful to be able to show Christ's love by helping others when they were suffering or when they were sick.

One of the most common ailments at our dispensary was the tropical ulcer, a big open sore that can form anywhere on the body. Tropical ulcers start with an injury or small sore but can grow, eating away flesh and leaving an open, smelly wound. Poor nutrition and a lack of good medical care keep them from healing. Sufferers often came in with their sores covered with leaves or with old rags tied around them to keep flies away. The smell was overpowering. At first, I thought that to be a good nurse, I should open the dressing and clean out the sore for the patient. But after encountering a few sores with maggots in them and almost losing my lunch, I decided on a method that would work better for everyone. I prepared a place behind our dispensary with benches where people could sit and clean their own sores. I also kept a fire going where they could burn their old dressings. Then I would slather the wound with a concoction of Vaseline and ulcer powder and cover it with a bandage, usually strips of old sheets. Sometimes we ran so low on bandages that we had to ask our patients to wash their bandages and bring them back the next time.

Along with bandages, we sometimes ran out of prepared medicine for tropical ulcers, since they were such a prevalent problem. Helen taught me a trick for making medicine which she had learned from a retired missionary to China. We would boil soap with sugar, making a poultice to put on the sores each day. Our homemade medicine worked. Soon we saw the pink flesh coming in and the sores healing up nicely. As Helen wrote, "Those scars of healed ulcers opened many doors for witnessing in the villages throughout the years."

Any time I had left was spent caring for my household, my husband, and my children. Especially in Tera, a good part of my days went toward home schooling. Back in Algeria, I had started to teach little Luann using the Calvert course, the only home-schooling course available at that time. I continued using the course with each of my children until they reached high school age.

Several times while our children were growing up we experimented with different educational options to see if the children could receive their education elsewhere. For example, while we were in Yantala, one of our missionaries, Phyllis Bacon, started a Christian Elementary School. Luann and Laya were both included in the first class of students at the French school, which became one of the most successful ministries EBM began in Niger.

Later on, we sent Luann and Denny to the government school in Tera. We wanted Denny to be able to learn French as Luann had done back in Niamey. Denny was only six or seven years old, and the first several weeks of school he cried every morning. We practically had to drag him to school. But eventually he became much braver and was able to learn to read and write and speak in French. Luann also did well in school and enjoyed being with her friends who, after rubbing her arm several times to see if she was black underneath, welcomed her to take part in all their fun and games.

We were happy with the progress Denny and Luann were making until we found out about some of the customs at the government school. Though the students received a good education there, the method of punishment in the school would astound any PTA. If the teacher asked a question and a child did not know the answer, the next child who knew the right response got to slap the face of the child who answered incorrectly. If a child disobeyed or talked in class, the teacher would call him to the front and switch his fingertips very hard with a stick. For those who constantly misbehaved, the teacher would tell the other children to spit on them at recess to humiliate them. These harsh methods may work in Africa, but we did not like them at all. Furthermore, students made fun of Luann and Denny for following Christ. We decided it would be better for me to continue teaching our children at home.

We spent many a Christmas in the desert, where it was up to us to make our holiday merry. There were only a few Christians in our area, but we always threw a big party for the village children, giving them little gifts such as candy and popcorn. Then our family would put on a little play to entertain the children and tell them the story of Jesus coming to earth.

At home we put our imaginations to good use for decorations. One year we made a fake fireplace around a bookcase with red paper for bricks and a drawn-in fire. Another year we decided to make a Christmas tree out of a thorn tree, one of the only green things in Niger that vaguely resembled the real thing. Our thorn Christmas tree, propped up in a bucket of stones, didn't look anything like the traditional spruce trees back home. But to me it was very special because it pointed to Christ, who wore a crown of thorns the day He died on the cross to save us. After that first year, our thorn Christmas tree became a part of our Christmas celebration every year.

We always enjoyed exchanging gifts, even gifts such as flashlights or head scarves bought locally in the bush market.

One of our children's favorite gifts was peppermint candy. The peppermint balls were sold by African lady merchants who sat on the ground at the market and counted the candy balls over and over again, rolling them around in jars or on their colorful cloths and handling them generously as they chose five or ten for each customer. Dal and I thought it would have been wiser not to let our children eat the peppermint candy, heavily handled as it was, but it was one of their most anticipated treats. No one contracted a horrible disease because of a peppermint, so Dal and I joked that the peppermints must be strong enough to kill germs.

The best Christmas was the year that Moses Oyinwola, his wife, Abigail, and their baby joined us for the holidays. Moses was of the Yoruba tribe, and he had accepted Christ as his Savior while attending the mission church in Niamey. Moses had already received some education and was capable of the heavy-load classes required of a pastoral student. Abigail was a sweet Christian lady and a splendid cook, with a wonderful chuckle of a laugh. We all loved being around her because she made everyone near her feel happy and welcome. Her infant son, named Baby Sunday because of the day on which he was born, soon became the joy and delight of us all, especially Luann and Laya. They were thrilled to have a real live baby to take care of and carry around on their backs like an African mother would do.

Our life in the bush became much more exciting because of this lovely family that lived on our compound. And our Christmas that year was special as Moses and Abigail and Baby Sunday took part in our celebration as if they were our own family. It was sweet to have a little baby to buy gifts for, even though the gifts we exchanged were very small. It was a gift to share the season with friends who could, along with us, lift their faces to heaven and thank God for his precious Son, and for the wonderful gift of salvation available to all.

LIGHT IN DARKNESS

I will bring the blind by a way that they knew not;
I will lead them in paths that they have not known:
I will make darkness light before them,
and crooked things straight.
These things will I do unto them,
and not forsake them.

— ISAIAH 42:16

After a few months of working in the Yantala dispensary, I began to think about the blind people we treated. It bothered me that a number of them were young children who had been born blind or who went blind from disease or accident. They had only a life of hopeless darkness to look forward to. When I would shop at the markets in Yantala or Niamey, I saw countless blind people there who had turned to begging because they had no other way to provide for themselves. Sometimes the blind were elderly. But many were children who maneuvered through the market by holding on to one end of a stick while a sighted child held the other end.

On market day, these beggars sat by the road with their dishes held out, calling for money so they could buy something to eat. Beggars do relatively well in Muslim countries since almsgiving is one of the five pillars of the Muslim religion. However, most children who beg must turn over their "earnings" to older family members or "owners" who are supposed to supply their needs. Sometimes these owners take advantage of their wards and take more money than they should. But some of the children are clever and learn how to keep a significant amount of their money.

At first, I pitied these beggars and wanted to give to them, but I was also afraid because they would surround me if I gave anything to just one. After we had lived in Africa a while, I began to think about them as opportunities instead of nuisances. Then the Lord started burdening my heart for the blind.

My first efforts to reach them were simple: I began by talking to blind beggars at the market, trying to make friends with them. I wanted them to get to know my voice. I also invited them to come to a children's class or other church activities where they could hear the gospel. But I knew it was difficult for them to come, because they had to be brought and taken back by someone else. Also, they could be severely punished for attending a white man's religious service.

However, several young blind men began coming to our church to listen to the preaching. They were very intelligent and could memorize scripture just from hearing it. When I saw their hunger and thirst for spiritual things, I began to think, *Oh, how I wish they could read the Word of God in Braille!*

One day I asked some of the children, "Would you want to learn how to read if there was a way?" They were astonished that I could even imagine such a thing. "But, Madame, that is impossible! We are blind! We can't learn to read. You are making fun of us!" Of course, they had never heard of Braille. When I told them that it was possible to read with their fingers, they thought I was talking about magic. I finally convinced them that I was not pretending and promised I would teach them how to read. "You just wait and see," I said.

Every year we were in Niger, we traveled to nearby Nigeria for a little vacation and a break from the desert heat. Most missionaries in the arid parts of Africa must take some time each year to rejuvenate themselves physically and spiritually. We always anticipated our times in Jos, Nigeria, a town situated on a high plateau where the weather is much cooler than the surrounding area. The land there is fertile, with lots of green grass and many fruits and vegetables that we could not get in Niger. Best of all, our hosts served lots of rich whipped cream over a fruit salad of papayas, mangoes, or bananas to make luscious desserts we only dreamed of in Niger. We especially anticipated attending the mission church in Jos, where the wonderful preaching (in English) and good Christian fellowship always renewed our spirits.

There was also a very nice hospital nearby, run by the Sudan Interior Mission (SIM), where missionaries could receive excellent medical care and treatment. This hospital was important to us as both Dal and Denny broke bones one year by playing sports too vigorously. I learned that SIM operated a large blind ministry in Kano, Nigeria, where they offered a teacher-training course in Braille. I wanted to take the course, even though I would have to transfer to French and Zerma when I got back to Niger. So while my family was on vacation, I spent the month at SIM learning to read Braille with my eyes. The missionaries taught me the Braille alphabet and gave me books and tablets for use in teaching. The tablets enabled me to write lessons by slipping paper inside and then making indentations in the paper with a pointed stylus or, in French, a *poinson.* Small dots or bumps appear on the other side of the paper, creating Braille writing. The missionaries at SIM even gave me an alphabet on a metal plate because they knew it would be difficult to teach the alphabet on paper in Africa. If my blind children had to use their fingers to rub paper alphabets over and over again, pretty soon they would flatten them out or dirty them too badly to use.

That metal alphabet plate became a prized possession.

Besides all the training I received at SIM, I also learned a little about the Frenchman Louis Braille. When Louis was a child, he accidentally punctured one of his eyes while playing with a sharp tool his father used in leatherworking. The infection that resulted from the puncture wound spread to the other eye and little Louis found himself blind at four years of age. Though he was of course discouraged at being blind, he seemed to manage his discouragement well and was known for his patient and uncomplaining attitude. He received education from a local priest and decided he would make the best of his life.

Later, when Louis attended a school for the blind, he realized that the popular system of printing books for the blind in huge raised letters was a good idea in theory, but inefficient and expensive. He set out to create another system of printing for the blind that would be easier to read and cheaper to produce. Amazingly enough, the very tool that ruined Louis Braille's eyes is the tool God allowed him to use to make his new alphabet. With a pointed instrument quite similar to the awl used in leatherworking, Braille invented the simple system in which the *poinson* creates raised dots that are easily felt by the fingertips.

I admired Louis Braille because he sought to do something profitable despite his limitations. From Louis I learned that God puts into our hand the very thing that gives us pain so we may glorify His name. Whatever situation we find ourselves in, God has planned it from the beginning of time and He has a way for us to honor Him. From what we know of Louis Braille, he seemed humble despite his eye problems. Perhaps he even recognized Christ as his Savior. In any case, God allowed a tragic accident in Louis Braille's life to encourage him to create an alphabet that would open the Word of God to people who would otherwise never be able to read it. Because God used Louis Braille, I was able to teach African blind people to read the Bible.

I returned from Nigeria with my new equipment and my new knowledge, ready to work "magic" on my blind beggar children.

When I arrived home I set up all my Braille teaching equipment in our little chapel so it could double as a classroom. I knew the blind children I would be teaching knew street French, like *"Donnez moi cinqs francs"* or "Give me five francs," but they could not speak French fluently. So I decided to begin by teaching them Braille in their tribal language, Zerma. But nobody had put Zerma into Braille, so before I could start teaching I first had to create a Zerma Braille alphabet. Fortunately, Zerma does not have as many variations as some other languages, though it has a few "strange" sounds. We were thankful that the New Testament had already been translated into Zerma, so we could use it as a resource.

Although creating a new alphabet may sound like a difficult task, it was not tremendously hard. Louis Braille developed an extremely simple cell system of dots. Six dots are possible in each cell. Some letters may have only one dot, some will have two dots, and so on. In Braille, it is possible to create 64 different letters or characters from only six dots. The system is sufficient to make an alphabet of any language. It can also be used to represent arithmetic numbers and figures as well as musical notes. Another advantage to Braille is that "A" is "A" in every language. So, there is no need to recreate dot combinations for the first 26 letters of any alphabet. The only new combinations I needed were for the few strange letters in Zerma.

Once I felt confident teaching Zerma in Braille, I gathered

together some blind boys I knew from the market and brought them to our little chapel to start Braille classes. What I didn't realize was that I would need to start by teaching the children the difference between left and right. Some of my blind students had been born blind and had difficulty understanding that the Braille cell has two sides: dots 1, 2, and 3 are on the left side and dots 4, 5, and 6 are on the right. To teach my students to recognize the location of the dots, I started them with little pieces of wood drilled with holes in the configuration of Braille cells. The students could put their fingers into the holes in the piece of wood to better comprehend the two sides of the Braille cell and where the six dots can be. Being able to feel on a larger scale what their fingertips would later recognize with ease helped the students to form a picture of the Braille cell in their minds, though they would never see it with their eyes.

In more eminent blind schools, teachers use pretty, round marbles to act as the dots on the wooden block, but I found that more common rough stones do not roll away from blind students like smooth marbles do. So I made a rule that each child had to bring six stones to class every day. This way we were not constantly losing marbles.

I was overjoyed to see how fast my students caught on. After they learned the Zerma alphabet, I was soon able to work with them on simple exercises in writing and reading. I wrote many of these exercises by taking a verse or a phrase from the Zerma Bible and writing those words in Braille. Though my lessons were basic at first, my boys had good minds and absorbed anything I gave them. I had my work cut out for me just keeping up with them.

After a while, I wanted my blind boys to get a real education. So I switched from Zerma to French Braille and ordered a series of books called *Les Six Points,* or *The Six Dots,* which was just like the primers young readers read. My students studied the Braille letters for French until they could read and write well in French. I also taught them typing, using some old portable manual typewriters that we had fixed up with Braille signs on the keys. After teaching them to keep their hands in position on home base by using drops of clear airplane glue on those keys, I could eventually take the Braille signs off the keys. All my students learned to be good typists.

I taught some of the boys for a long time, until I realized I had taught them all I knew. They had no trouble with either Zerma or French and wanted more and more to read. I considered buying more French books, but then I realized they could be taught over in Nigeria. So when I had taught them as much as I could, I signed them up to attend the Bible Institute for the Blind in Nigeria, where they were taught in English. This was a great advantage for them because they were able to get a good college education while participating in Christian circles, reading the Bible, and hearing good Bible preaching. One of these students from the Bible Institute went for further education in England and was admitted into law school, where he studied law in Braille. When he came back to Niger, the government used him in their legal offices, and he became well respected as a great asset to the country.

Although I was proud of my students and their successes, my goal was not just to expand their earthly horizons by teaching them to read. As Isaiah 42:16 says, I wanted to *bring the blind by a way that they knew not; . . . lead them in paths that they have not known; . . . make darkness light before them, and crooked things straight.* I wanted them to know the love of Christ, who, when He was here on earth, healed blind people who called for help. I wanted them to have the hope that their sight would one day be restored by

Christ. I wanted them to accept God's gift of salvation so that one day in heaven they could look into the face of Christ with their own eyes.

My work with the blind was also rewarding because it gave our mission a good name in the eyes of the Muslim government, which supported any effort to help the people of Niger. After Dal was appointed field director of the EBM Niger work and we moved to the mission house in Niamey, I resumed teaching blind students a few at a time. One day, as I worked with several boys on my porch, a government official visited our mission to see what we were up to. He was simply flabbergasted that blind boys were reading with their fingers. He had never seen Braille, and it was like magic to him, just as it seemed to the blind children at first. This official approached me and told me he was so impressed that he was going straight to the president of Niger, Hamani Diori, to tell him the amazing story of how sightless people could be taught to read.

Soon afterwards, I received an invitation from President Diori to come to the palace. "Bring your students this afternoon," his message said. "I want to see what you are teaching them." By the time I received the message, my blind students had already returned to their villages on the outskirts of the city, so we hurried to find them. We helped them get a quick bath and provided them with clean clothes to wear. We even shined them up with Vaseline to make their skin bright and polished, rather than parched and dusty.

When we arrived at the president's elegant mansion, an attendant ushered us into a room where we could set up our demonstration. Dal helped me carry all the typewriters, Braille writers, and reading books that each boy would use. I was so proud of my boys. They were not afraid in the least to

Clockwise from top:
A blind student types on a typewriter.

The president of Niger, Diori Hamani.

A blind student reads Braille for the president.

Learning Braille letters using a wooden block with six holes and six stones.

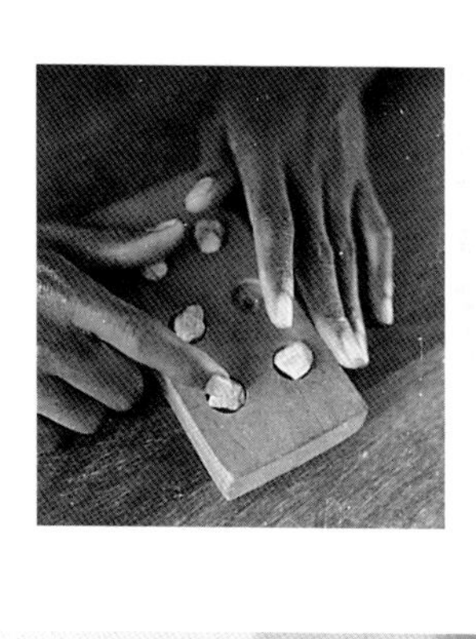

Muslim Day of Prayer in Niger: 20,000 pray at the end of Ramadan.

The imam, or Muslim priest, directs the Day of Prayer events.

A grenade is lobbed by a political enemy.

President Johnson and Ladybird invited President and Madame Diori (right) to the White House.

Laya as a bride.

Pastor David and Laya with their four children, Evodie, Timothé, David, and Prisca.

ABWE survey team.

Mother Weber joins the family in Greenville, SC.

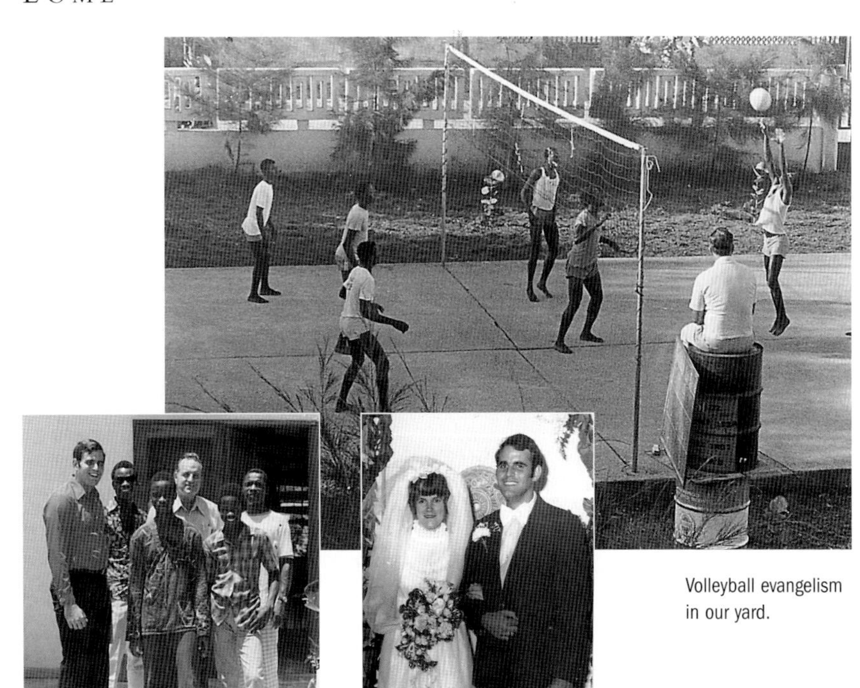

Volleyball evangelism in our yard.

Arrival in Lomé, Togo. Terry and Dal with first Togolese friends.

The wedding of Terry Washer and Sandra Fields in ~~our~~ home.

An early Togolese baptism in the ocean.

perform for the president. When President Diori entered the room, we all stood up to honor him, even the blind boys, whom we prompted at the proper time. My boys had hardly started their demonstration when the president became so excited that he called his aides to come and see what the boys could do. All the ministers sat around President Diori, and I was pleased to see their faces light up with interest as my students gave their presentation.

The first few boys read from the Bible in the Hausa, French, and Zerma languages, demonstrating how they lightly touched the letters with their fingers in order to read them. I chuckled at the amazement of the ministers, who had trouble believing that blind people could read from paper. Our next performer typed on a Perkin Brailler machine, which produces Braille text; and then another student wrote on a Braille tablet. The last boy typed a short French phrase on a conventional typewriter. After he typed, he read his note out loud to the president: *"Bonjour, Monsieur le President. Nous sommes enchantés d'être avec vous!"* or, "Good day, Mr. President. We are honored to be with you!"

We all felt honored that President Diori would be so interested in what we were doing. When my students had finished their demonstration, the president thanked me for coming and told me what a great hope this was for the blind people of Niger. Then he reached down into the front pocket of his long, flowing *boubou*, the robe that Muslims wear, and pulled out a thick roll of money. He peeled off several 5,000 franc notes, one for each boy. They were incredibly excited, for 5,000 francs was worth $25 in those days, more money than they would see in a whole year. As we left, the president thanked us again and told us he would like to help us so we could continue to teach his people.

I never felt led by God to start a blind school in Niger, though I continued teaching several students at a time during our ministry in that country. But I will always remember how sweet it was that President Diori offered to support me in starting a school. He seemed to be a very kind and gentle man.

ATTEMPTED ASSASSINATION

It makes no difference where He places me or how.
That is rather for Him to consider than for me;
for the easiest positions He must give me grace,
and in the most difficult, His grace is sufficient.

— HUDSON TAYLOR (Inscribed by Dal in his Bible)

When we lived in Niger, the missionaries on our field council asked for a documentary film to show their supporting churches so the people in America could see what our ministry was like. We also wanted to show what the African people looked like, how they lived, and what they did for work.

Though we sensed the great need for a documentary, we could not afford to hire professional photographers or filmmakers. I had done some photography work before, but only as a hobby. When we came back to the States on furlough one year, and my children were going to school in Greenville, S.C., I thought, *If I went to school and took some courses in photography and cinema while we're home on furlough, I could take some of the footage for the Niger film project!*

So I signed up for my first filmmaking course at Bob Jones University, and on each successive furlough I took more and more film and photography courses. Eventually, Dal bought me a very fine 16mm movie camera with a turret lens that could switch from telephoto to wide angle. This was the sort of camera press cameramen had used during World War II.

One year at school, I worked on the film *Flame in the Wind.* All cinema students were given assignments to work on props or to make things for sets on the sound stage. The assignment I am best remembered for was a disturbing scene where recently tortured Christians are lying in straw, surrounded by rats crawling over their bodies. The rats we used were actually white lab rats. Mrs. Stenholm, the director, said that since I was from Africa, I would not be afraid to handle the rats. So with great bravado I agreed to figure out how to turn white lab rats into brown wild rats. With huge gloves on my hands and a bucket of dye, I reached into the cages and caught a rat. Holding him firmly I baptized him in the dye, repeating the immersion until he was the correct color of a wild rat. I soon had cages full of brown rats. On the set we learned by trial and error that if we put females on the set first with a little food, we could release the male rats and know exactly where the males would run for optimum film quality.

In 1959, we were back in Niger, and the mission launched an evangelistic crusade. A floating mission station would sail down the Niger River for the first time, and our mission airplane was going to fly in and meet the boat on its maiden voyage. I was not a graduate in cinema yet, but I did know how to run my camera. So I decided to film the event from the airplane. The door was removed from the Cessna and I was strapped down on the airplane floor so I could lie on my stomach, looking down out of the airplane, to film the countryside of Niger and the boat going up the river.

I never would have attempted something so dangerous had Dal advised me not to. But he never kept me from doing something just because it was dangerous. In fact, Dal was on the boat while I was in the airplane. He had told me, "Now, if you fall out of the airplane, just drop the camera so I can get it safely on the boat."

The field council had wanted the film to introduce viewers to Hamani Diori, the president of Niger. While we lived in Niamey, I watched for good opportunities to film him, and one such opportunity occurred in 1965. Muslims in Niamey gather annually for the Day of Prayer, marking the end of Ramadan. Twenty-thousand men gather in a field outside the city, bringing their sons with them. Women come as well, although they sit in the back.

I had heard about this holiday, and also that President Diori would be at the Day of Prayer with his people. So I got out my camera and tripod, and I prepared to go. I even checked with the *Sureté*, the police department, who gave me a permit to take pictures and film the event. I couldn't have known beforehand that flying strapped to the floor of a Cessna was only moderately dangerous compared to filming the president of Niger on the Day of Prayer.

At the time, there was significant political trouble in the country. Enemies of the state were trying to overthrow the president, and there were many coups in those years. So precautions for presidential security had reached a high point. Just before President Diori's arrival, his guards picked up his prayer rug and shook it, searching through the sand for potential hazards, I suppose. Finally, the president arrived along with his sons, their limousine open to the sky. The family was surrounded by a bevy of security guards who let the president out of the car and then followed him as he walked to his prayer rug.

Hamani Diori looked solemn and distinguished in his Muslim robes and his white turban. He also had a golden band, indicating that he had visited Mecca. As he stepped onto his rug, he looked up and recognized me, so I knew he was aware of my filming. He took off his shoes as all Muslims do at prayer and, sitting sideways on his prayer rug, he pulled his prayer beads out of his *boubou* (robe), ready to recite the 99 names of Allah. But when he looked down at his feet, he realized that there was a big hole in the toe of his sock. As I twisted my telephoto lens to zoom in on the sock, the president reached down, surveying me with one eye, and tucked his sock under his toes.

The Day of Prayer begins by reciting the names of Allah while fingering prayer beads. Muslims in the Niger recite 99 names of Allah, because they say that only the camel knows the 100th name of God. The story goes that Mohammed whispered it in the ear of the camel long ago, and the camel has never told the secret. But I like to think that the 100th name of God, the one the Muslims do not know, is the name of Jesus Christ, our Savior.

As we all waited for the ceremony to start, I pointed my camera out over the crowd and panned slowly from one side of the field to the other. It was an amazing sight to see all those Muslims in their pale robes and turbans. What a pity, I thought, that they all gathered here to pay homage to the wrong person.

When the men had finished with their prayer beads, the imam, the Muslim priest, stood up to lead the prayers. I was situated very close, probably within fifteen feet of him. He gave the call to prayer over the loudspeaker so all could hear: "Let us all stand and make ready to pray." Just as he was about to begin, I realized I had to change my film. I tried desperately to change the film quickly, but I knew I wouldn't be able to complete the switch by the time prayers started. I was afraid I would miss the most important part of the whole day so, almost without thinking, I called out to the imam. *"Betu, . . . kana tilas ai gaba ka pepa berme"* (Wait a minute, I need to put more paper in my camera!), I said. Believe it or not, the imam listened to me and held up the entire cere-mony long enough for me to change my film.

I can still hear the eerie noise 20,000 men made praying at

once in Arabic. The imam, in a singsong voice, would call out a phrase, and then the crowd would repeat his words in perfect unison:

Allahu akbar.
God is great.
Annishhad innala illahu il Alla.
We witness that there is no God but Allah.
Annishhad inna Mohammadu rasul Illah.
We witness that Mohammed is the prophet of Allah.
Hayya alla salatu, hayya alla il falatu.
Come to prayer, come to the opening.
Assalatu abil il naumi.
Prayer is better than sleep.
Allahu akbar.
God is great.
La illaha il Allahu.
There is no God but Allah.

Several times during the creed, everyone lifted their arms in the air slowly and then lowered them. There was a constant wave of motion as hands moved gracefully up and down. It was at this point that a political enemy of the president's chose to make his move. He was in the back of the crowd but had situated himself directly behind the president. His plan was to lob a grenade over the people's heads, making it land on the president's rug. As everyone lifted their hands, he pulled a grenade out of his pocket and slid the pin out. But just as he swung his hand up, his arm got tangled in his robe, and instead of lobbing the grenade forward, he threw it sideways.

Everyone heard the explosion immediately. In my viewfinder I saw a burst of sand fill the air. The people panicked, but the imam commanded them to continue praying. He called out, "Get back in line! Pray, pray, pray." But people could only say, "Bomb, Bomb, Bomb!" The chant soon spread over the entire field, and people panicked, streaming off the field and scattering everywhere. But I stayed where I was, with my camera lens focused on the president.

To my right, I saw a group of people struggle past, carrying a man who had been hit by the grenade. He was bleeding profusely. Then another man went by, carrying a young boy across both his arms. The boy had also been hit by the grenade, and it must have caught him in his chest, which was drenched with blood.

Until this point, I was not especially frightened. I wasn't upset or shaking. It was almost as if I was not really there, as if the horrible sights were just part of a scene being acted out in front of me. The lens kept me at a distance. All I knew was that I had to keep filming. We were taught in film class that during an important event or historic moment you must keep filming, whatever the cost.

As soon as they could, the president's ministers circled around him reaching into the deep front pocket of their *boubous* to pull out their long-barreled handguns. In a manner that seems comical in retrospect, the president kept thrusting his head through the robes of his ministers or peeking through their legs, trying to see what was going on.

All of a sudden, camouflaged military men surrounded the place. Over the loudspeaker a soldier barked, "Everybody sit down! Anyone who moves will be shot." So everybody tried to sit down in the field, though they were extremely afraid. Police flooded the rows of people, jerking men up and searching their deep pockets for hidden guns or other weapons. Several times they pulled a man to his feet and ripped his clothes roughly. Eventually, a limousine came to remove the president and his sons from danger.

Denny was with me through the whole ordeal. I knew he loved to work the camera just as much as I did, so I said,

"Denny, here's another camera to use!" It was an amateur movie camera that belonged to a missionary friend. I told Denny to go shoot another scene. I was not worried about his safety because I could still see him, and he remained behind the barriers that separated the Muslim crowd from the European visitors and media. Denny discovered that the police had caught a man and were putting him on a truck. This man was the rebel who threw the grenade. He had been recognized as a member of the Sawaba Party, the group trying to overthrow the government. After ripping his clothes off, the police found another grenade, along with a gun, a dagger, and poison. He was insisting loudly that he had some medicine which, if swallowed, would turn him into a cat. The police disregarded his claims and continued beating him on the truck bed, while Denny, just thirteen years old, got it all on film.

Finally, things began to calm down. I stopped filming because I had gotten everything I could. When I had nothing else to do but wait, my mind began whirling with overdue worries: *Oh, I know they're going to take my camera and—oh no! They might even put me in jail!* The fact is, in Africa, the government can do anything it wants to do.

Dal was supposed to come pick us up, but he didn't know what was going on. So I waited, not knowing how I would get out, and the warning, "Anyone who moves will be shot," was still in effect. As I waited anxiously, a policeman came up and poked me in the shoulder, saying, "We want you to get on that truck there and go into town." I let out a deep sigh. I just knew they were going to take my camera, dispose of all my film, and then send me right to jail.

The police put Denny and me in a truck along with all our camera equipment. Then they took us to the corner by the mission in downtown Niamey. I couldn't believe it. Here I was at home, all in one piece, with my son *and* my film! I was so thankful. The first thing I did was to call the American Embassy. In a shaky, stuttery voice I said, "Can I t-t-talk to the ambassador? I n-n-need to talk to the ambassador. I was at the D-D-Day of P-P-Prayer!" When they finally understood me, they told me to stay right where I was. The entire city was under alert by this time, and they realized I was in no state to travel anywhere. So the Embassy sent a group of men down to see me. Only afterwards did I realize they were probably from the CIA. They sat me down on my couch and said, "Now, Mrs. Washer, you tell us who was standing next to the president." I was so flustered that I said, "I'm sorry, but I don't remember where anyone was standing!" I could not give them any report, but I told them that if they watched my film, especially the panoramic shot I took at the beginning of the day, they could see everyone and who was standing by whom.

The ambassador called me back later and said the Embassy wanted to take my film and send it to America to be processed. "How much do you want for your film?" he asked. I said, "Well, this film belongs to my mission—I was supposed to make a film—so I can't just give it away." The ambassador laughed and said, "Madame, we will make copies. Just give us permission to make copies."

"Oh, I see. You can make copies!" I still didn't understand what he was asking.

He said, "Well, what do you want for your film?" Of course he was talking about money, but I didn't catch on. I was unaware that my film was worth any money.

And I said, "I want two copies. And I need my original back. I have to have my original."

The Embassy took my film and sent it to Washington, D.C., with a courier. Copies were made there, and then the courier brought the film back to Africa. When the American ambassador received it, he called me and said, "Madame, we would like for you to come down to the Embassy and splice your film together so that we can project it." Fortunately, the Embassy had arranged for a smart young man to help me with the equipment that was provided. It took us awhile to splice the film because I had used several rolls at the Muslim ceremony. After we finished, the Embassy looked at it and decided they needed to show it at the president's palace. They invited the ambassadors, the military officers, and the police to come to the president's palace to see the film. They invited Dal and me to come as well.

Connected to the president's palace was a large terrace on the edge of the Niger River. It was a beautiful spot for gatherings, and as we arrived that evening we admired all the intricate stonework and the faintly rough stone floors. We had been to the palace for other receptions, when hundreds of people would gather on the terrace for *mishoui*, or lamb roasted on a spit.

We all stood when the president entered the terrace. He announced that, as part of the program that night, I would be projecting the film I took on the Day of Prayer. At the appointed time, the projector was started by the young man from the Embassy. The minute the opening panoramic shot lit up the screen, some police in the audience jumped up and said "Wait! We haven't got that one yet! We didn't get that one! Stop!" They could not identify the people fast enough. I rewound the film and rolled the first panoramic shot again and again until the police and government ministers identified all the people they possibly could. Once they pointed out those they felt were in the rebel group, they quieted down and watched the rest of my film.

After it ended, the president thanked me, saying, "Madame, you are a very brave woman. We want to thank you for your courage." He paused, and I saw an amused glint in his eye. "My photographer ran and hid behind a truck!"

A few months later, the American Embassy informed President Hamani Diori that President Johnson had invited him to America as his guest. Johnson wanted to celebrate the protection of President Diori and his ministers. By the time he was invited to the White House, we had come home to Greenville on furlough. We were honored to receive invitations from both the Niger Embassy and the U.S. Embassy to be at the White House when President Diori arrived.

We drove to Washington, D.C., and were met at our hotel by Esper Ajaj, a fellow EBM missionary and an Arab by birth, who was working with Muslims in Washington D.C. He drove us to the White House, and we waited in the lobby where we had to show our IDs and invitations before we could receive our name tags. Finally we were ushered into the garden. From our seats we could watch the greeting ceremony unfold as President Diori and his wife landed in their helicopter.

I decided to use my ever-present camera to capture the historic meeting of two presidents. At first, the White House security guards gathered around, asking, "What are you doing? Why are you filming?" I tried to give them a simple answer: "I'm from his country, Niger. I know him well."

The dignitaries and their escorts walked right past us down the aisle between the benches. But after President Diori had passed us, he must have realized who he had just seen. He stopped, turned around, and said, *"Bonjour, Monsieur, Madame!"* The entire procession came to a halt, even President Johnson. Hamani Diori shook Dal's hand, expressing his pleasure at seeing us. Then he brought his wife forward and she and I exchanged greetings in Zerma. We shook hands and said one greeting, then drew our hands back to our chests, then shook hands again with another greeting. The security guards and the Johnsons must have been puzzled to hear us jabbering in our own language. But Dal and I and the Hamanis were so excited to be speaking our African language and practicing our African customs that we didn't notice what was going on around us. Later, Dal said I was so excited to see President Diori that I forgot to shake President Johnson's hand! But I know I did. Dal was just joking.

We stayed in a fancy hotel near Pennsylvania Avenue and went to all the dinners. One was at the Senate building, and others were at hotels. I remember one evening reception in particular because the rooms were so ornately decorated and the tables were heaped with all sorts of elegant *hors d'oeuvre.* Shrimp were hanging on little trees and there were ice sculptures all over the place. Before or since, I have never seen such a beautiful banquet.

Several years later, I scaled down the massive amount of material I had about Niger and put together a film I called *Thirsty Land.* It explored the mission field in Niger, highlighted the landscape and the people, and emphasized the great need to reach the lost souls there. I added a brief section from my Day of Prayer footage to demonstrate the possibility of political problems in Niger. After making my film, I was eligible to graduate with a degree in cinema, which I did in 1971.

The Niger missionaries eventually gathered enough footage to make their own film. They used footage from many different sources, including some of my scenes, to make an interesting, almost journalistic, film that featured many personal conversations with the people. It was used as an educational tool in America and as an evangelistic tool in Niger. The dreams of the missionaries to have a film were finally realized, and the work that God was doing in Niger was at last documented to encourage and inspire the next generation of missionaries.

LAYA'S WEDDING

Being confident of this very thing,
that he which hath begun a good work in you
will perform it until the day of Jesus Christ.

— PHILIPPIANS 1:6

In the years since she had come to live with us, Laya had developed into a lovely young lady. She had smooth, milk chocolate skin and wide-set eyes. When she smiled, you could tell she was a little shy. Muslim men began to notice her, attracted to her external beauty, but I believe also to her inner beauty, which they did not recognize as the Holy Spirit. Laya had decided early on that she would not marry a Muslim. She did not want to be forced back into Islam, nor did she want to be one of many wives.

Ever since Laya had accepted Christ, her life was different. She wanted to take part in everything we did as missionaries and at church. She especially loved teaching Sunday school to the little children. This became an important part of her life, and while we were in Tera she traveled to Yantala and Niamey to teach special classes and workshops. When she was sixteen years old, she began working at the orphanage in Goudel.

While she was in Goudel, Laya attended church at the Evangelical Baptist Church in nearby Niamey. The Sunday school director there was a young man named David Allagbada. David came from the Nagot tribe, which lives on the West African coast, mostly in Benin. The Nagot are known for their good minds and their tall, slim build. Many are elite business people or well-educated teachers. One day in 1957 David accepted Christ after hearing about salvation, and the next year he was baptized in the Niger River. As it happened, Laya was also baptized there that very same day.

Soon afterward, David began taking night classes and correspondence classes. He also taught at the nearby French elementary school in Goudel during the day. The school employed only Christian teachers who taught the traditional disciplines along with Bible verses and Bible songs. Amazingly, the Muslim community supported the school because it had an honorable academic reputation.

During the summertime when school was out, David traveled up to Tera with missionary helpers to assist Dal in children's camps. Laya also helped with these camps, and I am sure her time spent in Tera continued to develop the relationship with David that had begun in Niamey. However, I was never conscious of them being together. Even if I had seen them together, I probably would not have encouraged them, because I was uncertain whether their two tribes were allowed to intermarry.

At one Niamey youth conference, Laya taught Bible visuals along with songs and verses, and David continued to watch her. One day he walked into her classroom and said, "Laya, I wanted you to know that I'm asking the Lord if I can marry you." Laya ducked her head shyly and then said, "And I am asking the Lord if I can marry you."

Shortly after this conversation, David wrote us a fine letter asking us if he could marry Laya. We had been impressed with David when he visited us in Tera. We sensed that he had dignity and the natural instinct to be a leader. We also knew his good business sense would serve him well as a pastor.

By the time we saw Laya again, she was talking about whom she would choose as bridesmaids and what she wanted her wedding dress to be like. I was surprised when she said she wanted a white dress for her wedding just like a missionary lady. I wasn't sure where we would get white fabric. Compared to Laya's faith in me, my faith in God to help me find the dress was quite puny. Yet God had already prepared to meet Laya's desire. Years earlier, when I was in America, a wealthy interior decorator friend, Mrs. Scribner, had given me a bolt of white satin with little flowers embroidered in it. She had wanted me to use it for drapes, but I couldn't bring myself to do that because it would get so dirty in our dry climate. It was still wrapped in plastic in one of our barrels. When I got it out, Laya was thrilled. "This is perfect!" she said, her eyes sparkling. "This will make a beautiful dress!"

Laya wanted a fitted gown in the European style, so we found a woman in Niamey to sew the dress. The only thing we lacked was a veil. Fortunately, we had an abundance of mosquito netting, which we edged with pretty ribbon. Dressed in curtain fabric, with her veil of mosquito netting, Laya looked like an exquisite flower on her wedding day.

Though we had given our blessing to David and Laya, it was of course necessary for Laya's Muslim family to approve the match as well. So David traveled out to her village alone to gain her family's approval. He talked with Laya's mother (her father had died) and her family, who agreed to the marriage. However, just before the wedding, some of Laya's relatives sent word that Laya would not be allowed to marry David because a young Muslim priest wished to marry her. Messengers from her village threatened to take Laya back with them if she insisted on marrying David. They even sat in the church compound near our house and recited Muslim prayers all day long, insisting that we stop the marriage. But God protected Laya so she could obey His will and marry a Christian. Though our nerves wore thin with the presence of the messengers, we knew David had already received permission from Laya's mother and her family, so we believed we were in the right.

The day of the wedding was spent decorating the church yard in Niamey, since we planned to have an outdoor reception after the wedding. Even though it was the hot season of the year, Laya had an abundance of beautiful flowers. According to a sweet African custom, guests brought flowers to the wedding in tin cans, pots, and baskets. That day, as I sat in our church and watched our African daughter married in a Christian ceremony, I rejoiced that the Lord had brought her to us. Dal and I were especially thankful that Laya's family did not cause any problems or disturbances. Not long after, her mother sent a goat as a wedding present for the newly married couple.

Several months after their wedding, Laya watched proudly as David was ordained by the church at Niamey. David then took a job with Sudan Interior Mission as a writer for their magazine *The Champion*. SIM held great respect for David and Laya, and the editors of the magazine arranged for one cover of *The Champion* to feature a picture of Laya herself, while an article inside gave her testimony. It was rare in Africa to see young Christians who kept their lives pure and dedicated to God, especially youth who came from Muslim backgrounds like Laya did.

Laya and David lived in Nigeria for three years until God brought a church-planting work their way. Earle and Winkie Watson, whom Laya had stayed with in Niamey, were starting a work in Dahomey (present-day Benin) and invited David and Laya to work with them in their current work in Cotonou, the capital. While in Cotonou, David and Laya raised four children—Evodie, Priscilla, Timothie, and Daniel—all of whom have accepted Christ as their Savior. When the Watsons moved, David became the pastor of the church in Cotonou.

I look back on how God brought Laya to us, and I marvel at how much He has done in her life since then. He has made her into a godly woman, given her a godly husband, and helped her raise children who will glorify the Lord. Our family was so blessed to take part in God's work in her life. As David said, "Our road has passed by some moments that were difficult but the Savior has held us up. We give praise and thanks to God for this."

LONG FURLOUGH

Of his bounty, the Lord often grants not what we seek, so as to bestow something preferable.

— ST. AUGUSTINE

In 1961, when Luann turned fifteen years old, Dal and I began to think seriously about our children's higher education. There were no high schools for missionary children in Niger, and the nearest secondary school was at Bouacké, in the Ivory Coast. And political trouble was brewing in the Ivory Coast.

A number of our fellow missionaries had sent their children to Ben Lippen Academy in Asheville, N.C., and everyone we talked to assured us it was a wonderful place for missionary children. Dal and I hated the thought of being separated from Luann, but boarding school seemed the only option. Many missionary children were sent away much younger. We felt we had been fortunate to have everyone at home for so long.

The weeks before Luann left passed in a flurry of activity. We made arrangements for her to fly back to the U.S. with one of her adopted "aunties," Gladys Gilson. But the day of our separation arrived too soon. The whole family piled in the Land Rover and drove to the Niamey airport, where Gladys met us. She greeted us cheerfully and did her best to make us comfortable. Dal and I were confident that Luann would be well taken care of. But we weren't so sure we would survive the trip back home—much less the long months ahead—without our daughter.

At last evening came, and it was time for Luann to board

the plane. Dal and I, the boys, and Laya stood on the dusty tarmac and watched her climb the steps to the plane. Tears were streaming down my face, but I didn't care. I felt Dal's arm tighten around my shoulder. Looking over at him, I saw he was crying too. We stood together, watching the lights of the airplane disappear into the night. "O Lord," I heard him pray, "that's my precious little girl. She's my alabaster box I am breaking and pouring out for you. Please take care of her."

In 1963 we began planning another furlough so we could be near Luann. We were looking forward to having all our children together again. We were also glad that we would be able to celebrate Luann's graduation, as the date of the ceremony fell right in the middle of our furlough. After Luann graduated, she joined us in Greenville, S.C., where we were renting a house.

Luann had decided that she wanted to go to college at Bob Jones University, where she would prepare to be a teacher. It was exciting for her to start college, but it was also tremendously hard to say goodbye again after our wonderful summer together. We put off leaving for Africa as long as possible so we could spend time with Luann. But, finally, it was time to go. As we drove away, leaving our precious Luann to walk to her dorm room alone, my tears starting coming, faster and faster. My heart cried out to be with my little girl. It was not easy for Luann either; she told us later that she climbed into her bunk bed and cried for a few hours. We were sad to leave Luann again, but the Lord blessed her with wonderful roommates who helped her get adjusted.

In 1967, when our next furlough came around, we felt we had to make a decision. We believed in the importance of a good education, and we also believed the unity of our family should be preserved. As our three boys were nearing high school age, we had to decide whether to stay on the field and send them to school alone or leave the field and keep the family together. Although our hearts were dedicated to our work, we also knew Satan's desire to destroy the family, so we decided to return until our boys' schooling was finished.

We settled in Greenville in order to be near Dal's mother, who was elderly and needed our help. Lillian, or Mother Weber, now in her 80s, was a widow once again. Dr. Weber had died some time earlier, after they returned from Africa to the United States. She lived with her grandson Larry in a little house near Bob Jones University, and her health was failing. It was our responsibility—and our pleasure—to care for her. Her health continued to deteriorate throughout our stay, and we spent many hours with her in doctors' offices and hospital rooms.

We started out by renting a house, but after a year went by, the landlord died and we were able to buy it. Ron and Terry were still in elementary and junior high school, and at the time we felt comfortable sending them to a public school. Denny, however, was ready for high school, and we wanted to send him to a Christian school. Since we lived within walking distance of Bob Jones University, sending him to Bob Jones Academy seemed like the best plan. Dal and I knew very little about Bob Jones University when we moved to Greenville. However, the more we heard about it, the better we liked it. Their beliefs were in line with our own, and their academic standards were very high. We were thankful we lived so close to the school.

When the school term began that fall, not one but three Washers enrolled at Bob Jones. Denny was in the Academy, Luann was a senior in the University, and Dal was taking classes in secondary education. At the time he was preparing to help high school missionary kids with their correspondence courses. I also took a class here and there in cinema, sewing, and French—whatever interested me. Ronnie was my French tutor, since he was taking French classes at the same time. After several years, I realized I was very close to earning a degree in cinema, so I went ahead and completed my final film project and graduated in 1971. If it had not been for the help of my family, I could not have gone to school at all. They were very kind to help with the dishes and housework.

During our first year in Greenville, EBM suggested that Dal be a representative for the mission, traveling to churches and representing Africa and other fields that EBM covered. Dal loved his job, especially when he could challenge young people to serve the Lord in Africa or wherever He led them.

After a year, our furlough was technically over, and our churches, which had a policy not to support missionaries delayed in the U.S., had to discontinue their support. We fully agreed with this policy; we would not want to take support away from a couple who were on the field. We knew we had to depend on God to meet our needs. He knew we felt responsible for our children who were still in grade school, and also for Mother Weber, whose condition continued to decline.

One day, soon after support from our churches had ended, we were walking to chapel at Bob Jones University when we noticed Dr. Bob Jones III behind us. He tapped Dal on the shoulder and asked him to come see him in his office. After a time of friendly chit-chat, Dr. Bob III asked Dal if he would consider teaching French and Bible in the Academy and missions in the University. Of course, Dal agreed immediately. God had provided overwhelmingly for us.

Our years in Greenville were happy ones, especially as we watched our children make important life decisions. Luann, for example, met a young man named Joe Whitaker, who also wanted to serve the Lord in education. They were married in August 1968. Ronnie went forward at a missionary conference to dedicate his life to be a missionary. I was a little surprised since he had not talked much about wanting to do mission work. But when he heard the message that night, he must have realized he knew well the need on the mission field, having lived there for many years. These and other decisions were answers to the prayers Dal and I prayed every day on our knees by our bed. Our greatest hope was that God would use our children in His service.

Though we were happy in America, we never felt like we were home to stay. I refused to invest in good furniture or spend much on our little house. After all, we were just home for a long furlough; Africa was still our goal. Many times I would sit in my American home and weep as I thought of Tera. I would think of our Muslim neighbors there, and I would tell Dal, "We need to be in Tera! There is no one there to tell them of Christ!" Our thoughts were never far from the few who struggled to stay faithful to their newfound Savior. Yet God had given us four children. They, too, needed us at this time in their lives.

By 1972, after we had been in South Carolina almost six years, all of our children had graduated from high school. Unfortunately, Mother Weber's condition had worsened so much so that we could no longer care for her ourselves. Our friend Dr. Dreisbach, who visited Mother Weber every day to check up on her, advised us to find a good nursing home where she could receive 24-hour care. Our ties to the U.S. were loosening, while our desires to resume mission work were as strong as ever. We believed that our desire to be back in Africa was the Holy Spirit speaking to us. We allowed ourselves to begin dreaming of our return to Africa.

Our relationship with EBM had discontinued, not because of problems or antagonism, but simply because we had stopped receiving support while we were not on the field. We considered resuming service with EBM, but we were not ruling out new mission boards. One day we received a phone call from our good friend Dr. Masteller, who knew we wanted to return to Africa. He told us that the Association of Baptists for World Evangelism (ABWE) was planning to enter the field of Africa, but that they wanted to begin with a veteran couple rather than new recruits. Dr. Masteller asked if we were interested in being that couple. It seemed like a perfect opportunity for us. We would be their pioneers.

On November 27, 1972, two ABWE board members, Harold Amstutz and Robert Reese, flew to Africa to do preparatory surveys to determine where ABWE would begin its work. As their chosen pioneers, Dal and I accompanied them. We were fairly sure that we knew where we would work: the northern part of the country of Dahomey, home to the Zerma-speaking Dendi tribe. In Niger, we had worked extensively using the Zerma language, so we felt Dahomey would be a good match. Also, we knew that EBM had always wanted to start a mission station there.

After a grueling flight across the Atlantic, our survey team landed in the capital city of Cotonou. There we had a joyous reunion with Laya and David and their family. Laya was as beautiful as ever, but I couldn't believe how big her children had grown. We also had the privilege of worshiping in the church David pastored. Sitting in that service, surrounded by believers and listening to David's message, our hearts praised the Lord for sending Laya to us all those years before. What an incredible return on our investment!

While I remained behind, the men flew north into southern Niger to survey the Dendi area. Dal was in his element among the Dendi people. His Zerma flooded back to his mind as he spoke with them. They, in turn, were thrilled to meet a white man who spoke their language so well. They listened with interest as he told them of the love of Jesus Christ.

Our local missionary friend Jim Brock introduced Dal and the other men to the native pastor he was working with, an old man named Talibi, who proudly showed them the simple mud church his congregation had built. The congregation greeted their visitors warmly. Bob and Harold were particularly impressed by their knowledge of scripture.

Dal came back to Cotonou full of plans for our work. The people were Muslim, much like those we had already worked with. The language was not identical, but Dal found that he could make himself understood with minimal difficulty. Settling in Dahomey would be like coming home.

We expected Bob and Harold to share our enthusiasm, but they were more cautious. They had spoken with missionaries already in the area. Some of them, such as the man who had taken them into Dendi country, were in favor of our coming. Others were more hesitant, feeling that a new mission board would complicate rather than help the work in the country. Some thought another mission board would create tension with an already unstable government and confuse the issue of government registration. The leadership of one board claimed they had already planned to begin work among the Dendi people. Their director asked that we allow them to follow their plans and find somewhere else to work. With heavy hearts, Bob and Harold conceded to their request.

When they told us the news, Dal and I were crushed. We had been so sure that God was calling us to work with the

Dendi Muslims. We had worked eighteen years among Muslim people. We were well qualified to open this field. With troubled spirits we submitted to the decision and set out to survey another country—Togo.

Togo was unfamiliar territory to us. It had a much smaller Muslim population than Niger and the people spoke primarily Ewé (eh-vay), a language we did not know at all. We were unsure how well we could minister in such a new place. But we admired the character of this new mission board when one of their representatives, Bill Pierson, wrote to us, "We are more convinced than ever that the field is the world and that we must be prepared to move into a country when the Lord directs." We waited to see what the Lord would show us.

During our years in Niger, neighboring missionaries would occasionally travel to the coast in Togo, sometimes called the "armpit" of Africa due to its appearance on the map. Missionaries enjoyed seeing the ocean and they enjoyed the people as well, even though they were idol worshipers, because it was easy to talk to them about Christ. We had also had occasional contact with several Togolese Christians who taught in our elementary school in Niger.

But our vague familiarity did not prepare us for our first visit with Bob and Harold. The survey of Togo took our breath away. We rented a car and drove from Cotonou to Lomé, Togo's capital, spending four days in a survey of Togo's southern area. After eighteen years in Muslim Niger, we were used to stony indifference or blatant rejection. So we were overwhelmed by the openness of the Togolese. They eagerly accepted literature we passed out and requested Bibles in their own language. Children and young people mobbed us as we handed out tracts. They inquired with interest into our religion and welcomed us warmly into their villages. They wanted someone to teach them about the God who was stronger than the evil spirits. While labor among the Muslims had been exhausting preparatory work, the field of Togo was white and waiting for harvesters.

This is not to say there were no other Christian works in the area. There were many different churches, but we heard little of salvation through Jesus Christ. The majority of the people remained pagan animists. Especially out in the bush, where people were untouched by Christianity of any stripe, there were many areas that had no church at all. There was much to be done.

In Togo we found a comparatively stable and progressive government. When we had the opportunity to speak with the minister of the interior, Dal dispelled the man's initial coolness by addressing him in Zerma. In speaking with the government, our team was very honest. They told the government that Dal would be doing church planting, visiting villages, and leading Bible studies. They told how we planned to help with literacy and how I was able to teach the blind. When the government officials understood what we wanted to do, they welcomed us, though they could not commit themselves before their president, Eyadema, approved the plan. Soon we had full permission to begin.

The disappointment Dal and I had felt in having to let go of our dreams to serve in Dahomey now turned to thanks that we would be privileged to work in such a friendly, delightfully tropical country. In a matter of a few days, God placed the Togolese on our hearts. From the fetishers in the capital to the Muslims in the northern bush country, the nation was calling for the gospel.

Lomé

I beseech you therefore, brethren, by the mercies of God,
that ye present your bodies a living sacrifice,
holy, acceptable unto God,
which is your reasonable service.

ROMANS 12:1

Though we knew God wanted us in Togo, there was a lot to be done between our survey trip in late 1972 and our return early in 1974. Since we had been away from the field for six years, we had to go on deputation to raise monthly support. We prepared diligently so we could accurately and earnestly describe the new field of Togo and the goals we hoped to achieve there. Many churches that had supported us in Niger generously supported us again, and we added a few more churches as well.

But even after we had raised 100% of our support, we did not leave immediately. Though everything seemed to be ready, Dal was hesitant to leave. He lacked his usual excitement about going to Africa. It was not difficult to figure out what was weighing on his mind—the health of his dear mother, whom he would have to leave in Greenville. Even though Dal knew that God wanted us in Togo, he struggled about leaving. Finally, Luann and Joe stepped in and volunteered to take care of Mother Weber. They assured Dal that they would watch over her with as much tenderness as Dal himself would show. Dal was relieved and began to feel confident that we could leave. As the days drew nearer for our long trip, it even seemed that Mother Weber was improving a bit and becoming stronger, perhaps due to her excitement for us. Nevertheless, our goodbyes were bittersweet.

On February 2, 1974, Dal, Terry, and I approached Togo in an airplane. We were thrilled to have Terry with us for this first year in Togo. As Lomé, the capital city, came into view beneath us, we were surprised to hear that we would have to circle the airport to allow another plane to land. So for an hour or so we took an airplane tour of Togo and parts of neighboring Ghana and Benin. We found out later that we were waiting for Togo's presidential plane, their equivalent of Air Force One. Our plane honored the president by allowing his plane to land first.

We soon learned the history behind the Togolese presidency. Togo had been a French West African colony for many years until 1956, when it was proclaimed autonomous. Years later, the Togolese army took power under the leadership of Lieutenant Colonel Gnassingbe Eyadema, and he soon won the campaign for the presidency. His election was due in large part to a startling event just before the election, in which Eyadema's touring plane dropped out of the air and crashed because it was flying too slowly and too low. Although several people died in the crash, Eyadema survived by going to the back of the plane. The people of Togo viewed Eyadema as immortal. He was elected president by a landslide, and all over the country groups of young people gathered for special dances and celebrations to honor him.

The second day of February was later named a holiday celebrating the "triumphal entry" of Eyadema after his brush with death. For us, it was a special day as well, as it was the date of our own "triumphal entry" into Togo. In years to come we would always have a little fun on that day, pretending that

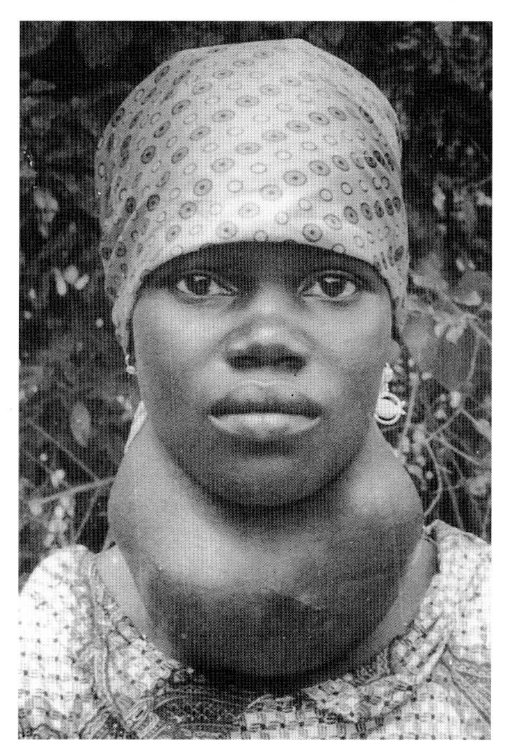

Clockwise from left:
Girl with a goiter; John and Paul, Dal's faithful helpers; the Yopé Baptist Church; the chief of Yopé and Dal.

Baptism of Chief Assah and his wife.

The Blind in Lomé

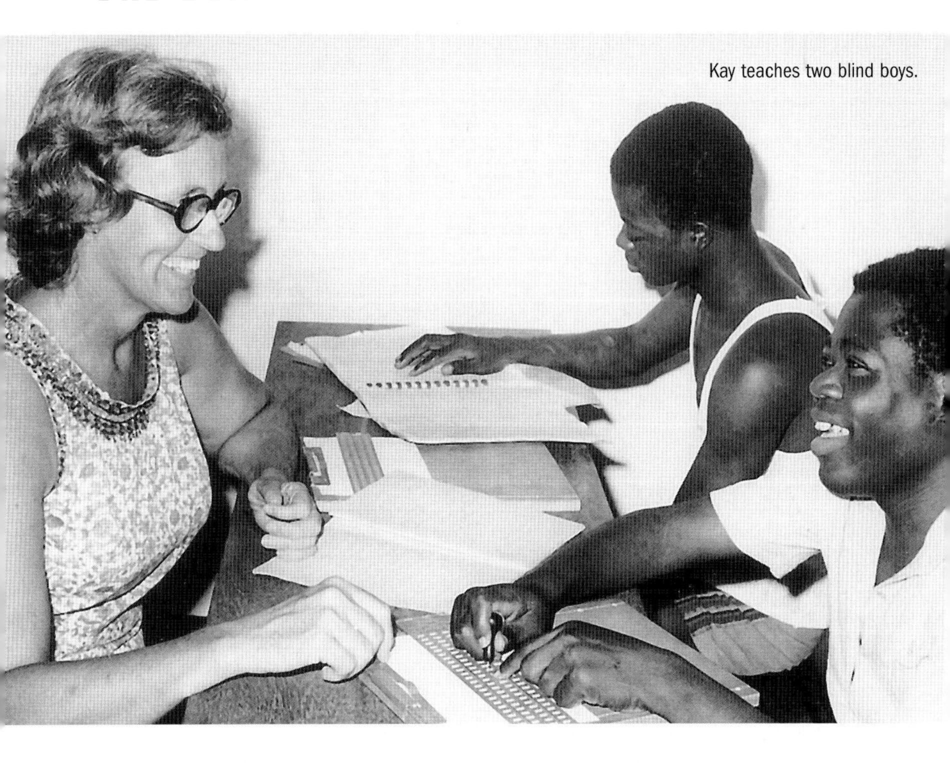

Kay teaches two blind boys.

The African market sells fish, crabs, and beautiful fabric.

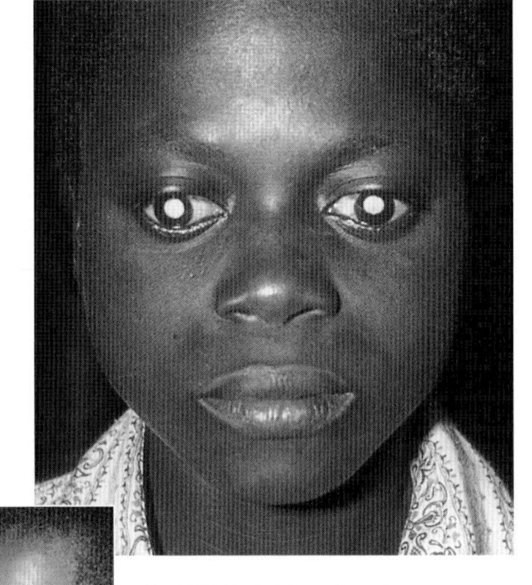

A child blinded by cataracts.

Many children become blind from measles, cataracts, glaucoma, birth defects, and accidents.

Above:
Ewé language lessons taught by Dr. Hargis (formerly Dr. Collins).

Da Pauline by Dal's grave.

Melissa Washer loved to be carried on Da Pauline's back.

Cooking for blind students.

Da Pauline teaches a blind student to weave baskets.

First Ewé language lessons. Dr. Hargis (formerly Dr. Collins) teaches while James translates.

Making a movie of James' life.

Above:
James leads the choir.

Below:
Dal preaches in a village and James translates.

the holiday marked our own arrival into the country, not just Eyadema's.

All three of us felt just a little out of place in Togo, since we had not secured a place to live, much less perfected our plans for working in a new country. We did not even expect to be met at the airport and were fully prepared to find our own way into the city. Naturally, then, our mouths dropped open when we saw David and Laya waiting for us at the airport! They had come from their home in Benin to meet us because they did not want us to be alone. Not only that, but they had already reserved rooms for us at the Seaman's Hotel near the port of Lomé.

Our first ride into town was quite stimulating—a heart-stopper, as a matter of fact. There were no lane markings on the road, and no traffic lights, but traffic flowed just as freely as in a busy American metropolis. There seemed to be an unspoken code of the road in which only three items on a vehicle were absolutely necessary: headlights, horn, and turn signals. Of those, the horn and turn signals were equally important, since each was used to communicate the intentions of the driver. The use of brakes, we learned, was incidental.

Lomé sits right on the edge of the Bay of Benin. We came to love living close to the ocean and enjoying fresh fish, shrimp, and even lobster. Fishing is a big enterprise in Togo. It was beautiful to watch a man as he tossed his net into the air like a lasso, letting it fall gently so it cut a perfect circle into the water. The weighted net settled down to the bottom, catching fish inside.

Our house was close enough to hear the ocean's roar at

night and feel the refreshing breeze. But the moaning sound of the waves also made us sad. If we let our feelings get out of control, the ocean could make us extremely homesick because we were all alone in a foreign city with only one of our four children. We knew our other children were far across that ocean, but it did comfort us to know that they looked on the same moon and stars that shone so bright above us.

The breaking waves would keep Dal awake at night. I knew he was thinking about his mother, wondering if he had done the right thing by leaving her. I would remind him how much Mother Weber enjoyed Luann and Joe and their children, Jeffrey and Jennifer. But Dal still felt a great sadness, perhaps because he felt he would never see his mother alive again.

Just a few weeks into our makeshift surroundings, we got a telephone call from Luann saying that Dal's mother had passed away. Dal decided he would go back to Greenville alone, since we had just arrived. Those nights I spent in Togo without Dal, thinking of how he was suffering greatly, were sad nights. But I was thankful that Dal's trip home eased the pull of responsibility that had somewhat overshadowed our new ministry. Dal himself said that his mother's homegoing lifted a burden off his shoulders and brought closure to another era of our lives. He felt he was finally able to face our new life in Togo with complete dedication.

To stick it out as we began the work in Togo, we had to brush aside the inconveniences and setbacks and continually remind ourselves to keep the gospel on our lips. We prayed that God would intensify our burning desire to communicate Christ's love to the people of Togo. We had to face reality and remind ourselves that these lovely, friendly people were going to end up in hell, forever separated from Christ, if we did not share with them God's gift of salvation. Our time in Togo was not about ourselves, but about obedience to Christ.

I believe the one thing that keeps young people from the

mission field today is this reality of sacrifice. It seems harder and harder for young men and women to commit to being missionaries now unless they grow up in a family or a church where they are taught the importance of missions from an early age. Perhaps there needs to be more emphasis on the concept of sacrifice, not to scare people away, but to instill in our youth the importance of doing without the comforts of America in order to minister to those in need of Christ. A successful missionary need not live in the most uncomfortable of situations. What is most important is that the missionary makes the decision, before ever reaching the field, that he or she will never say no to God, no matter what He asks.

The Togolese people are kind and lovable and often open to the truth. The country was, and still is, a field white for the harvest. We were amazed at how hungry many were to hear the Word once they trusted us. Not everyone accepted the Lord, though. The older generation in Togo, for the most part fetishers or animists, was especially hard toward Christ. These fetishers worship idols and fear the spirits of their dead ancestors. They also believe in the necessity of blood sacrifices. For an animist, every animal killed for food must first be sacrificed to idols and cooked in a special sauce before it can be eaten.

Because of this resistance from the older generation, we decided it made sense to target the youth of Togo with the gospel. They were more likely to accept the truth, and they were also more likely to win their older relatives to Christ by living out their testimony in the home. The children loved to hear our Bible stories and wanted to receive tracts and Bibles to read.

One of the most popular weekly activities we used to interact with the Togolese youth was volleyball on the court in our yard. Even I played volleyball in those days on the court that

Dal and Terry built. Word soon got around and boys from all over our part of the city would come to play volleyball with us, even if they didn't know how. We had fun teaching everyone. Some of the boys became terrific players.

After the games were over, Dal would encourage the boys to take a rest with him and sit on the edge of the court, where he would lead them in a Bible study. Most boys would stay and listen, unless they had to get back to a job or their family. This volleyball court was an exceptional tool that God used to attract many Togolese young men so we could share Christ with them.

Like many of the young men, Paul Assignon and his brother Damien came from a Catholic family, though their Catholicism was mixed with rituals of traditional spirit worship. So when Paul began to be enthusiastic about Dal's Bible teaching, his family was not very pleased. They wanted him to adhere to his family heritage, not to follow after some strange new God. But despite the objections of their family, Paul and Damien eventually accepted Christ as their Savior. Dal baptized them in a bay area of the ocean where the waves would not rush in too fast. Soon afterwards, they began praying that the rest of their family would follow in their footsteps. Dal and Terry and I became good friends with the Assignon family, since we lived just across the street, and we often joined Paul and Damien as they prayed. Even after we moved away from Lomé, the Lord continued to answer our prayers, and Paul and Damien's mother accepted Christ. Eventually, several other members of the family were saved as well.

Emile was another boy whose family mixed Catholicism and idol worship. Emile and his family lived towards the particularly heavy area of Lomé in a suburb called Bé. His parents opposed his coming to our meetings, and when his father found out he was still coming to meetings and Bible studies with us, he threw away all of Emile's belongings and would not allow him in the house. Emile had no place to sleep so he made his way back to us. We helped him find a place to stay until his father allowed him back into the family home.

Emile continued to come to our activities, despite his parents' disapproval, and soon he accepted Christ as his Savior. As a new Christian, Emile's conscience was very sensitive and he felt it was wrong to eat the meat his family sacrificed to idols. It was Emile's own decision and conviction, and his father put him out of the house again. We were concerned for Emile, but at the same time we were proud of him for taking a stand for Christ in his own family.

He continued to attend our church services and our Bible studies after volleyball, and he, along with Paul and Damien, also met with Dal every morning from 7:00 to 8:00 to study the Bible. After several months of these classes, the boys learned to witness, pray, and study God's Word on their own. They became strong disciples of Jesus Christ, and we prayed they would, in the future, be Christian leaders among their own people.

Today Emile serves the Lord as a pastor, a glorious trophy of God's grace in the midst of difficult trials. Paul was led by God to become an evangelist.

YOPÉ AND ADANGBÉ

For the Lord is great, and greatly to be praised:
He is to be feared above all gods.
For all the gods of the nations are idols:
but the Lord made the heavens.

PSALM 96:4–5

Even with all his activities in Lomé, nothing could keep Dal from venturing out into the bush villages on the outskirts of the city. As soon as we were settled in our house, Dal began to visit villages on Sunday afternoons and weekday evenings. They could only be reached over rough roads, but happily, a small station wagon had been made available for us upon our arrival. This Renault 12 had a small engine that, with gasoline up to $1.25 a gallon at that time in Togo, was a godsend.

As he visited villages, Dal often took the young men under his discipleship with him, including Paul, Damien, and Emile. Everyone would pile in the Renault with their equipment and supplies. It was Dal's goal to use the village ministry to help these boys to grow strong in the Lord. Eventually, he wanted them to preach and witness on their own.

When the men arrived at a village, each had a special role to play. They would begin by setting up a movie projector and amplifier, tying a bed sheet to the side of a building for a screen. Then Dal would show a gospel film, an immensely popular event in Togo that would instantly draw a crowd. Paul would translate the words so everyone could understand. Many Africans had never seen a film before and were absolutely enthralled. Afterwards, one of Dal's helpers would lead in a time of singing, and another would teach a Bible lesson using a visual aid. Finally, it was Dal's turn to preach a sermon, translated into Ewé by Paul or one of the other young men.

Since Africans often feel they have not learned unless they ask many questions, Dal followed his preaching by answering question after question. From these discussion times he was able to start Bible classes for those who wanted to be trained. We saw a number of young men progress from studying in these basic classes to becoming pastors with successful churches.

On his trips to the villages Dal would often come across a person who was confused about a doctrinal issue or who clung to a cultural practice that kept him from accepting Christ. At times, these issues were ones Dal had never even considered.

One minor issue was the seating arrangements of church congregations. In Togolese churches the wives sat on one side of the church with their squirming children, while the men sat on the other side where they would not be bothered. But as Dal preached on marriage and how the family should be maturing in Christ, some men began to sit together with their wives and children, listening to the sermon as a family. To us, this was a breakthrough. It showed that real Christian families were starting to develop.

Dal was also able to teach his congregations the difference between infant baptism and dedicating a baby to the Lord. Many couples who joined our church were only familiar with the Catholic practice of infant baptism. In fact, the word for "baptism" in Ewé means "God's water on the head." We tried to help parents separate in their minds their baby's salvation from the promise they gave to raise their child in a way that honors God. It was thrilling to see Dal perform many baby dedications as couples were saved and brought their children to be dedicated.

One Sunday, Christianyo, an older blind man, and his wife came to church with their new baby dressed up for dedication. Dal asked them to come forward so he could pray for them and their child. They did so, placing the child in his arms. Dal began to pray, "Lord, bless this little life and bless the parents who brought it, and may it grow up to serve you." All of a sudden, the baby started to wet. Now, the people in Lomé do not put diapers or underwear on their children. Even when a child is all dressed up, the mother or father just hold it over the ground in the event of an accident. Christianyo's baby, according to custom, was wearing no diapers, and a stream of liquid made its way down the front of Dal's suit. He couldn't get rid of the baby in the middle of his prayer, and it was too late anyway, so he just held the baby over the ground and finished praying. Soon after that, Dal learned to wrap a cloth under the baby to protect himself from a sudden shower.

The primitive village of Yopé was the first we focused on while in Togo. About an hour and a half from Lomé, Yopé lies toward the border of Ghana, far back in the bush. Prosperity to the people of Yopé is subsistence living to us—having enough corn to eat and some animals. They have no real chance or hope of improving their lifestyle, and many resign themselves to staying where they are. In their hopelessness, the villagers had turned to witchcraft and spirit worship to give their lives a sense of meaning. It was in Yopé that we first saw intense idol worship. The people there believed they would have protection from evil spirits if they made blood sacrifices from chickens or other animals and poured the blood over the heads of their idols. It was also not uncommon to see signs of curses, such as a snake draped on a forked stick in a doorway.

Before Dal and the boys could begin sharing the gospel, they had to formally introduce themselves to the chief, who sat in his compound in a big carved chair. When Dal and his helpers arrived there, they bowed politely. The chief, thankfully, seemed to be sweet and kind, despite the evil practices going on in his village. He shook hands with Dal and the others and allowed them to begin their gospel program. After a few visits, Dal found that he had better attendance on weekdays since people were not busy with their fetish ceremonies, so he started a schedule of visiting Yopé on Tuesday evenings.

One day, I went along in order to build relationships so I could teach a children's class in Yopé. I chuckled to myself at the reaction of the villagers seeing a white woman for the first time. They stood apart discussing among themselves how I must be the white man's wife since I looked like a woman. All the children ran screaming to their mothers, saying they were afraid of the "white ghost." In a funny sort of way, I found it hilarious to see what a ruckus I caused.

On the other hand, I was just as curious about the people of Yopé as they were about me. Many Togolese wear Western-style clothing, but in Yopé, the dress was more traditional. It was not rare to see children playing with no clothes at all or clad only in underwear. Neither was it rare to see women around the village wearing only a long, brightly colored skirt. Once a Togolese girl reaches her teens, her legs are seldom uncovered, but the upper body often goes unclothed. Togolese women are modest, but their idea of modesty was a bit different than mine!

To help the women become accustomed to me, I said a few words to them in Ewé, like, "What is your child's name?" After a few visits, I was able to start children's classes. The village children would sit in a circle around us on the mats we brought for them. We would lead them in songs and teach them a Bible story.

After the first few visits, I noticed a young girl named Charlotte hiding just inside the door of a nearby hut. She wore a head scarf that covered her head and her neck. We tried to get acquainted with her, but she was shy. It was several more weeks until we realized why.

Charlotte had a goiter on her neck that had grown to the size of a coconut. The deformity embarrassed her and baffled her parents, who had no idea what to do. Dal and I wondered if there was something a doctor could do, so we asked her family if we could take her to the French hospital in Lomé. They agreed.

The old French doctor there said he would operate to remove the goiter, but Charlotte would lose a lot of blood. We managed to convince several members of her family to make the long trip and give blood for Charlotte so the operation could be performed. Thankfully, it was successful. In fact, when Charlotte came home from the hospital without her goiter, the whole village of Yopé thought we had done a miracle. At first they just stood and stared at her. Then they brought chairs for us to sit in, and they filed past, bowing and taking my hand in theirs, saying, *"Yakpeloo,"* which means "A big thank you!" My answer was, *"Akpe na Mawu"* (Thanks be to God).

After everyone had thanked us for helping Charlotte, a bowl was passed around for all of us to take a drink as a symbol of friendship. I took one look at the dirty water and my health training brought me visions of oodles of microbes invading my insides. I did, in fact, see a hair floating in the water and I panicked. After all their kindness, I passed the bowl to Charlotte without even taking the smallest sip. Despite my faux pas, the people of Yopé seemed to overlook my actions: Charlotte's father told me that Charlotte was my daughter now, too.

Though Yopé was far off the beaten path, it had been heavily influenced by Catholicism, and it was this influence that kept the chief from spiritual change. The staunch Catholics in his village vowed that if their chief left their church, he would not be buried with the normal honorable ceremonies. This made it hard for the chief, but he was eventually saved.

Shortly after, he asked to be baptized along with his two wives, both of whom had also accepted Christ as their Savior. Dal struggled with the chief's request. Finally, after much prayer, he took the position that the chief should have only one wife in order to be baptized, but that if the chief kept both wives, he would still be saved. The chief, to be obedient to the scriptures, sent one wife back to her family's village, while continuing to care for her financially. Dal and I were proud of him. This was the first of many times that he chose to honor Christ even if it meant breaking long-standing village traditions.

After Charlotte's successful operation and after the chief announced he had been saved, many more people came to church and to Bible studies and children's activities. By 1976 we were conducting classes for 100 or 200 children each week. We also started in-depth Bible classes specifically for college-age youth.

Years later, the chief of Yopé gave us a tract of land on which to build a church. We had graduated from meeting under a tree or in the chief's compound to meeting in a large grass chapel. But the chief was eager to have a real church building in his village. Every Sunday, at services in the grass church, the chief encouraged his people to give money for a permanent building. Though the villagers had no good source of money exchange (they usually bartered instead of using cash), they always put something in the offering plate, even if it was a very small coin. The little bit of offering every week would never have built a church, but God provided in other ways and we built a simple cement structure with a tin roof. The gospel preached there erased the misery and dissatisfaction that had afflicted the people of Yopé for ages; it filled their emptiness with the satisfaction they had been seeking for so long.

I still have a picture of Dal sitting beside the chief of Yopé. The chief, an old, shriveled man with short, closely cut gray hair and no beard, wears a crimson robe. Dal is in a short-sleeved suit and is very tan. The picture was taken at dusk, and the bulb was just enough to light up Dal's face against the reds and browns of the Africans crowding behind him. Characteristically, Dal has a Bible in hand and smiles as if he is listening to something being said. The picture documents Dal's great passion: to take the gospel to villages that had never before heard of Christ. I believe God gave Dal a special gift of befriending and winning chiefs to Christ. Perhaps because he was older he could more easily gain their trust. God knew it was important to win chiefs to Christ, because a saved chief makes a huge difference in the spiritual direction of a village.

The village of Adangbé was another early site of our ministry, and God had a roundabout way of getting us there. After about a year in Africa, Terry befriended a young man named John, who had come to Lomé from Adangbé. John understood English and was interested in spiritual things, so Terry spoke with him about Christ. To John, who was raised Catholic, the gospel Terry spoke of was different than anything he had ever heard. Soon, John accepted Christ, and became the very first person to do so while we were in Togo.

After his conversion, John returned to Adangbé and led his

own father to the Lord. Then he rejoined our ministry as a song leader and began to study the Bible. He also asked Dal whether he had considered starting a work in Adangbé. We had heard about Adangbé—it was teeming with fetishes and idols, and its villagers practiced some of the most disturbing ceremonies in all of Togo.

Dal, however, viewed this as a challenge, not a threat. So he took John and several other young men and started visiting Adangbé. Upon entering the village, the men passed idols that looked like big, red-mud snowmen. The idols' eyes, noses, and mouths were made of cowry shells and many were covered by a grass-roofed shelter to keep rain from washing them away. Clay pots filled with water were placed in front of the idols in case the spirits became thirsty. These idols were believed to have power over sickness and death.

Amazingly, despite Satan's clear claim to this village, the chief and the "big men" of Adangbé gave Dal permission and land on which to erect a large grass shelter for their Wednesday evening services. But the fetish worshipers and the Catholics were not happy about the Christian presence in their village, and each time Dal and his helpers arrived they found new obstacles. One week the tom-toms and ceremonial dancers whipped up an uproar about fifty yards away. Another time the Catholics started a big soccer match and insisted that all children had to attend. Once a crazy man came to a service and made a lot of noise. People would send their pigs running through the village, and Dal finally had to put up barriers around the grass church so the animals wouldn't tear it down. One day the children even threw gravel and dirt as Dal drove the Renault home.

Finally, on one wonderful Sunday, God gave us the chance to show His love to the village. An old woman was very ill, probably with pneumonia. The family had gathered to await her death. They had made many blood sacrifices to their idols but she was no better. So we asked if we could take her to the government hospital in Lomé. After much discussion they agreed, as long as a family member accompanied her. As we made a bed for her in the back of the Renault, villagers gathered around the car to watch us. We prayed that our actions would serve to glorify God and show the people that we loved them for Christ's sake. Sure enough, the old woman improved under hospital care, and God continued to help us reach the "village of idols."

Miraculously, in spite of all the opposition, the work grew. Children's classes expanded until ninety children were coming every week. A few adults who attended church services also began Bible correspondence courses. We were thrilled that we had the privilege to fight for the souls in Adangbé.

THE BLIND IN LOMÉ

I will bring the blind by a way that they knew not;
I will lead them in paths that they have not known:
I will make darkness light before them,
and crooked things straight.
These things will I do unto them,
and not forsake them.

ISAIAH 42:16

I loved going to the market because it is such an exciting place. If there is anything going on in a town, the market is where it is happening. The government in Lomé had constructed large buildings for its city markets, and vendors could rent little stalls for their wares. In the seafood area, fish were laid in rows to dry, and clay pots overflowed with live snails and crabs caught from rivers and the ocean. It was not uncommon for a prodigal crab to knock the lid off his pot, crawl out, and run away down the street, chased by a string of children. A person with a sensitive stomach would be wise to stay away from the fish market because of the smell. In another section of the market, women sold clay pots for cooking and storing food. It was amazing to me that some pots were as tall as I was. These giants would be used to catch rainwater from the thatched roofs.

The market's beautiful fabrics, in a rainbow of distinctive African colors and designs, were no less impressive. I loved to wander among them, for I enjoyed sewing clothes from the lovely cloth that was made from beautiful long-fibered cotton grown in West Africa. It can be washed in the river and laid on a bush to dry. It's also wrinkle-resistant. Women who sell fabric in Africa often become fabulously wealthy by African standards. In Togo we have a name for a woman like this: *Nana-Benz*. (*Nana*: mother; *Benz*: Mercedes Benz). A *Nana-Benz* is easy to spot: just look for a heavyset woman with a fat purse who comes to the market in a chauffeur-driven Mercedes Benz. These women have beautiful houses and eat all the food they desire, sure signs of wealth.

The market in Lomé was open every day, and most people went at least twice a week since food does not last very long in a tropical climate with no refrigeration. If you bought fish on Tuesday, you had better eat it on Tuesday, unless it is dried. Vegetables, fruits, and bread might last a few days. I also went to the market often because it was interesting to watch the people in such a lively atmosphere. I could always find someone new to talk to and make friends with. Though the same kinds of vendors worked each day, they were not always the same people. Every time I went, it seemed that a different crowd of children was improvising games in the sand. Sometimes they were so absorbed that they were oblivious to me as I passed by. At other times my tall white form would catch their eye and they would shout a greeting to me in French.

Every so often, I would spot a blind child in the market. As in Niger, my heart was burdened for those in both physical and spiritual darkness, and I soon found the blind in Togo to be as numerous as those in Niger. Unfortunately, in Togo there was very little professional medical help available for them.

Any child whose eyes have scarred or clouded over or been spoiled by infection becomes an outcast and has no value, because he is believed to be cursed. The Togolese insist that only a medicine man or witch doctor can remove the curse or evil spirits that caused the blindness. Most families go to great expense to regain their children's eyesight, subjecting them to a number of pagan ceremonies. When the ceremonies do not restore sight, as is most often the case, the ashamed family will usually send their child away to be cared for by relatives deep in the bush areas of Togo, where living is less expensive.

As a Christian, I knew that these blind people were under the influence of a disease even more serious than their blindness—sin. Their physical darkness would become eternal spiritual darkness were it not for Jesus, the Light of the World, their only hope. For this reason, shortly after we arrived in Lomé, I resolved to invite some of these children to come to Braille classes in the little grass hut in my backyard. I planned to introduce them to the love of Christ, who could "make darkness light before them" (Isaiah 42:16).

It was no coincidence that, just as I was beginning to think about starting a Braille class, God led me to a boy named Koffi. I met him at the hospital. His eyes had been burned in an explosion, and he had gone blind. As he sat on his bed, he told me how he had been to school in Ghana, where he learned Ghana English. I asked Koffi if he would like to learn Braille so he could help us create a Braille alphabet for the Ewé language. He said he would enjoy that very much.

As soon as Koffi was released from the hospital, he began to study Braille with me. By the time he learned the French alphabet in Braille, I thought he would be able to start reading Ewé. Just as with Zerma, though, there was no complete Braille alphabet for Ewé, much less complete books in Ewé Braille. So Koffi and I set to work creating a Braille alphabet for his Ewé people, a process easier said than done. Ewé has seven extra letters that need their own Braille combinations. But, slowly, we began to translate parts of the Bible into Braille to make our Ewé primer.

While Koffi and I were beginning work on our Ewé Braille alphabet, my Braille class started to grow. I enjoyed teaching my small group out in our *piote*, the grass hut in the backyard, where the breeze crept in from the ocean. I limited the class to children since young fingers are generally still sensitive enough to feel the Braille dots. After a person reaches thirty years old, his fingers are not usually sensitive enough to learn Braille.

I began by teaching my students the Braille alphabet using the French primer *Les Six Points*, just as I had in Niger. Soon they were able to move on to using the *poinson* and the Braille writing frame. The students soon became experts at fitting the paper in the writing frame, making sure it snapped when the paper lined up correctly. The frame held the paper beneath a grid of rectangular cells and on top of a series of tiny depressions. To write a Braille symbol, students made indentations in the paper by poking the *poinson* through a rectangular cell and down into the little depressions.

My class grew rapidly, and it became necessary to rent a small building to accommodate all the students. An empty shop building became the first Blind School in Togo. Overnight, it seemed, I went from teaching one or two students to juggling the different paces and levels of twelve. I took every chance I could to witness by telling Bible stories or having them learn verses and songs. These first students were the ones who gave me the nickname that has continued to stick for many years—*Koklonaw*, which means "Mother Hen." My blind students liked to imagine I was their mother hen and they were chicks safe under my wings.

This sweet African custom of giving people animal names became precious to me. When the children first started calling me "Mother Hen," many people wrote me, saying, "Who wants to be called an old hen? Aren't you insulted?" I tried to explain to them the characteristics of a mother hen: she protects her babies, puts them under her wings, fights wild animals or snakes for them, shows them where to peck on the ground for food, and even dies for her chicks if a fire comes. When I began to understand the meaning, I thought, *Am I really worthy of this name? Would I fight for my children, or die for them?*

In most African nations the government does not have a program to care for handicapped people, so in Togo the government encouraged us to do whatever we could for the blind. They were pleased we were doing something for these neglected people.

One day as I was in the middle of a Braille lesson at our storefront near the ocean, a government official stopped in to see what I was doing. This official had heard about our classes but had never seen Braille and was amazed that people with broken eyes (as he put it) could read by passing their fingers over little dots on paper. He told the minister of health about our little school and brought him back to observe how I taught the students. The minister was extremely pleased with my students' progress and encouraged me to make the school available to all visually impaired children throughout Togo.

At that point, I could not imagine tackling such a gigantic project. I was concerned daily for the dangers my blind children faced on their journey to school. The narrow alleys and roads were dangerous for the sighted, and even more so for the blind. If a relative was not able to bring the students to school, they sometimes braved the obstacles of the trip alone. On one visit the minister of health said the president thought a Blind School in the interior would allow the children to be safer. In fact, he offered to give us land for a school. "We will help you get the land you need, anywhere in Togo," he said. I thanked the minister for his encouragement and told him I very much appreciated the president's offer. But I was experiencing a struggle inside. I did not feel qualified to start a school, much less to direct it. I also feared that government backing would have the adverse effect of making the school a social work only.

Throughout our time in Lomé, the Holy Spirit seemed to be urging me not to make teaching the blind my first priority. It was as though the Lord and I shared a secret. He would have something special for me to do with the blind later, but I felt He wanted the Togo ministry to begin with a solid foundation of preaching and starting churches. I helped build this foundation any way I could, and I trusted that God would not forget my burden for the blind, and that He would make my way clear in the future.

DA PAULINE

Blessed are they which do hunger and thirst after righteousness: for they shall be filled.

MATTHEW 5:6

I always looked forward to hospital visitation because I loved medical work. With the help of Florence, my Togolese translator, I would round up a record player and some salvation messages and venture into the wards. We would play the records and sick people would listen from their beds. After listening, many would ask about Jesus. Though African people have a great respect for God as Creator, they do not know Jesus Christ as Savior, so I was pleased to hear questions about Him.

After we made sure that people understood what they had heard on the record, we would lead them in a song, either in French or Ewé. Then we would close our meeting in prayer. When we got to the prayer time, many would ask for me to pray over them the prayer of *tsitre*, which means "get up" or "stand up." I did not feel comfortable praying this prayer of healing, because I did not want them to look to me as having miraculous healing power. Instead, I prayed with them that God would work in their hearts and bodies.

One day at the hospital we found a lady who had been in a car crash with a taxi while traveling to Benin. In Togo, taxis are actually trucks with little benches where as many people as possible squash in. The drivers speed around in them recklessly, causing many accidents. This particular accident was so severe that all but this one lady had died. She was badly hurt and groaned continually from her pain. Her sister was caring for her when we arrived. She introduced herself as Pauline. I had learned enough of Togolese manners to know that since Pauline's hair was still black, I should address her as Da or Dada Pauline. Had she been older, with white hair, I would have called her Mama Pauline. My manners were improving.

Da Pauline invited us to come near the bedside and pray for her sister. So I prayed for her and the sisters were grateful. Then Da Pauline asked us to tell her about Jesus. We played a gospel record in the Ewé language and she listened intently. When we left for the day, we gave Da Pauline a few tracts. She said she could not read, but that she would find someone to read them to her.

After that, we visited the sisters often and noticed that Da Pauline made herself useful at the hospital. One day we found her helping long-term patients pass the time by learning how to make baskets. Other times we noticed her helping others with sick family members. There is much to do in an African hospital because patients are cared for by their own family. Medicine comes from the government, and the hospital personnel perform operations and give injections, but the family must do everything else. They must walk to the pharmacy to buy medicine and bring it back to the hospital for a medical person to administer. The family must also supply and change the bedding, bring in food, and feed their sick relative. Da Pauline was always sensitive to the needs of others, and she made many friends at the hospital by working hard to make other people's lives easier.

After a few months of teaching my blind children, I decided I wanted them to learn a trade so they could earn their own money. We desired our students to live a full, happy life both physically and spiritually. Sedou, one of our translators, was able to teach crafts, such as weaving chair seats with sea grass and making leather purses. But I remembered that Da Pauline had excellent basket-weaving skills. I went immediately to find her at the hospital.

When she saw me, Da Pauline's smooth ebony face glowed with a smile. She expressed great happiness that I had sought her out and that I would actually pay her to teach blind children to weave. Then she pulled a tract out of the basket she was holding. This was the tract I had given her, and people had read it to her many times. With tears of joy in her eyes she said she wanted to receive this Jesus who had died for her sins. Holding up the tract, she told me, "This is what I want."

Soon after she accepted Christ, Da Pauline started praying for her lost family. In her first effort to witness to them, she asked Dal to visit her village and tell her parents about Jesus. We all decided to go down that first time, but her family was not ready to accept Christ. Later, Da Pauline surprised us by bringing her mother to our house in Lomé. After we had eaten, Da Pauline said, "Now, tell her how to be saved." Dal explained salvation to her, and the mother became a follower of Christ that very day.

Da Pauline especially desired salvation for her son, her only child, so when she invited us to her compound to meet Methode, we agreed immediately. Da Pauline brought her son to Dal, and Methode bowed in a casual sort of way. We could tell that he did not seem interested in God or the spiritual help we wanted to bring to him. Even when Dal put his hand on Methode's shoulder and said, "I love you and I want to tell you about Jesus," it appeared that Da Pauline's son heard nothing of what was said to him.

Methode attended the University of Togo, but because the Togolese have no electricity in their homes, it is difficult for students to study at night. The Southern Baptist mission saw the need and built a study room with electric lights, tables, chairs, and a small library of Christian literature. One day, Methode ventured into the study room. He said he felt his heart becoming curiously interested in spiritual things. He looked around the shelves and found a French volume called *The Evidences of Jesus Christ*, which he started to read. Through studying this book, Methode realized his need of a Savior and was wonderfully saved. The Southern Baptists were able to disciple and counsel him, and today he is a pastor in the Southern Baptist Church. He has matured into a good man, a faithful pastor, and a wonderful preacher, making his mother very proud and happy.

When our ministry in Togo was a year and a half old, we excitedly welcomed another experienced couple to Togo, David and Elwanda Fields. They established a new work in the east end of the city, an area called Bé, the Lomé suburb where fetish worship was especially strong. The people there were imprisoned by idol worship, blood sacrifices, and spiritism. Nearby was the "Sacred Forest," where witch doctors practiced their trade. Right next door to David's and Elwanda's house was the compound of a witch doctor who carried much credibility in the area. From his yard the drums sounded every weekend and every day he slung a fresh, bloody, sacrificial chicken above his door.

But the Lord blessed the work in Bé, and we were all amazed by how well David and Elwanda did in spite of such spiritual warfare. They connected with young people by inviting them into their home and getting to know them. Since Elwanda was musical, she taught the young people Christian songs and how to play the guitar, the accordion, and the organ. The Africans, already musical at heart, picked up these new instruments with ease and agility. Elwanda even taught them how to write music. Dave preached strong messages every

Sunday and taught the young men Bible courses, giving them a firm foundation in the Word. We heard wonderful reports of the good times at the Fieldses' house, studying the Bible and learning fine music, as well as sharing simple fellowship over tea and banana bread.

Soon after, Dr. Grace Collins (now Hargis), a linguist from Bob Jones University, also came to Lomé to help us learn Ewé. She spent most of a month helping us with the sounds, grammar, and vocabulary of the language, and she taught several Africans to be language helpers. By the time she left, Dr. Hargis had given us practical methods to continue learning how to speak the language. We were grateful for her help. To speak Ewé well would allow us to more easily explain the way of salvation.

After David and Elwanda arrived, Dal began to feel the Lord leading him to expand the work further inland to reach Togo's interior with the gospel. The Fieldses were happy to stay in Lomé and absorb our work into their own growing ministry. So we corresponded with ABWE and shared some research with them on Kpalimé, a town of about 30,000. It was centrally located in a string of villages, about eighty miles north of Lomé in one of the most scenic regions of Togo, and we believed it would serve us well as our first inland mission.

As Dal continued to go into the mountains on village trips, he began to look around for a house to rent in Kpalimé. As soon as he found a suitable one, we set about moving. About this time, Da Pauline confided to me that she had a husband. She was, in fact, one of many wives who lived together in a harem. The husband would choose one wife each night to cook for him in exchange for the privilege of staying in his compound for the night. Da Pauline told me that each wife tried to outperform the other wives in cooking and in sexual pleasures. There was much jealousy among them.

Da Pauline believed the harem system was wicked. She knew that her new "Master Jesus" would not be pleased with this part of her life. One day she came to me very upset and said, "Oh, Madame, when I try to go to sleep at night, I have all sorts of evil thoughts in my head. I take my Bible and I lay it open on my chest because I want God's words to go into my heart and take all the wicked thoughts away." I was touched by Da Pauline's desperate desire to live a holy life, and by her childlike faith that God's words would take away her bad memories, though she could not even read her Bible yet.

After we had prayed about her troubles, she asked if it would be right for her to leave her husband. She felt he wasn't happy with her, mainly because she had borne him only one son. Da Pauline wanted me to go to her husband and ask him if she could leave his harem. Though I wanted to help Da Pauline, I hesitated a long time because I didn't want to get involved in the problems of their marriage. But when we were about to make the move north to Kpalimé, I gathered my courage to ask Da Pauline's husband if she could come with us. I felt it would be less serious than to ask if she could leave permanently.

When I spoke with him he was quiet for a moment and then told me he really didn't need her anymore. He remembered she had given him only one son and he mentioned what a great expense she was. So he agreed to let her go, but only if I would promise to pay her and take care of her. Dal and I were quite willing to support Da Pauline in return for her help, so she left her husband and came to live near us.

Da Pauline was not the only dear friend who joined us in Kpalimé. Our son Ron, his wife, Ann, and their daughter, Melissa, arrived in January of 1979 to help us with the new work. At that time, Melissa was just a tiny baby and Da Pauline cared for her as if she were her own daughter. She loved to carry her around according to tribal custom, wrapping her up in a cloth and tying her on her back. Ron and Ann fell in love with Da Pauline, just as Dal and I had, and they were glad to have such a gentle nurse for their little one. As more and more missionaries came to Togo, Da Pauline became the beloved grandmother of all the little missionary babies.

When Da Pauline would pray, we couldn't help but keep our eyes open because it was so interesting to watch her pray. She would start out talking to God softly and reverently, as if she were speaking with a king. But she would get louder and more excited as her prayer went on and she would always end with a resounding AMEN!

We quickly began taking the gospel to the people of Kpalimé. Through church services in our house, we met a young builder named Kwadjo Paul, who helped us find and buy a piece of land on the main road that stretched through Kpalimé. We first poured a cement slab on this land, forming a basketball court to use as a ministry tool for the young men in the village. By 1980, about a year later, our house became too small for church services, so we used the cement slab as a foundation for our first church building in Kpalimé. The church members donated twenty-four teakwood trees for the roof supports, and the men in the church worked together each Saturday until they finished the small mud structure with a grass roof. It was just large enough to seat two hundred people, giving us plenty of room to expand. Our first meeting happened to be on Easter Sunday morning, a perfect day to make a new start in a new place.

Dal and Ron worked hard nurturing the young church and holding services in other villages. A number of young men in the village wanted to study the Bible, so Dal began leading them through advanced courses. Ron started classes for new believers who wanted to follow the Lord in baptism. The work in Kpalimé was growing by leaps and bounds.

Da Pauline's official jobs were teaching basketry, cooking, and helping me with the blind ministry. But she did much more than that. With her evangelistic spirit, she was a perfect candidate to visit other villages. When she and I visited together, I loved to watch her as she gathered the women and children, encouraging them to sit down and listen to the Bible lesson. She would often translate the lesson into Ewé, and then help the illiterate women and children to pray. Afterwards, she would talk with each mother to find out if anyone was sick. Even when she grew older and her hair was sprinkled with gray, Da Pauline was known to stay up all night with a sick person. And every Sunday she brought a spiritually needy friend to church to learn of Christ's mercy and forgiveness.

About a year after we had moved to Kpalimé, Da Pauline convinced her father and mother to come for a visit. Even though the trip was long, they agreed to come. We were all excited about the visit and prayed that God would grant Da Pauline's foremost desire—that her father would be saved. Dal talked to him for a long time in our living room, and at the end of the discussion, her father prayed a prayer. Only God knows whether his heart turned completely to God. We have a picture of Da Pauline and her parents from that day. Her mother is hugging Dal and her father stands in the stately African way, holding the Bible Dal had just given him. The picture also captures the joy in Da Pauline's face, which is wet with happy tears.

Da Pauline, or Mama Pauline, as she is called now that she is older, was just one of many African people who helped us in our ministry in Togo. As missionaries, we leave the work in the hands of the godly African people whom the Lord has sent to continue His work in their own land. We thank God for people like Da Pauline, whose life is an example of the power of the gospel to change a heart from one who worships Satan to one whose master is Jesus. Da Pauline's sacrificial love for others was as beautiful as a rare jewel. Only Christ's love can produce such a jewel.

Maitre Awou Kwasivi, director of the elementary school, and his wife, the kindergarten teacher.

Below: Audience with President Eyadema, who gave approval for our students to attend secondary school.

Blind students "Braille" their exams.

Ann Washer teaches music to blind children.

Dal baptizes a young Christian.

Above:
The old grass *Chapelle* and the new *Eglise Baptiste* in Kpalimé.

Left:
Worshipers fill the new church.

Language study for the new missionaries: Mary Ann and Chris Thompson, Dallas Washer, Pastor Paku, national helpers, Ron and Ann Washer, and Annette Williams.

The Woumé chief died and Dal was chosen to preach at his funeral.

Above:
The Woumé chief became a follower of Christ.

Right:
The Allston family helped in the churches.

Woumé Baptist Chapel: Christians built their first meeting place, where Dennis and Diane Washer taught them God's Word.

The Village of Light was built with donations from Hampton Park Baptist Church and the generosity of many others.

Students enjoy a good meal thanks to U.S. Aid and donors who helped buy food.

Our fetish neighbors in the palm forest.

Village of Light students in redesigned uniforms originally donated by McDonald's.

JAMES

They're saying things that are not true
O blessed Lord, what shall I do?
He answers, "What is that to thee?
Thy duty is to follow me."

ANONYMOUS; BASED ON MATTHEW 5:11

We first met James in Lomé, when we were trying to renovate our house and yard. A man would walk past every now and then, and one day he ventured up and astonished us by opening his mouth and speaking English—very good English, as a matter of fact. He introduced himself as James and asked Dal if there was some work he could do.

Dal was greatly interested in this man who spoke such good English. He learned quickly that James was also very skilled at gardening. He knew how, what, and when to plant, as if he had worked in a fine garden somewhere. Dal gave him work around the house and yard and also installed him as a night guard, though we did not feel especially at risk.

So Dal and I slowly became acquainted with James. It was not easy to get to know him at first, because he was withdrawn and not interested in talking about himself. We could tell he must have had a hard life and that something had made him fearful. But, eventually, after much patience and nurturing of our friendship, we found out that James had been a schoolteacher in Ghana. He was about 30 years old and had been next in line to be chief of his village. Later he told us that he had a wife and three young children back in his village. We wondered what had made him come so far from home.

After a while James did not mind talking, so long as it was not about himself. We asked him many questions and improved our knowledge of West African customs and culture. But whenever Dal told James about the gospel, James became troubled. He finally confided to Dal that he and his whole village in Ghana had worshiped Satan. He had been deep into fetish and spirit worship.

By right of birth, James would be chief of his village and his major responsibility would be to lead his people in fetish religious practices. He would also initiate the drinking of palm wine, the smoking of a special herb which causes people to fall into a trance, and calling upon the spirits to commune with his people. But James did not want to do these things. His heart was disturbed by the evil workings of spirits in his village. But he was just as afraid that villagers would kill him if he refused to be chief. Fears encircled James on all sides, like carnivorous birds closing in on their prey.

Knowing he had to get away from this terrible life, James left his village and the school where he taught and came all the way to Lomé. The trip was difficult, as his village in Ghana was quite far inland and Lomé was on the coast, but he felt that if he could get lost in the large capital city, he would be safe. He looked forward to the day when he might bring his children to live with him, too.

Each morning, Dal held a Bible Study for our workers. He would discuss a verse and lead a hymn. James was able to sing the songs very well, so well that we wondered if he had heard them before. During these times, James also began translating Dal's words so the workers could understand everything.

As time went on, James became more intrigued by the gospel. He showed a sincere desire to understand the Word of

God. Dal gave James a Ewé Bible that he could read for himself and started him on a Bible study course which demanded close study. James did well with whatever Dal gave him, and he seemed to think deeply about spiritual things.

It was not long until James joined Dal on his trips to the outlying villages of Lomé. Dal set great value on James' help because he could translate English into Ewé, allowing Dal to preach in English rather than French. Before he would set foot in an unfamiliar village, though, James had to be sure it was out of the range of where his family visited. He was always afraid someone would discover him in such a public place.

Sometimes I would go along with the group to a village, and during the drive, Dal and I enjoyed getting to know James better. One day we discovered that, for some reason, James no longer had a wife. He was now the only parent for his three children, a girl named Kwasiwa, and two boys, Kudjo and Kwami, and was arranging for them to come and live with him.

During these talks, James seemed comfortable and almost relieved to tell us his story. We were glad he considered us friendly enough to share his fears, and we did our best to point him to Christ, the One who can remove fear.

One day, James knocked on our door. When Dal appeared, he told him, "Pastor, I would like you to explain this thing for me. Last night I read John 3:16 but I couldn't follow exactly what it means."

Dal smiled. He had been praying for this moment.

James continued. "Can you tell me now about this Jesus?"

"I'd be happy to talk to you about the Lord Jesus," Dal said. "Let's begin where God begins—with sin. It's very clear in Romans where we read, *'All have sinned and come short of the glory of God.'* To receive salvation through Christ, man must realize that he's a sinner."

James let Dal's words hang in the air for a moment. "Sinner. Yes, I see that." He paused. "If I followed Christ, would I be able to serve Him along with the evil spirits?"

"No, you wouldn't be able to serve both God and the evil spirits. And you wouldn't want to. Once you have the power of God in your life, you wouldn't want to go back and recognize the evil spirits."

James nodded. "Now, when a fellow accepts the Lord as his personal Savior, can he be free from the evil spirits he served and worshiped before? Or can they follow him?"

"Well, we have to realize the power of God. When we accept Jesus Christ as our Savior we have God's power on our side. James, by simple faith in the Lord Jesus Christ, you can be saved and go to heaven."

James touched his forefinger to his lips in thought, then said, "Pastor, I served the evil spirits for a long time and I know that they do exist. I'm afraid they will still worry me. I've used them and I know their power. But I like the spirit of love and the peace I see in the missionaries."

Soon after this conversation, James claimed the Lord Jesus as his Savior. But he continued to have many questions about the spirits that haunted him. Whenever he would talk about how powerful the evil spirits were, Dal and I would always tell him that the Holy Spirit was even more powerful, but also good and loving. We would remind him that the blood of Jesus Christ forgives all our sins and covers the Christian completely. Evil cannot take over what Christ has already claimed.

In 1977, when Dal and I were due for a furlough, we left our ministry in Lomé with David and Elwanda Fields and two new missionary families, the Neufelds and the Plunkitts. James continued to go on his own to the villages, and when we came back to Togo in 1978, we discovered that he had suffered much persecution for his preaching against polygamy and idol worship. We, too, spoke out against these things, but the people expected us to do so. They did not, however, appreciate one of their own people taking a stand on such things.

Around this time, the story of James' life had spread to the United States as a result of our prayer letters and deputation meetings, and our mission decided they would like to make a film about James. We did not know how James would react to this idea, so we were pleasantly surprised to find that he not only was in favor of the project but also wanted to write most of the script. He was even willing to play himself in the film, called *Enlighten My Darkness.* James was a natural actor, and his performance was realistic and compelling. His story was a tribute to the mercy and grace of God, who brought light into his dark soul.

When we moved to Kpalimé in 1979, James chose to help us with our new ministry. His three children also joined James there, and we were overjoyed to meet them at last. For several years, James participated in Dal's Bible studies and the church services in Kpalimé and continued to translate Dal's sermons into Ewé when they visited other villages.

But one day, out of the blue, James began acting strangely, as if he were regressing into his fearful moods. He began ascribing puzzling motives to Dal's ministry. He claimed that when Dal held his Bible in his left hand while preaching, he was actually putting curses on the church members. To James, the large gold graduation ring on Dal's right hand seemed suspicious, especially when he brought his hand down on the Bible to make a point.

James made such a big deal out of his claim that the Kpalimé police felt it necessary to summon Dal, who tried to explain how bizarre James' story was. He did not deny that he owned a big French Bible and showed them the graduation ring on his finger, but he made it clear that he knew nothing about curses. "I have not come here to give curses," Dal said. "I've come to preach the Word of God."

That evening, and many afterwards, Dal returned home with a broken heart. Though Dal tried to reconcile with James, asking him to stop telling stories about us, our relationship with him became strained. To our horror, church members started to take James' side against us and against God. They began to think, *Maybe this white man has another motive for preaching the gospel. Maybe his real reasons are evil ones.* Dal was discouraged over the state of affairs, and I would often come home crying after a frustrating conversation in the market. It seemed that Satan was killing our work with these strange, impossible tales. All we could do was pray that God would reclaim James' heart and protect His church, while we continued living Christ-like lives.

Dal led a worship service each Sunday for those who still believed we were in Togo for no other purpose than to teach the Word of God. After a while, things calmed down at the church, but attendance was still low. Many village people who were not yet strong in the Word either believed James or thought we were strange to allow someone like him to fellowship with us. So Dal finally had to make the hard decision to ask James not to come to church or work for us anymore until he could change his words and his behavior.

James respected our wishes and left Kpalimé, saying he was going to look for a place where he could buy land and start his own farm. While he was gone, he left his children with us in Kpalimé. We knew James would come back eventually, but we were not sure when, or if he would come back to church when he did return.

While James was searching for land, the Lord renewed the church in Kpalimé. There were still many who believed we were not trying to curse anyone. The church was rebuilt more wonderfully than ever, and it seemed that God was working through the Christians there even more powerfully since they had come through such a trial. The young men who remained faithful were translating and leading music in our churches in Kpalimé and in other villages. After James left, God blessed us with many new families who wanted to be baptized and who quickly matured in the Lord.

In 1980, just after we had left on another furlough, James suddenly returned to Kpalimé. The church members insisted that Dal was a man of God and that he would be forgiving. They advised James to talk to Dal when he returned from America. When we finally arrived, it was only one day until James was at our front door. Dal knew there was a change in him as soon as he answered the door. He could tell by his friendly smile and the tears in his eyes that he was remorseful and desired forgiveness. Before James could even open his mouth, Dal put his arms around him and hugged him. When James was able to speak, he said, "I have sinned against you, Pastor and Madame, and against God, and I beg you to forgive me." He said he had wept over all that he had done against us. Dal told him we would forgive him joyfully and that we had been praying for this day to come. We were so thankful that God had brought James back to us like a prodigal son, humble and repentant.

James took up his old position as a member of the church, going on trips to outlying villages, translating for Dal. In his spare time he farmed a small piece of land he had rented. He was proud of his children, who had grown tall in his absence. Kwasiwa especially had matured into a fine young lady, and she helped our mission by working for new missionaries who came to help us, cleaning their houses or taking care of the children. She was a great asset.

Then, one day when I was standing in front of our house, James approached me and said, "Madame, I'm afraid something will happen to me."

I didn't say anything, not wanting to encourage this train of thought.

James did not seem to notice my silence and continued, "There might come a day when they will find me and take my life. I want you to promise me that you will take care of my children."

"James, we can pray for the Lord's protection over your life. You keep close to God and God will take care of you." I could not promise him a long life, but I encouraged him to trust God for his strength and health and life. "But James, you know we will take care of your children. You know we love them."

At various times over the next two years James would disappear, only to reappear and tell us he had been looking at other villages for land. I believe he was truly searching for land he could call his own and leave to his family. But he never seemed to find the perfect property to buy. Finally, he vanished into the hills and we did not see him for a long time. It seemed he had forgotten all about his church and his family in Kpalimé. Fortunately, his children were older now and could take care of themselves.

Then one day, Da Pauline told us there was a man in the hospital who had been brought in from the mountain villages. He had supposedly been beaten with stones and cut with *coupe-coupes* (machetes), but, amazingly, he was still alive. No one in the area could identify this man. Da Pauline said,

"Madame, I think it is James. Let's go and see if it is James." My heart sank like a heavy stone within me, but I took a deep breath and went with Da Pauline to the hospital.

When we arrived, the nurses told us that the man had already died, and because of the extreme heat, they had already buried him in an unmarked grave. So we were not able to identify him. However, the hospital attendant brought out a picture they had taken of his face, which was puffed up with bruises. Da Pauline said the face looked like James, though she couldn't be certain, due to the disfigurement. Then the nurse showed us the man's belongings, which were tied up in a piece of cloth in the African way. Inside the cloth bundle were a few clothes, some green bananas, and a Bible. When we saw the Bible we knew that the man who died was James, because the Bible had been given to him by Dal.

We left the hospital very sad, knowing that James was dead, but not knowing the whole story. We never went searching for the explanation, but it came to us anyway, having passed from village to village by word of mouth. Supposedly, James had been traveling on the plateau north of Kpalimé where villagers were having a big celebration, complete with dancing and palm wine. James must have been wandering for a long while, because he looked unkempt and dirty, with long hair and a long beard. James tried to outskirt the celebration, perhaps fearing that someone in this village might know him. However, some of the village children spotted him and began to tease him about his tattered looks. In response, James reached out and took hold of one of the boys to make him stop. The adults assumed he was attacking the child and began to chase him, swinging their *coupe-coupes* and driving him down into a ravine where they stoned him. James was found alive in the ravine after his accident, but he died soon afterwards at the hospital.

By the time we got home, the children knew their father had died, and we did our best to comfort them. Though I had promised to be responsible for James' three children, I never thought the responsibility would come so soon. Since they were older teenagers by now, we felt they would be safe in some rented rooms near us where we could watch over them. We were thankful that their father's death did not deter them from growing up into fine young people who chose to give their lives to the Lord's service.

Dal and I and the entire church membership mourned the tragic end of James' life. We preferred to remember him as the man who taught us about African culture and who could preach the Word of God so well. We believed he evidenced spiritual fruit that showed him to be a true follower of Christ. We hoped that his mental condition was only an earthly burden and that in heaven his mind would at last be made perfect.

The Village of Light

The people that walked in darkness have seen a great light.

ISAIAH 9:2

When we moved from Lomé to Kpalimé, one of my goals was to continue working with the blind. And, soon enough, the Lord provided a two-room house for us to rent and begin holding Braille classes. Our school was situated on a patch of farmland, surrounded by tall trees with beautiful yellow flowers. It was especially comfortable compared to our building in Lomé since it had electricity to power a fan. Eventually, we planned to build a new school and church together on the same property.

As I prepared for my first lessons, I imagined sweet little children with innocent faces coming to learn in my school. But to my initial disappointment, my first student was a large, disfigured boy. His name was Dieu Donné, which means "God-given" in French.

Although he had been born blind, Dieu Donné was so rambunctious that his mother couldn't keep him from shimmying up tall coconut palm trees with a large machete to cut down coconuts. But one day he fell out of a tree and landed on his face. The impact of the fall deformed his face, causing his upper teeth to stick straight out. From then on he was not able to close his mouth completely and had trouble eating and speaking.

But Dieu Donné seemed eager to learn to read and was quick to grasp new things. At first I worried that his fingers would not be perceptive enough to feel the Braille dots, but he was soon reading Ewé. We also began to see that he had an amazing gift for memorizing scripture. At church on Sundays, when the pastor would call out a reference for someone to look up and read, Dieu Donné would recognize the verse by its reference and stand up and recite it from memory before anyone could look it up. He also enjoyed going with Dal on village visitations, where he would exercise the wonderful gift God had given him by sharing the Word of God with people who could not read.

As I grew to love Dieu Donné, I wished something could be done about his misshapen face. Though his deformity did not seem to affect his upbeat character, it did inconvenience him. Eventually, Dal and I agreed that we would see what a Lomé dentist could do about his teeth. We rejoiced when the dentist said he could do a reconstruction of Dieu Donné's mouth, and he would do it for a discounted price. First he pulled the teeth that were sticking out, and then he reconstructed his other teeth, straightening them with braces. Finally, he fitted him with dentures so he could close his mouth completely and chew food properly. Seeing Dieu Donné smile with happiness after his surgery was a beautiful thing.

As the people in Kpalimé became acquainted with us, they were amazed that I loved their blind children enough to set up a school for them. But some parents gave me the impression that they expected me to heal their children, not educate them. Unless a blind person could be healed, the African people did not think he or she had any value. Only the *Yovo*, the white man, had any use for a disabled child, or so they thought. So some parents tried to give me their blind children for good, but we stressed that they must take their children back at the next vacation.

Soon, children appeared on our doorstep out of thin air, brought by parents or relatives who had heard of our school by word of mouth. Word of mouth is powerful in Africa. When a woman goes to market, she is not going just for food, but also to hear the latest gossip. Someone who had a blind child was almost guaranteed to hear about the school in Kpalimé that taught blind people to read and write with raised dots on paper. From as far away as Ghana and Benin, parents appeared with blind children in the hope that we could help them.

Soon we outgrew the little building on the farm and rented a larger house nearer to our church. It was then that I began to pray for permanent facilities. I had never considered myself an "education person," and had never dreamed that my classes would develop into a school. But as the numbers increased, I felt the Lord leading me to develop a real school with classrooms, dormitories, and a staff.

The wonderful progress of our school also made me think about making our school official with the government. During our first few years, God sent us some excellent students who grew spiritually and also had the potential of following a full French curriculum. We knew that if these boys were to qualify as educated and to fill jobs, they would need to follow the same program as students in the government schools. My helpers and I began to create a government-approved curriculum, Brailling books on science, history, math, geography, grammar, and Bible study. From the very beginning we made it clear that our school was Christian.

It was not enough just to follow the official government curriculum. To have an official school in Togo, we needed permission from the president himself. Fortunately, President Eyadema regarded education highly, so Dal and I worked to secure an audience with him. A date was fixed and we traveled to the capital to meet him at his palace. We were ushered into an elaborately furnished office, more like a small auditorium with rows of seats. President Eyadema sat at the far end of the room at a marble desk.

When he recognized us, calling us forward to present our case, he generously allowed us to spread pictures and documents all over his desk. We explained the progress that had been made and our desire to be recognized as official. We made it clear, however, that we were trusting God to supply our financial needs. Although he never seemed to understand the concept of reading Braille dots on paper, President Eyadema liked our plan. He was pleased that someone was helping the blind people in Togo. Before we left, he assured us of his approval and reminded us that he would give us land for our school. We exited the president's office thankful for the favorable response we had received. We felt that God was throwing open the door to a giant opportunity and inviting us to enter with confidence.

After our meeting, Dal and I began to think seriously about the president's offer of land. We knew that we needed our own property, somewhere with lots of room for our school to grow. But every time we had received an offer, Dal and I graciously refused, remembering the advice of a dear old African doctor. "Don't ever take land from the government," he had told us when we first arrived in Togo. "Always pay for what you get."

After our pleasant meeting, though, Dal and I decided to accept the president's offer of land. We asked the government if there was any available near Kpalimé for a Blind Center. The president and the minister of health both gave their approval and asked local authorities to locate some land.

With the president himself behind us, we found the local officials quite willing to help us. They showed us one piece of land after another. Some were too small for the ministry to be able to grow. We liked one piece of land on a hillside very much, but word came back that it was selected for a military base.

One day a local official took us up to the foothills. There he showed us a beautiful piece of property, a forested valley at the foot of the lush green mountains running between Togo and Ghana. The land was dense with majestic mahogany trees. There was even a stream running through the property.

"This land has been designated for a school," the official told us. "A school for the blind would qualify. You could have this land."

Dal and I began to seriously consider this property. It was right off the tarred road, just a few minutes away from town and supplies. It was also near the church Dal had started in Kpalimé, which was good since we wanted the school to be under the authority of the church. But it wasn't large enough, we decided. When the official heard, he quickly offered to add to the property.

"But doesn't that land belong to anyone?" we asked.

"No, no," he assured us. "The government required anyone who lays claim to a piece of property to have it surveyed and paid for. The deadline has passed and no one has paid for this land or even had it surveyed. So it all belongs to the government."

After additional negotiations, we agreed to accept ten hectares of land (about twelve acres) for our school for the blind. In our minds we could already envision the beautiful campus we would build for our students. Eager to get under way, we hired a retired German architect to draw up plans.

However, word about our property soon spread, and almost immediately we began hearing disturbing rumors. Certain individuals made it obvious that they were not pleased with the government's decision to give us what they believed was their land. The persistent rumors, though few, disturbed us, and we approached the local government with our concerns.

"Don't worry," the official assured us. "There is no substance to these rumors. The land belongs to the government to be used as we see fit. Everything will be perfectly legal."

Since we were scheduled to take a furlough, we decided to wait on construction. Back in the States our home church had promised to match whatever we could raise from other supporting churches and individuals. On our furlough, God allowed us to raise $7,000, which Hampton Park Baptist Church matched for a total of $14,000. Construction in Togo is not expensive, and labor is relatively cheap, so we had plenty of money to start building.

When we returned to Kpalimé, the disputes seemed to have died down. Since the government paperwork was complete and we held the deed to the land, we felt comfortable moving ahead. The first step was to clear some of the land. I cringed at the thought of cutting down the ancient mahoganies, but we did not want to build a school just to have it flattened by a falling tree. I watched eagerly day by day as the men built cement block walls, added an aluminum roof, and poured cement floors. Instead of painting the walls, the men faced them inside and out with beautiful rough-cut stone slabs that would not become dirty as the blind children felt their way along. The mahogany trees were cut into planks, and the beautiful wood was used for doors, window frames, desks, tables, and chairs.

At last, the final sheet of roofing had been laid and the last screen had been installed. Dal and I walked through the buildings, completely awed. The main building held an assembly hall, a classroom, and a smaller room we could use for a library. After years of teaching in rented houses, I felt like we were moving into a mansion.

We decided to call our school The Village of Light, or in French, *La Ville de la Lumiere*. The name refers to helping the blind escape their prison of intellectual and social darkness. But, more importantly, it refers to Christ, the Light of the World, who brings spiritual light into a life.

At first we wondered if we should advertise the school on the radio or in the newspapers, but soon we found out that wasn't necessary. Every so often the government would broadcast a short program about our school on the radio, describing how children learn to read by touching dots on paper. Along with word of mouth, this brief program on the radio sufficed to spread the news all over Togo and even to other countries that did not have schools for the blind.

There were no application forms or registration fees required for a child to attend our school. There were, however, some restrictions. We would not take epileptic children because the African people believe epilepsy is caught by touching, or even by looking at, the person. Even though this is obviously not true, we believed it was better to avoid the problem completely. We also had an age restriction. We liked our very youngest children to be at least five or six years old and able to eat, dress, bathe, and go to the bathroom by themselves. I learned from experience that some parents may say a child is older than he really is. To counter this problem, I found that if a child can reach his hand over his head while standing straight up and just touch his opposite ear, he is definitely at least five years old.

Our students loved all the disciplines, but their special joy was to learn mobility, which we taught them as soon as they arrived. We had a rule at the school that the students must walk with a cane so they would not fall or bump their head against a wall. Since we could not afford expensive canes, we cut bamboo sticks, smoothed the rough edges, and put tape around the tops for handles. Older students received a store-bought white European cane. Our students learned how to carry their cane properly and how to move it from side to side, feeling the gradations of the path or the nearness of steps. It was exciting to watch a student come to love his cane. "It is my eyes," one said. "It tells me where to go."

It always amazed me to see children run around our campus paths as if they could read the path, whether it was smooth, like our stone terrace, or bumpy, like steps. Down by the dormitories where it looked as if God parted the sea of grass, leaving a path of dry land, the children could find the path easily by feeling the grassy edges with their hands and feet.

Our students learned to move by sound as well, and they were sensitive to the movement of air and the sound of their voice echoing off nearby buildings. Sometimes they would talk or whistle to themselves, their ears telling them a building was nearby. Even at night, when I could not see anyone, I would hear a little voice call, "*Bon soir*, Mother Hen! Where are you going?" I could not hide from my blind children. God sharpened their senses to make up for blind eyes.

Half of our teaching staff were blind and half were sighted, a good balance in a school like ours. A visually impaired person can do many things that a person with sight cannot do. For example, a blind teacher can read in Braille much more quickly than a sighted person. They are also more sensitive to their students' needs because they think like their students. And, for the most part, our blind teachers were blessed with excellent classroom skills. They could lecture well, and they could also walk around the room to help students who had questions, reading what they had written or feeling the Braille cubes used in their mathematics lessons.

However, the need for trained teachers was continual. God helped meet that need by sending us an older man who had become blind while he was the director of a public school. *Maître* (Master) Awou Kwassivi came to our school with his wife, who cared for him as he took special classes to learn Braille. He also accepted our invitation to visit the mission church where, after several months, he repented of his sins and trusted Christ as his Savior.

As he improved in Braille through the years, Maître Kwassivi became an excellent teacher. We found him to be a faithful Christian and an honest man, as well as an accomplished teacher who understood his students. Eventually, we put more and more responsibility on him, and in 1989 we asked him to become the director of the elementary school. His capable oversight of the younger students took a heavy load off my shoulders. His wife was also an outstanding teacher. With a sweet, soft voice and a skillful, professional demeanor, she worked wonders with a class of kindergartners or a group of teachers in training. We were so thankful to the Lord that he sent us the Kwassivis, two excellent teachers with beautiful, loving spirits.

For many years we were able to teach only through elementary school. If students progressed beyond that level we might educate them in Bible correspondence courses and crafts. But I felt it would be profitable for them to continue on through secondary school. From the many different possibilities I decided the best idea would be to integrate our students into the Kpalimé secondary school. If they went there, they would be able to go on to a university. So Dal and I requested an audience with President Eyadema to ask for permission. To our meeting we brought some of the textbooks we had translated into Braille, as well as photos of the school and the students. We presented the president with a special Braille copy of the alphabet in his language, Kabiyé, as well as the Gospel of Matthew in French Braille.

President Eyadema was impressed with our ideas. He sent his minister of education to make an official visit to our school. The minister's visit, organized by local officials, turned into a big event for the town and was even covered by the press and a television crew. The people of Kpalimé were excited to see an important national official and his impressive entourage drive fancy cars solemnly through the town and onto our Blind Center campus. We prepared a tour for the minister of education so he could see that the students were proficient in Braille and all the necessary subjects and could adapt to the secondary level. In addition, we explained to him the role of "resource teachers," who would help the students read the blackboard or translate handouts and books into Braille. The resource teacher would not necessarily have to be in the classroom. If the student was careful to receive all his materials, his resource teacher could put them in Braille or even read the information aloud on tape.

The president soon granted our blind students permission to go on to secondary school if they so desired and to graduate by writing the same government exam as the sighted students. He also agreed that Togo would help pay the salaries of some of our resource teachers. We praised God for paving the way for several of our blind students to enter the school system of Togo.

Once we secured this permission, we had to help the government give the exam to blind students, since in Africa the government administers all exams. Togolese students are notorious for cheating on exams, so police must monitor every room while the exam is given. The government set up the same system for our blind students, and all questions were kept secret until the last moment. The difference was that the blind students were put into a special room with Braille writers and typewriters. The students worked out their answers in Braille and then copied them by typewriter in French for the sighted inspector to correct. There was no room for cheating with the Braille system; nonetheless, a policeman hovered over the students to make sure. It was a wonderful testimony to the government that our students were honorable.

In 1982, the first year the government exam was administered at our school, the two blind students who took the exam finished first and third out of eighty students in the area who took the exam. The news spread like wildfire, and many dignitaries came to congratulate the students. The blind students' accomplishments were even announced on the radio. The people in Kpalimé could hardly believe that our students had scored so highly, and they sent sacks of rice and beans and other gifts to honor their great achievement. Students at the Blind Center gave testimony that it was all of the Lord.

We are thankful for the strong testimony God has given our school through opportunities in Kpalimé and throughout Togo. Many visitors to the Blind Center have exclaimed, "I thought blind people were sad. These are all happy!" Truly they are. As Acts 26:18 says, it is Christ who is able *to open their eyes, and to turn them from darkness to light, and from the power of Satan unto God, that they may receive forgiveness of sins, and inheritance among them which are sanctified by faith that is in Me.*

AT THE FOOT OF THE BLUE MOUNTAINS

All things bright and beautiful,
All creatures great and small,
All things wise and wonderful,
The Lord God made them all.

— CECIL FRANCES ALEXANDER

The country of Togo was named after a village on the bank of Lake Togo. *Togo* means "water's edge," and, in our eyes, the country was unquestionably on the brink of receiving the Water of Life. Dal and I were honored to show them to the Water's Source.

Before Europeans colonized the country, African tribes existed according to "the survival of the fittest." The strongest tribes ruled, while the weaker tribes kept on the move, always seeking to avoid conflict. As people moved from east to west, ethnicities mixed and the land that would become Togo grew diverse, with many dialects and people groups. There are currently twenty-one tribes and ethnic groups in Togo, and the Ewé tribe is the largest.

Under the reign of Ago Koli, an oppressive king, many Ewé tribespeople scattered into the bush in search of peace. Some of these founded the village of Kpalimé around 1720. Eventually, the people of Togo turned from a monarchy to the clan system, in which numerous chieftaincies ruled the tribes, creating a semblance of democracy. Perfect equality among the tribes was never attained, though, since some tribes were always stronger than others.

The first Europeans to settle in Togo were German missionaries from the Evangelical Mission of Bremen. Later came merchants and traders of Brazilian or Portuguese origin. Many family names in Togo can be traced to these early European traders. During the colonial period, when European powers began struggling for control of Africa, the German empire prevailed upon a number of Ewé kings to sign the Treaty of Protectorate in 1884. The weaker tribes welcomed the Germans, but the protectorate lasted only thirty years, until World War I ended and the Treaty of Versailles divided Togo between the British and the French.

The French certainly left their mark on Togo. As the official trade language, French is still widely spoken. Virtually all official business and teaching is carried out in French. France did much to develop Togo's educational system, bringing literacy to about fifty percent. France also helped strengthen Togo's military, and the president now has an army to protect his country. The British contributed to the country by developing Togo's medical resources. Hospital facilities are not supported by tax money, so British medical personnel, with their modern medicine, have done their best to meet health needs.

After World War II, Togo was given over to an international trusteeship. But in 1956, the Togolese population voted to end the trusteeship and became an independent nation. The people were jubilant in their new freedom, and the Togolese thought that because they were under their own rule everyone would be rich. April 27, 1960, is now recognized as the official Independence Day of the Republic of Togo.

Togo is a long, thin country, about the size of West Virginia, with a tiny span of shoreline and a length of 260 miles stretching north. The country has a population of over two million people, making it one of the most densely populated areas in all of Africa. Kpalimé is located eighty miles inland. Though its population—about 30,000—would classify it as a small city, the people in Kpalimé are farmers who export products such as cocoa, coffee, cotton, peanuts, bananas, tobacco, and cane sugar. But an average farmer's income is only $150 per year—just enough to survive.

Visitors will find the lifestyle to be similar to that of a century ago. Many Togolese live in mud brick homes with conical thatched roofs, while others live in houses made from split palm branches. A few have solid concrete houses with metal roofs. Land holds great value for them, as almost every Togolese has a garden or a field somewhere.

Though many wear Western-style clothing, just as many wear traditional bright-colored dress. In the north, the flowing white or light-colored robes and baggy pants of Muslims are more prevalant. In the small villages, children play with no clothes or clad in only underwear. It is also common to see women in the village wearing only a skirt. Slacks for women were once worn only by prostitutes, but are now growing in popularity through Western influences.

The Togolese value their families. Uncles and aunts and cousins are important members of the "immediate" family and are treated as, and even called, brothers and sisters. It is not uncommon for everyone in a family to live in a single hut.

Visitors to Togo always praise the beauty of the country. In contrast to the brown colors of Niger, Togo is green—luscious green. One of our favorite places to take visitors was to the nearby waterfall at Kpalimé. During the rainy season, it poured a white, misty stream over a three-story cliff, while in the dry season, it was hardly a trickle. We loved to picnic there and rest in the rain forest under the tall mahogany trees that are hundreds of years old. Looking up into the dense canopy of the forest, we could often watch monkeys jump from one tree to another, jabbering and screeching about the strange white people below.

Although there is some grassland in Togo, the majority of the landscape is rain forest, with tropical trees in thick green layers that let in only spots of sunlight. Along with mahogany trees, there are cocoa, palm nut, mango, and teakwood trees. Even in town, fruit trees grow generously, reminding residents that their earth is anxious to bear fruit. The earth is so fertile that if we cut a branch and stuck it into the ground it would grow into another tree in no time.

The flowers in Togo are also magnificent. One of my favorites was the frangipani, which is used in Hawaii to make leis. It blooms in pink and peach and yellow, among other colors. In Africa, the frangipani is commonly planted over graves to keep them supplied with fresh flowers. Also growing wild are the bright bougainvillea, the striking bird of paradise, and the lush hibiscus. At Christmastime, wild poinsettia turns from green to red.

The fertility of the land is increased even further by little streams that run through our area. The little stream on our Blind Center property became a large river in the rainy season, and we used its water when our water pumps failed to work. The rainy season also creates small mud holes wherever the land is low and, in the bush, people wash their clothes and cars and, animals in these ponds, making the water unfit to drink. All the activity does not seem to bother the hundreds of frog inhabitants, whose voices tinkle like chimes on different notes. Their music, though pleasant, kept our visitors awake at night.

We spent so many years calling Kpalimé home that we became used to things that we once found strange or distasteful. I cannot say that we ever got used to the spiders, though they were frequent guests. As Dal wrote in a letter,

> A few nights ago a large tarantula was on the wall. As I struck at it, it jumped, surprising me, for I never knew a spider could jump. Kay laughed watching me try to avoid it landing on me and yet make sure it was killed. I hesitate to mention this as it may reduce interest in Togo by prospective missionaries.

It was usually only when visitors came that we remembered just how foreign this land really was. In August of 1978, the Project Compassion Team, a group from Bob Jones University, came with Dr. and Mrs. Dreisbach, whom we had met in Nigeria. The team taught VBS and took part in medical work at the government dispensaries. Dr. Dreisbach also assessed the need for a mission hospital.

The four nurses, two lab technicians, and one seminary student on the team adjusted moderately well to lizards in the kitchen, spiders on the walls, and cockroaches scuttling along the floor. They had less success sleeping. The first night they were kept awake by two crying goats that made sounds alternately resembling a child being cruelly punished or someone sick and vomiting. The next night, when tom-toms started beating for a funeral, they thought they had been chosen for a human sacrifice. But after only one week, they made wonderful progress, no longer taking a flashlight to search in their beds for spiders or insects. We knew we had finally won them over when one team member said to an insect on his plate, "Get out of there, bug, you can't eat my cake."

Living in a rain forest, we were often troubled by poisonous snakes. One night at prayer meeting in our little grass church, a slimy creature that seemed to want some fellowship slithered down the aisle. Another time, a big black cobra appeared next to our water pump. Someone screamed, "Snake, snake!" and those who were nearby grabbed sticks to hit him. As the cobra tried to escape he rose up and spread his hood. Even the African boys screamed in terror. Finally, a strong young man crushed and killed the cobra.

We prayed daily that the blind children would be safe from snakes. Once, as I walked down the path by the water faucet, I saw one of the little boys filling a bucket of water for his bath. By his feet I saw a large black cobra coiled up by the faucet. One of the workmen near me saw it too, but we did not make a sound since any noise could cause the snake to strike. Finally, when I was just about to faint from holding my breath so long, the boy picked up his bucket and left, without a care in the world. The workman ran out quick as lightning and killed the snake. In this same way, God has often protected our children who cannot see the snakes to avoid them. We have killed hundreds of snakes on our land. That no child has ever been bitten is a sweet testimony to the Lord's care for His little ones.

Another intriguing aspect of Togolese culture is the food. The Togolese generally eat a starchy root with a sauce of tomatoes, onions, and fish, or, on occasion, meat. The starch may be corn, yam, cassava, plantain (cooking banana), or taro. The Togolese also love vegetables such as okra, peppers, onions, and spinach, as well as fruits such as tomatoes, oranges, grapefruits, bananas, and avocados. For snacks, they might eat sugar cane, bread, canned mackerel, sardines, or peanuts. My favorite snack to get at the market was fried plantains. The vendor cut them into small slices, salted them, and dropped them into a pot of hot oil. After fifteen minutes they had caramelized and turned brown. They were served in sturdy paper and it was hard not to burn my fingers as I eagerly ate the plantain pieces, crisp on the outside, soft and sweet on the inside.

The Togolese eat all sorts of meat. The forests are home to game like agouti, antelopes, warthogs, and buffaloes. On the coast there is fishing, but many people also breed farm animals such as cows, pigs, goats, sheep, and chickens. In Togo, people eat almost every part of an animal, down to broiling the kidneys or pickling the intestines of a cow or pig. The people feel there is nothing wrong with eating animals like monkeys and snakes. In fact, they prepare an excellent snake stew, which I tasted when some men killed a big viper at the school. The meat, which resembles stringy chicken, was tough since it comes from the snake's muscles that slither when it moves.

The Togolese are also fond of making meals out of bush rats, which eat only herbs and leaves. For Africans, eating rat is not abnormal or dirty. It's just meat. African bush rats are not filthy like most American rats. However, they are very big. Our carpenter would put traps all over the Blind Center property and he was always so happy to catch a nice fat field rat. The blind children loved to hang around him in hopes that they might get a rare rat treat. The rats are either roasted whole, hung up by their tails over a fire, or skinned, cleaned, and cut in pieces for use in a spicy meat sauce. I have tasted rat once or twice, so I could say I have eaten it. It has not become my meat of choice, though.

Watching a Togolese woman cook is like watching an artist at work. Everything has to go in the pot at a certain time, and there are many rules about which foods may be served together. For example, couscous is a popular starch, but it is usually only served with lamb, just as rice and corn mush have their proper partners. And each dish has its own particular sauce.

When we planned a big dinner at our house, it would often

turn into a "Bring your own *ignam*" party. The *ignam* (ee-nyahm) is a starchy, yam-like root vegetable, often as long as two feet, which most Togolese grow in their farms and gardens. I would let the girls from the village know that we would be having dinner at our house and they would bring *ignams* to make *foofoo*, a dish similar to mashed potatoes that was sure to please a crowd. One of the best things I ever did was to get a food pounder, a round wooden log on a pedestal, all carved from one piece of wood. Women would take turns pounding the hot, boiled *ignams* with a large wooden pestle until they reached the proper consistency, forming a round ball. It was entertaining to watch, especially when three ladies would gather and pound their pestles in harmony, keeping perfect rhythm.

Inside, I would make a special chicken sauce over our kerosene stove or bottled gas fire to serve over the *foofoo*. The sauce must be a thin, watery gravy because the *ignam* absorbs all the liquid. We did not want a thick gravy because the *foofoo* itself is very filling and sits heavily on the stomach. The sauce was just for flavor. When all the food was ready, we gathered around the table to thank God for providing for us.

Any visitor to Togo while we were there will remember "coffee break." This tradition goes all the way back to Biola, when Dal and I would sit with others after a long day and fellowship over a cup of coffee. Years later, in Togo, we kept our appointment together as regularly as clockwork, and we became known for our "coffee break." I would come home at 10:00 in the morning from working at the Blind School and if Dal was in the area he would return from the village he was visiting or a Bible Study and we would sit together on stools at our kitchen counter. At "coffee break" we were able to touch bases with each other, to hold hands, to give encouragement, or just to listen. It was a time to find out what we would be doing next. Seeing each other for just a few minutes gave us renewed spirits to return to work again. Our life together was sweet, because Dal had his work and I had mine, but we made time to meet each other every day. My granddaughter Melissa began coming for "coffee break" when she was just a tiny girl. She always wanted to drink the coffee that was left in our cups. Eventually, I gave her a little child's cup with a painted face on it and made her "coffee," which was really a little bit of coffee with lots of milk and sugar.

Above:
The termite mound that indicated where to drill for water at the hospital site.

Right:
Village chiefs at the hospital dedication ceremony.

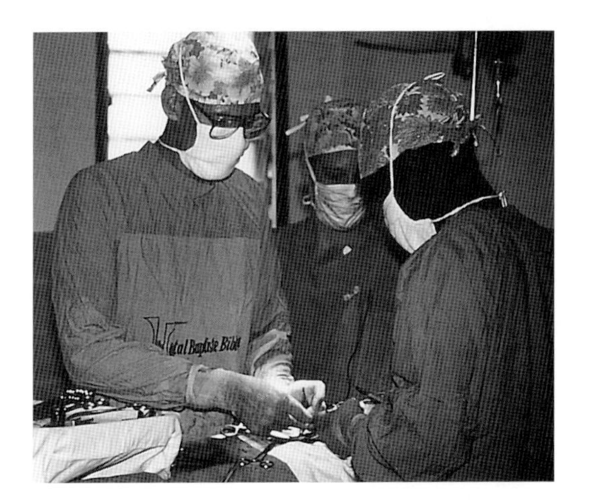

Dr. Clutts, who designed and directed the building of the hospital and served as the first doctor.

Dr. Cropsey, his wife Shirley, and their children.

Kay teaches Baby Daniel's family how to feed him with a baby bottle.

Lydia is carried by Jane.

Baby Noelle, whose mother died at birth.

Baby abandoned on the school's doorstep.

Dal and Kay's grandson Jeffrey Whitaker, 1969–1987.

Dal Washer, 1921–1989.

Some of those who came to Christ under Dal's ministry gather around his grave.

Pastor Yearick, from the Washers' home church, preaches at Dal's funeral.

Sons and pastors carry Dal's coffin.

The Kpakope church, built with resources from Dal's Memorial Fund.

Bob Jones University conferred an honorary degree on Kay. Left to right: Kay's daughter, Luann Whitaker, Kay, and son Dennis.

Jane Hankin, LPN, the new director of The Village of Light.

Ann Washer and Grandma Kay with grandchildren Melissa and Bradley.

59/50

If God places me in great perplexity,
must He not give much guidance;
in positions of great difficulty, much grace;
in circumstances of great pressure
and trial, much strength.
As to work, mine was never so plentiful,
so responsible, or so difficult,
but the weight and strain are all gone.
His resources are all mine,
for He is mine.

— HUDSON TAYLOR (Inscribed by Dal in his Bible)

By the early 1980s, our ministry in Kpalimé was in full bloom. Tears and laughter mixed with hard labor and prayer as the Lord brought rich blessing for our church and its congregation. Ron and Ann continued to be a great help. Our little grass church, which Ron pastored, was starting to fill to capacity every Sunday, and God worked in hearts as he preached. We looked forward to reuniting with our oldest son, Denny, and his family, who were planning to plant another church in northern Togo.

After Ron took over many pastoral duties in Kpalimé, Dal had more time to pursue his passion: to bring the gospel to the unreached villages in Togo's interior. Dal made it his business to see that God's Word was preached in the fifty-nine villages that stretched along the fifty miles of road from Kpalimé to Atakpamé. Dal's dream came to be called the 59/50 plan and our supporting churches began praying excitedly for its success.

Dal's plan was to visit a new village each week, revisiting

one more time, and then moving on to the next village. He came home excited after each village visit because the Togolese were so willing to accept tracts and to listen to his preaching. As he had done with village visitation in Lomé, Dal would bring along a group of young men who had been studying the Bible. Village visitation gave them experience witnessing for Christ, preaching, and translating for Dal. They grew quickly and deeply in the things of the Lord.

In pursuit of his 59/50 plan, Dal soon became incredibly busy with village visitations. On each trip, Dal and his helpers would visit at least one village, gathering people to hear songs and preaching about God's saving grace. In the daytime, villages might also be treated to a Bible story with visual aids. At night, Dal and the men would set up a screen and projector to show Christian films, which were as popular with the Africans as ice-cream trucks are with Mississippi children in midsummer. The numerous villages lay fertile for the seed of God's Word, and many trusted Christ as Savior.

Sundays were especially busy but blessed, as Dal would say. He would rise at 6:00 a.m. and drive north to a village such as Avého, where the people were waiting when he arrived at 7:00 a.m. for an early service in their little grass shelter. God was doing a marvelous work in people's hearts in that village: people were being saved, and there were nine in Dal's disciples' class after only a few months. Soon the men in the class would be able to lead the Sunday activities in Avého. It was not long before they built a grass-roofed church, and then a larger church building.

Dal stumbled upon the village of Kpakopé after people in another village did not want him to meet with them. Situated in a beautiful valley surrounded by hills, Kpakopé had never had any sort of church. The people welcomed Dal to their village, and soon Sunday morning attendance grew to one hundred people. The villagers quickly developed a desire to have a church building. Their little grass chapel was built entirely by Christians and was for a long time the only church for miles around.

The hearts of the Kpakopé people were extraordinarily tender to the gospel. One day a man with many idols and fetishes expressed his desire to be saved. He knew that God did not like idols so he decided to burn them. Many church members went with him to his hut to help him find all the idols and fetishes. Some were in the house, some were tied to the poles of his roof, and some were buried in the ground. When all the idols and fetishes were gathered together, they poured kerosene over them and burned them up completely. While the idols were burning, the Christians shouted, sang, and praised the Lord. It was a great victory in a church when someone got rid of his idols, so the Christians made a great deal out of it for encouragement. This same man had two wives, who were impressed by the difference the gospel made in their husband's life. Eventually, both wives decided to follow Christ. In a situation like this, our missionaries wanted the Holy Spirit to teach the man what to do about having more than one wife. Often the husband will let one of his wives go, while still providing for her, but sometimes he will keep both, knowing that he may not become a leader in the church.

Woumé was the third village Dal visited as part of his 59/50 plan. Home to over 2,000 people, the village was spread out and its inhabitants lived either in mud houses with grass roofs or cement block structures roofed with rusty aluminum sheets. Cornfields and gardens surrounded the homes.

As in the first two villages, Catholicism had reached the

people of Woumé long before Dal did, and Satan was using a strange combination of animism and Catholicism to hinder the preaching of the Word. Dal first approached the chief and asked permission to preach from the Bible to his people. The chief called his village council together to hear Dal present his desire to preach, but the Catholics expressed great opposition to Dal's visits. To keep the peace, the chief told Dal he would not be able to preach. Dal was discouraged, but he trusted that the truth of God's Word would triumph, one way or another.

It was not long afterwards that a young school teacher from Woumé, Kossi Hedzo Wawotu, attended a meeting in our home and began taking Bible courses with Dal. By God's grace, Kossi just happened to be the son of Woumé's chief, and, on a visit back to his village, he told his father about the *Yovo* who taught the Bible. He must have been convincing, because shortly after the chief sent word that he wanted us to come again to his village. Dal and I were thrilled. God had obviously brought Kossi to us as a means to reach Woumé, and Kossi was not even saved yet!

When Dal arrived in Woumé this time, the chief required all his elders and wise men and all his people to be present as Dal spoke from the Bible. The attendance at this meeting was beyond anyone's expectations: 350 people came to hear Dal preach outdoors. Woumé was a poor, primitive village, and most of the people seemed to be loving and friendly. When Dal and his helpers returned a second time, bringing the Blind School choir to sing and give testimonies, they were greeted with welcoming shouts. The people applauded the program to show their appreciation. In subsequent visits to Woumé, Dal recorded in his journal that he and his men distributed seven New Testaments and seventy-nine Gospels of John.

About this time, Kossi accepted Christ as his Savior, to our great joy. He immediately began helping Dal minister in Woumé, assisting in the Bible class that Dal had started with four people. The class soon grew to sixteen, many of whom professed Christ as Savior. To our delight, these people left their worship of idols. This weekly class continued with long hours of questions after every meeting. Kossi also helped Dal with those interested in Bible correspondence courses. When a VBS was held with help from a team led by Dwight and Anna Clark, many children responded to the gospel.

Dal began to feel close to the people of Woumé. While he was sharing Christ among them, he was also learning about their way of life, and it saddened him. The evil ceremonies in this village had become deeply rooted in the culture there. At the same time, Dal was also encouraged by what God was doing in the life of the chief, who seemed to show a real love for the Word of God. I suggested that he give the chief a Bible. We knew the chief was illiterate, but we hoped one of his elders could read it to him. So Dal made plans to present the chief with a Bible the next time he visited Woumé.

In Africa we had learned that you may not just hand a gift to a chief. You must first give it to one of the chief's attendants, who will describe your gift to the chief, after making sure it is not intended for harm. So when Dal arrived in Woumé, he told one of the village elders that he had a gift for the chief. The elder presented Dal to the chief as he sat on his chief's chair with his feet on an animal skin. This meant he was in "office" and would receive visitors.

The chief wore his usual outfit: a yellow cap, a necklace of yellow beads, and a short-sleeved, loose, striped shirt over black striped pants. He was an older man with a wrinkled face and a nicely trimmed white goatee. Dal approached the chief and bowed politely before him. The chief extended his hand, a sign that Dal could move forward and shake his hand. Then the elder said, "The white man has a gift for you," after which Dal took his cue to tell the chief that the gift he was about to give him was a gift from God—the Bible, the Word of God. The elder moved to take the Bible, signaling that Dal would not be allowed to give it to the chief directly. So Dal bowed and the elder received the gift in his two hands and repeated the words Dal had spoken to the chief. Bowing, the elder gave the Bible to the chief, who also received it with two hands.

Dal was not prepared for what followed. The chief reached up to his right shoulder where he wore a long, colorful, woven cloth signifying his leadership in the village. He slid this cloth off his shoulder and wrapped it around his waist like a servant so that his chest was bare on top and he wore only a cloth around his waist. When Dal told me the chief humbled himself in this way, it reminded me of Christ, who washed his disciple's feet with a towel wrapped around his waist. The old chief stood up, holding the Bible in both hands, and bowed before Dal, saying, "I have waited a long time to have this book. Now I have it in my own hands. *Akpé na wo. Akpé na Mawu!*" (Thank you. Thank you, God.)

It was only a few months later that the growing group of Christians asked Dal to lead a Sunday service so their families could learn God's Word. Dal was, of course, delighted to hold Sunday services in Woumé. He was not always the one to preach there, but when he did, I would sometimes accompany him.

There were always good crowds. The chief attended church regularly and instructed his wife and family to attend the services as well. It was so sweet when his wife accepted the Lord. Such a good response to the gospel made it easy to see why there was soon a strong knot of believers in the village, more than enough to warrant a church building.

The chief decided to make a bold move and give a gift of land for the church. This gift demonstrated the strength of his belief in Christ. After accepting salvation through Christ, the chief also turned away from mistresses, alcohol, and idol worship, and he went a step further by encouraging his villagers to serve the one true God.

The day the new church was dedicated was a day of rejoicing for all. The Africans decorated their new building with palm branches and flowers and invited many guests, packing the church to overflowing. The chief came to church in great state, not wanting any of his people to miss his presence at the first service in the new church. Many elders accompanied the chief, carrying the train of his robes. Shortly after the building dedication, Dal led baptismal services for new Christians.

Though a core of believers was growing in Woumé, many villagers were upset that someone was teaching people to turn to Jesus Christ. They feared what would happen if they left the idols their ancestors had trusted in for centuries. So when the chief lay dying a few years later, the unbelievers in the village did not want Dal to bury him. They wanted a burial in the African manner, complete with a pagan ceremony. But when the chief was on his deathbed, he expressed to Dal and to his family the desire to be to buried as a Christian. He asked Dal to perform the ceremony, wanting his body to be buried immediately after his death and covered with cement so the unbelievers in his village could not perform their own ceremony or dig up his body.

After the chief had died, large crowds came from many villages to pay honor to him. Many people from our churches attended the funeral ceremony. The Blind School choir sang in their uniforms. A number of government officials also came because the chief had ruled the village for many, many years.

Dal preached in French, and his words were translated into Ewé. The chief's faithful followers dug his grave and lined it with cement blocks to house the handmade coffin. Then they lowered the coffin, covering it with dirt and palm branches. Through the chief's strong witness, many people came to Christ.

The church in Woumé continues to be faithful today in spite of persecution from a liberal church nearby. The church has grown and the pastors are faithful to the Word of God. Many women bring Bibles to the services, which is rare for Africa. It means these women had learned to read over a period of years. Any church where the women start to read is a strong church.

Though his plan was to go at least once to each of the fifty-nine villages, Dal faced a delightful "problem" when villages readily accepted the gospel and hurdled to the next step—Bible studies and discipling groups, bringing Dal and his helpers more often. To meet the great discipleship needs, Dal and Ron decided to start a Bible Institute similar to the one Dal had organized in Niger.

By 1981, Dal and Ron had started a small institute in Kpalimé for those who wanted to study the Word of God more seriously. That year, they each taught fifteen students in classes like Bible Synthesis, Homiletics, and Eschatology. With interpretation into Ewé, the classes lasted an hour and a half and were usually offered at night. Dal was overjoyed as God continued to send him young men who wanted to learn the Bible. By 1985 there were thirty-five people taking classes through the Institute. Dal added classes in Hebrews and Romans.

Knowing that the relatively small number of missionaries could never reach every village in the country, Dal realized that training national pastors was the key to growing the work. He believed that the young men he taught would be the next generation of Christian leaders in Togo. The combination of motivated temperament and the challenging training they received, allowed many of Dal's students to plant strong churches where God's Word was preached and where God's people were encouraged.

When Ron and Ann left for a much-needed furlough in 1982, Dal regained the pastoral duties of the church in Kpalimé. Because of the workload increase and the beginning of the rainy season, Dal had to put aside village visitation temporarily. It was hard for him to put his plans on hold, but he prayed that a solution would be worked out so the "dear people out in the bush" would be able to hear the good news.

During the delay, God gave us the joy of seeing the grandfather of one of our blind teachers come to Christ. This man was an old village chief who was almost blind, and he invited Dal to bring the gospel to his village. Dal went along with several helpers from Kpalimé, our Blind School choir, and the chief's grandson, who preached a moving gospel message. That day the love of God was communicated clearly to 300 adults, all of whom listened attentively. After the service was finished no one wanted to leave—the people gathered in groups to ask questions and hear more about the Lord.

Dal was also encouraged during this time by the "All African Conference," a culmination of the first stage of growth in Togo. The conference took place in October of 1982 and was attended by missionaries and new Christians from all the churches and chapels established since Dal and I arrived in Togo eight years earlier. Dal wrote of this conference with great enthusiasm:

> If we had known eight years ago that we would have, from the three we started services with in our home, 300 converts meeting together from all phases of our missionaries' combined work here in Togo, we would have been dumbfounded.

On December 29, 1986, Dal celebrated his sixty-fifth birthday. I joked with him that it was not fair that he could retire but I couldn't yet! But Dal did not want to retire and neither did I. We were both perfectly happy in the work God had given us to do and we remained in good health, in part because we were working hard, walking a lot, and eating well. Mostly, we did not have time to think of our wants, as there were so many who needed us. The last thing on our minds was to retire, go home, sit in a chair, and do nothing!

We felt that Dal's sixty-fifth birthday was a special milestone in his life. To thank the Lord for years of safe travel, I decided to start an Evangelist Travel Fund among the local churches to help with the travel expenses of evangelists as they went from village to village.

Instead of preparing for retirement, Dal and I made the choice to anticipate eternity in heaven. We looked expectantly not to a cushy retirement on earth, but to a welcome rest with Christ. We longed for the day when we could gather in heaven with all those who came to Christ through Dal's faithful witness and introduce our American friends to their brothers and sisters in Christ.

Mother Hen: A New Nest

Fear thou not; for I am with thee:
be not dismayed; for I am thy God:
I will strengthen thee; yea, I will help thee;
yea, I will uphold thee with the right hand
of my righteousness.

ISAIAH 41:10

Before we built the Blind Center, we noticed that behind our property there were several mud-thatched huts sitting in the forest among the palms and cocoa trees. This compound, connected by small paths, surrounded an open area where inhabitants practiced spirit worship, healing by witchcraft, and African medicine.

In Lomé, we had come into contact with fetishers and spirit worshipers, and we knew these people were especially needy. But I must admit I was not excited to have a voodoo compound practically in our backyard. I reminded myself that when we moved to Tera in Niger we had settled on allegedly spirit-inhabited land. It would not be the first time that God had given us the opportunity to call upon His help in the face of evil.

After the school was built and we had lived on the property for awhile, God impressed upon my heart that I should take an interest in my fetish neighbors. I began speaking at first with the women and children nearby. For a long while, I was hesitant to open a conversation with Papa, the fetish priest and chief whom I would see working on his farm, attending to his palm trees or gathering plants to make fetish medicine.

One day while I was in our yard I noticed Papa rooting around nearby for herbs and plants. I summoned my courage and approached him, though I did not know exactly what I would say. I started out simply, with a traditional greeting, *"Ndi na wo!"* (Good morning to you!)

The chief nodded to me, but remained quiet.

Then I asked, *"Mi ele nuie?"* (Are you all well?) *"Davio, wole nuie?"* (The children, are they all well?)

He responded, *"Wo fau."* (They got up.) This meant his children were healthy.

"How good God is for making your children well!" I said. The chief was silent. I went on to make a comment about the plants he was gathering and then, rather awkwardly, I asked the chief, "Do you believe in God?"

Papa looked up, a little startled. "Yes," he replied, then threw a question back at me. "But who made the stars?"

I said, "Well, God did."

"And who made the moon and the sun?"

"God did."

"And who made the angels?"

"God did."

"And who made Satan?"

I hesitated because I hated to say this. "God did."

"You see," he quickly replied, "that is why I worship Satan, because Satan is one of God's sons."

I was saddened to hear of the immense power Satan held over our neighbors, but I continued to pray for them. Everyone at the Blind Center prayed to see this chief saved. He heard the gospel many times from our blind students and many visiting friends gave him Bibles to read. Eventually, one of his sons, Dodzi, did accept Christ, and his salvation reminded us that God has more power than Satan.

As we built our school and dormitories, there were many sleepless nights because of the tom-toms from our neighbors' ceremonies. Palm wine stirred the people into a frenzy of dancing, and many acts of madness would occur. As the drums accelerated, we could feel the throbbing vibrations in our bedrooms. Our blind children would cry out in fear because they had experienced what happened at these ceremonies. Almost all of them had been taken by their parents to the local fetish priest or medicine man to try to regain their sight. Many endured painful ceremonies to appease the spirits. Some had traditional, harmful medicines poured into their eyes while others witnessed the slaughtering of an animal as a blood offering for the idols. We understood why the children were afraid, and we did all we could to comfort them.

One night we were invited to the fetish compound because a child we knew had died. The deceased young girl had come often to the mission compound for classes, programs, or sports that we hosted. But we were not looking forward to visiting the compound. We knew what we would find there.

We had to follow a small path leading through the forested area and, as we followed the path, we passed under a rope hung with bones, feathers, and pieces of dried animals. Not knowing exactly what they meant or what power they possessed, we felt very uncomfortable. Also along the path and throughout the compound we saw bowls filled with offerings to the spirits.

We approached the fetish compound with extreme caution, trusting God to preserve us from evil spirits inhabiting the place. The drums were beating as local people gathered. The family showed us the child propped up in the corner of a room, bound in a grass mat and ready for burial. The priest, her father, was dressed in ceremonial clothes—a white robe with a red and black turban and sashes. Above his head he waved his scepter of wood covered with animal skin. He looked so fearful and mystical that I thought he might be demon-possessed. He was so different from the easygoing man I had spoken with earlier.

A dancer dressed in a red cloth twirled and shouted as the drums increased their tempo. At this point the drinking of palm wine and other strong drinks started, so we felt we should leave. On our way out we told the mother that she could cry out to the God who wanted to help her. Though she had lost many children during her lifetime, we could see she was still dealing with deep pain and grief. We hoped this tragedy would turn her to Christ for comfort.

Years later, when I had retired and was back in America, I received news from Togo that our neighbor, the chief of the fetish village, had died. My heart was sad to know that Papa would not have another chance to be saved. His sons said there was a time when he told them he was going to follow Jesus, but he never seemed to get around to doing it. To my knowledge, he never turned from the worship of Satan and was now in hell with the demons that he had served.

One of my most treasured memories from my blind students is going to chapel with them each Friday morning. Chapel was a time for students and staff to join together to sing, pray, recite verses, and listen to a message from God's Word. One of our classes would also present a special song, testimonies, and verses to show what they were learning.

I was usually in charge of welcome and announcements for chapel. As in Lomé, my students in Kpalimé called me *Koklonaw*, or "Mother Hen." Occasionally, instead of saying *"Bonjour, mes éléves!"* (Good morning, my students!) as I stepped in front of my little flock at chapel, I would begin with a "Cluck, Cluck, Cluck," and my students would giggle and answer me, "Peep, Peep, Peep!" Their enthusiastic reply was music to my ears. Once we had been in Kpalimé for awhile, the whole village began calling me *Koklonaw*. Only if it was serious business would they say "Madame Washer."

I was not a perfect "Mother Hen" by any means. But I worked hard to provide for the upkeep of the school and for the care of our students, many of whom came from faraway villages. Since we did not require registration fees due to the poverty level of most students, it was nothing less than a miracle that we had enough food. For a long time we fed our students with donations from the World Health Organization, distributed through the American Embassy in Togo. We would store the corn, rice, and oatmeal in big drums to keep it safe from insects and mold. The families of our blind students also added to our food supply by bringing gifts when they could. We supplemented the donated food with food from our gardens. After our first building project was complete, Dal made sure to plant fruit trees near the buildings so the fruit would be available to hungry children. He planted banana trees, citrus trees, coconut palms, and mangoes, his favorite.

Clothing was sometimes a problem, as the families did not always send their children with enough clothes to last for an entire school year. But God kept us supplied, sometimes in odd ways. For instance, in the 1980s, a thoughtful lady in the United States asked the McDonald's chain if they would donate their old uniforms for needy children in Togo. McDonald's agreed, but only if Togo had no McDonald's restaurants, which it did not. The lady and her friends then changed the pants into skirts for the girls and altered all the tops to sizes that would fit our children. When they received the uniforms, our students could hardly contain themselves. They were so excited to have new clothes, and they were especially impressed with the white hats. When the school choir sang at Togo's official opening of "The International Year of the Handicapped," they emerged onto the platform dressed in light blue shirts and ties, with navy blue skirts or pants, courtesy of McDonald's. As the students sang, I saw many people wiping tears from their eyes as they saw and heard what our young people could do.

Going on to universities to further their skills was something that our blind students did not believe was possible. It was therefore a big step for us when, during another visit to President Eyadema, we asked that our secondary school graduates be permitted to go on to further schooling. We informed the president that we were aware that our students would have difficulties in the university and that they would require assistance by resource teachers. We already had resource teachers helping our high school students attend the local private school in Kpalimé, so we knew the concept worked. And I had great confidence in Maître Kwassivi, so I recommended that he assume the position of *conseillé*, overseeing the entire university program.

The president graciously gave our blind students permission to pursue advanced degrees and also encouraged us to train resource teachers for them. In the years afterward, several of our students attended the University of Togo at Lomé. One of them was the very first Togolese blind person to graduate from a university. Most blind students who went on for higher learning chose English, German, or French as their major field, as blind people are good with languages.

For each of our blind students, whether they pursued advanced degrees or trained to be pastors, our deepest desire for them was that they do work profitable for eternity. There would be many obstacles along the way, but God would go before them, smoothing the road and lighting their paths.

Eventually, as our school began to average fifty students a year, our growing teaching staff felt that our curriculum needed to mature. We wanted to give our students every possible advantage while they received their schooling, so that they would be well prepared to continue their education. Part of our curriculum growth was adding many more books to our library.

But we also decided to look into having books translated into Braille. Because we wanted to translate so many books, we found that we could not afford to have everything done professionally. So after some deliberation, we decided to set up our own print shop and translate books ourselves.

The process took a lot of time and energy from many workers. A sighted reader would read printed text aloud while a Braille typist transcribed the text using a Perkins Brailler, a specialized typewriter with only six keys. Then, a thermoform machine duplicated the paper copy by melting a piece of heated plastic paper on top of it. The plastic copy was then bound into a volume.

The students who helped us translate books into Braille considered it a great honor as well as a profitable occupation. Since the translation work was never-ending, they could earn a good wage, either by the job or by the page, whichever they chose. As early as 1981, through our in-house printer, we had translated the Psalms, the three Epistles of John, and *Won by One*, a doctrinal primer written by ABWE missionary Mel Lacock.

Another exciting, though simple, development in our curriculum was our use of "touchboards" instead of bulletin boards. On these touchboards we used string to hang objects that the children could learn about by touching and reading Braille captions. We used our touchboards for everything from leaves and bark and seeds to identify trees, to plumbing parts and different cloths and fabrics. The touchboards were not always beautiful for sighted people to look at, but they were windows to the world for our blind students, who otherwise would have been unable to learn about many objects.

All children, whether young or old, progressed through the academic subjects taught in elementary school if they stayed long enough. After students finished, the teachers would evaluate them to decide what would be best for each one. Sometimes we encouraged a student to concentrate on becoming skilled in a craft instead of continuing in the secondary program. No matter what level of aptitude a student exhibited, we did not send anyone away unless they had a serious physical or mental condition.

For those students who identified more with crafts, God blessed them with a special teacher, Fiavi, whose name means "Little Chief." Fiavi was a kind, gentle man who worked quietly with his students, teaching them how to weave a mat or part of a chair or stool. Fiavi was partially blind himself, so he was even more patient with his students. He never raised his voice; instead, he nearly whispered as he instructed them how to ready the weaving rope, or how to count the widths of rope or fiber that must go in a mat or basket. He taught both their hands and their minds.

When our students were not working on academics or crafts, we provided many extracurricular activities to keep them busy. For example, we enjoyed taking our students on annual field trips. One year, the twenty students who had signed up said they wanted to touch three things: an airplane, a boat in port, and the ocean. It was quite an undertaking, but we managed to squeeze everything in. Everyone we visited gave us the "red carpet" welcome. While at the airport a big

DC-10 came in and the students were allowed to go inside. They all ducked down thinking the cabin was very small. On the other hand, they could sense the enormity of the sea and, when we arrived there, they were frightened at first. They thought the never-ending waves and ripples might just eat them up. Eventually they grew to love it, and as we stood on the pier touching one of the ships, it thrilled the children by blowing its horn loudly.

More routine activities included hospital visitation and evangelistic choir outreach. Our Blind School choir was exceptional: the students sang excellent four-part harmony. The Africans seem to sing parts innately. From the smallest to the largest child, their hearty voices blend together in exotic melodies which intertwine to create a distinctively African music that is difficult to write down or even translate. My favorite piece was a song based on Isaiah 51, one of the loveliest poems in the Bible. There were so many parts and so many voices that my ears could not separate one note from another as all joined together into a shimmering sweep of sound. I wish more musicians could study the music of Africa so that more people could appreciate its beauty.

The choir looked forward to village visitation night as "their night." This was their time to have complete charge of an open-air meeting in a distant village. When our Volkswagen truck pulled into the Blind Center for an outreach night, the air grew charged with excitement. As the vehicle moved through Kpalimé, they began to sing. And they continued to sing all the way to their destination. This always attracted crowds of people in each village. They would stare in amazement as a blind student showed pictures while telling a Bible story. They marveled when a young man read the first sixteen verses of John 3 without hesitation. Then the children would give testimonies that brought tears to the eyes of their hearers. Some told how they once tried to kill themselves because they hated being blind, but now were thankful that God sent the blindness so they would find the light of salvation. The climax of the evening was usually an evangelistic film in French. For those who lingered, tracts, Gospels of John, New Testaments, and Bibles were available. The blind students were eager to share verses with the inquisitive ones, hoping to show them how to know Christ as their personal Savior.

With all the attention we gave to educating our students academically, we also made sure to keep them physically active. Blind children are no different than any other children whose little bodies overflow with energy. Dal became their hero because he introduced new and ingenious ways to play the sports they never dreamed they could play. One of the first he introduced was beeper-ball, using a ball with an electrical beeper in it, allowing the children to keep track of it as they ran after it in a nearby field.

Later I learned that visually impaired people can run well if they are helped along at first and provided with a special track. Dal took on the task of building this track for our students, with an outer edge of gravel and an inner edge of dirt where children could land safely if they tripped. As the children first learned to run, they held on to a sighted person's hand. Soon they could run all by themselves. They loved to have races to see who was the fastest.

My favorite lighthearted activity was our weekly fun night. Dal and Ron and I gathered together a bunch of combs, reeds, wires, and tin cans so the children could make them into African instruments. Many also brought their own homemade instruments to blow or drum or ping. When everyone got together, Dal or Ron directed them in a big orchestra with all the kids playing their funny little instruments. The men clowned around as much as the children.

Dal always insisted that we have popcorn shipped over because he got such a kick out of feeding it to the blind children, who thought it was the most wonderful food they had ever eaten. We eventually got smart and bought plastic bags from the market so each child could carry their popcorn in a bag instead of in their shirts or pockets. Sometimes they tried to take more than popcorn home: we couldn't help but laugh when one child tried to save an ice cube.

We were constantly reminded that the time we had with our blind children was fleeting and therefore very precious. We had only a short few months to make a difference in their lives with the gospel. Most students came from non-Christian homes and were torn between their parents' teaching and the teaching they received at the Blind Center. Before they would listen to what we had to say, we had to win their confidence by showing that we cared for them.

Da Pauline continued to be a valued part of the spiritual work at the Blind Center. God gave her talents in relationship building, and under her sweet influence many came to know Christ as Savior. As her hair turned gray, she became known as Mama Pauline, but she never grew too old to care for the children. She especially loved the tiny girls from faraway villages who were homesick. Many did not speak Ewé and felt all alone with no one to turn to.

At night, when the students had hopped into bed after their evening cold-water baths, I enjoyed peeking into the girls' dormitories to watch Mama Pauline lead an evening prayer time. She would sit surrounded by little girls and would tell them a story or read the Bible or help them memorize a verse. Then they would choose a song they had learned in the Blind School choir. Their beautiful singing could make me cry, knowing that it came from hearts that could see God.

Afterwards, Mama Pauline would quiet everyone and talk to them about what they would like to pray for. The children especially liked to pray for their families. Mama Pauline would help each one to fold her hands and say a little prayer to God. In this way, she helped the young girls develop their prayer life, and prayer became precious to many of them.

Some of the sweetest sounds I've ever heard are those that reached out to the African night as my blind children sang in beautiful harmony, praising and thanking God for another day. I would often go to sleep saying, *Thank you, Lord, for making this possible. Thank you, Lord, for each life we've touched that now loves you. Thank you, Lord.*

Togo

I always look forward to the happiness of springtime,
when all the fruit trees blossom—
the beginnings of fruit forming on the branches.
The first trees to give ripe fruit are the wild mangoes,
a small and stringy fruit,
but the kids love them
and eat them like popsicles,
squashing and sucking on them
as the juice runs down their elbows.
My blind children have learned
to shake the branches
to make the mangoes fall
and then to pass their feet gently over the ground
until they feel the fruit.
Shrieks of delight echo through the trees
as they fill their baskets
and lick their hands.

— ALISON GRAY

A GOD-SIZED PROBLEM

Preach the gospel daily. If necessary, use words.

— ST. FRANCIS OF ASSISI

One day the fetish priest's wife came to me carrying one of her children. She begged me to give the baby some medicine, for the child had the raging fever that comes with malaria. I crushed up an anti-malaria pill, added some aspirin to take the baby's fever down, mixed it with water, and spooned it down the child's throat, hoping the fever would soon diminish. Then, I wanted to pray with her and for her child, so I asked her if she believed in God. She told me, "We know there is a God but we do not worship Him anymore. We used to worship *Mawu*, the Creator, at the Catholic church, but when we called on God for our sick children, they still died. So we began to call on the spirits and to bring sacrifices to the idols instead. Now that we worship Satan, we have some grown children. When we worship Satan, we have more power to get the things we need."

I told Dal about my conversation with the fetish priest's wife. Ever optimistic, he was excited that she seemed comfortable enough with me to be honest about her beliefs. He reminded me that God had placed us right beside a community for the specific purpose of reaching them with the gospel. But I longed for some way to minister to the people's physical needs, too.

Toward the beginning of our work in Kpalimé, Da Pauline and James would go with Dal and me up into the mountainous villages of the Danyi Plateau. Dal and James would preach to anyone receptive to the gospel and Da Pauline and I would work with women and children. We grew to expect that mothers would bring their sick children to us, and we were often shocked at the indigenous medicines they were given. Da Pauline and I did all we could to help them. If a person was in danger, we would try to save the life, or we might locate a rickety taxi to carry them to a distant hospital or clinic. We might even use our own car if there were no other alternatives. From our experience in Niger, Dal and I knew that medical care spoke to people's hearts more clearly than any words. What better way could we represent God's love for them?

One afternoon on our way down the mountain, we stopped for a picnic lunch. Our favorite place to eat was off the main road and down a path shaded by trees. As we ate, looking on the villages spread over the foothills below, we talked about the many sick people we had noticed. We had already begun to realize the great need for doctors, nurses, and a clinic to care for those who lived far from any hospital. Most of the villages in the populous 59/50 area were prohibitively far from a hospital or clinic, so Africans often waited too long—until it was too late for medical help.

There was a government hospital in Kpalimé that did its best to treat the many who came there, but the care it provided was inadequate. There was also a German hospital on the way to Lomé and another in Atakpamé, but they were both jam-packed and deficient. Our hearts were saddened as we looked at the many medical needs in Togo. We didn't know what to do.

So we did the only thing we knew: we stopped eating and prayed. *Oh God, these lost people need medical help. Please send us nurses to meet this great need.* Nurses alone wouldn't be enough to meet the need, but it was a start.

I began writing letters to our mission office back in America to inform them of the great medical needs. They helped us spread the news, and it was not long before God sent us several nurses who worked out of our houses in Kpalimé. As they began to learn Ewé, they also visited villages, but they had no center of operations and their work was limited.

As the months and years went by, we became bolder and braver before God. We had, up to now, been praying for nurses. Now we prayed for a clinic, a doctor, a surgeon, and a hospital where people could be restored to health.

In 1978 God sent us a medical-evangelism survey team led by Dr. David Clutts and Dr. Linc Nelson, both gifted surgeons. We told them our vision of reaching villages with the continuing gospel witness of a medical ministry. Dr. Clutts and Dr. Nelson encouraged us with their extensive research into medical missions. In Bangladesh, nearly every church leader came to Christ through the hospital ministry. In addition, hospital ministries in the Philippines were a decisive factor in forming over 150 local churches.

While we had formulated the philosophical foundation of our proposed medical facility, the word must have spread. A chief from the village of Adeta invited Dal and Dr. Clutts into his village and promised them a large tract of land if they would build a hospital on it. The land he offered was in the foothills, central to the region where hundreds of thousands lacked adequate medical care. The area was called Tsiko (Chi-kaw), or Water Stones. We were amazed, not only that God would throw the door open toward building a hospital, but also that the land included the very place where we had enjoyed our picnic and had prayed for a hospital. No one knew where we had first prayed—no one but God.

There was only one problem with the land we were given: there was no good source of water. A little stream trickled across the land, but it was not enough to provide for an entire hospital compound. Dr. Clutts, characteristically confident in God, asked Dal to find someone who would drill a well while he left to raise funds for the hospital. Dal found a mission in Togo that did drilling, but they had only a small rig and would try a certain number of times for a fixed fee. We were not concerned because we thought it would be easy to find water. But the drill went down and brought up only white powdery sand, no water. Over and over the rig drilled, until our chances were up. The well-digger said that either there was no water in the area or his drill bit couldn't go deep enough. We were discouraged. We thought we would have to give up the land and start over.

Then God sent a new American ambassador to Togo, a woman named Miss Johnson. She was an experienced politician, but also a compassionate woman, the kind who took her handicapped sister everywhere with her. This ambassador noticed that one of Togo's biggest problems was bad drinking water, which caused a host of diseases. Miss Johnson wisely put two and two together and realized that deeper wells and cleaner water would equal less sickness. So she arranged for big rigs from America to be shipped over to the mountains of Togo to drill wells. The American Embassy office created a complicated application with specific criteria for those who would get a well. It had to reach a certain number of people and it could not be for private purposes. Schools qualified, villages qualified, and hospitals qualified. When we asked the Embassy if our not-yet-built hospital qualified, they said yes.

The day the huge American rig came to our land, we were

thrilled. We thought surely such a big drill would hit water easily. We waited eagerly as the rig was set in place and began to drill but, again, the only thing that came up out of the ground was white, powdery sand. The rig was moved several times, even down into a river bed, but with no success. If there was any water in the land, it was certainly hiding its secret well. The Embassy had done every test imaginable to find water, from aerial photography to divining, but over and over the drill came up with nothing but dry white sand. Finally, the Americans told us they could only drill once more. And we had to make the decision of where that would be. We cried out to God for this big decision.

I don't remember who had the idea, but someone said, "Look at all those termite mounds—some are over two stories high! They must have water to keep their mud castles sticking together." Another person said, "You're right! Let's make a map of all the termite mounds, then draw lines from one to the other to see where the lines cross. Perhaps there will be water there!" When this was done, the lines, sure enough, all crossed at one point, which we hoped was the source of water for the termites. The rig was set up and the drill went down for the last time. If there was no water there, we could not build our hospital. This needed to be a miracle.

It wasn't long before the drillers called us to see moist soil coming up out of the ground. They continued to drill deeper and brought up more wet soil and even water, but the man in charge said the source would not be enough yet. So they kept drilling, until they pierced through a thick layer of stone. Below, they found a deep cavern that held an abundance of water. The crew tested how much water would be available, and the amount astounded even the supervisor. He said, "This is enough for a hospital. This is more than enough."

This one source of water has supplied the hospital and all

its patients, staff, and workers for over twenty years now. It has never run out. The stone cavern is a clear demonstration of the marvelous grace of God.

We decided to keep our hospital small and simple: just twenty-five beds. And our outpatient clinic would treat up to 150 outpatients each day. Only a small number of missionaries would live at the site, while most workers would live in neighboring towns. Even as a medical mission, we felt our priorities should be based on biblical goals: winning and training people in the ways of the Lord.

By the time the mission headquarters in America began to raise money for the hospital, God had already called two highly specialized doctors to Togo as missionary doctors. Also on their way were four more nurses and a lab technician. These were in addition to the nurses already working in Togo who continued to work on their language skills as they operated clinics. God eventually filled our staff needs completely. When our hospital opened in 1985, we had a marvelously talented group to welcome our first patients.

It did take a while to build the hospital, though. I remember Dal spending many hours driving a dump truck with sand and gravel for the foundation. But during these years of construction God sent many short-termers who came for weeks, months, or years just to work on the hospital. Some were carpenters, others were plumbers or electricians. Without these generous people, the hospital could not have been completed, nor would it be as beautiful as it is.

Finally, after six and a half years of planning and construction, the Karolyn Kempton Memorial Christian Hospital was dedicated on June 12, 1985. It was named after the wife of ABWE's president, Dr. Wendell W. Kempton. Karolyn had passed away in 1980, just as plans for the hospital were getting off the ground. She was a loving, compassionate lady who had greatly encouraged her husband, as well as many missionaries, including our own family.

On the day of the dedication, God, as a special benediction, sent us ideal weather. Although it was the rainy, windy season, God sent a gentle rain the night before and sunshine and cool breezes for the dedication.

Togolese people came from miles around to participate in the celebration. Many were dressed in vivid African robes and headdresses. An entourage of thirty village chiefs arrived, wearing colorful ceremonial caps over their graying hair. Representatives from the local and national Togolese government, the American Embassy, the Peace Corps, and other American mission organizations were also present. An estimated 1,500–2,000 people poured into the hospital complex to dedicate the new medical facility.

Under the shade of tents and palm branches, visitors first heard singing from our Blind School student choir. Then it was time for speeches. I was honored to contribute a short speech, telling the story about finding the plentiful source of water on our hospital property. Dr. Kempton and Dr. Clutts also delivered addresses to the crowd. The attaché of the minister of health and social affairs in Togo gave a speech of praise and thanks to the United States and the ABWE Mission. Then he asked everyone to stand and observe a moment of silence in memory of Karolyn Kempton, for whom the hospital was named. The poignant hush was soon dissolved by the local chief of Tsiko, who gave a rousing political speech to which the Africans responded in Ewé.

After the ribbon was cut, all the dignitaries and guests toured the wards, laboratories, operating rooms, and private rooms of the hospital and the clinic. There were endless opportunities to give God the glory for building, stocking, and staffing our new hospital.

At 3:00 that afternoon, Dr. Kempton asked the missionaries and the American guests to meet in the women's ward. There he reminded us of our main reason for being in Togo: reaching the lost for the Lord Jesus. He asked all the men to kneel on the cement floor for a private dedication of the hospital to the Lord. Dal and several other men prayed, and our hearts were united in asking God to bestow his blessings on the hospital so that many souls would come to know Christ as Savior because of this wonderful new tool of evangelism.

Soon the hospital grew larger than anyone could have expected, both in size and in range of influence. One of the most important additions occurred in May 1995 when a Nursing Education Program for Togolese students was begun under the tutelage of nurse Annette Williams. Classes are offered in obstetrics, endocrinology, tropical diseases, and basic nursing skills, while nursing students gain essential experience at the hospital. In its first ten years, the nursing program graduated dozens of nurses, many of whom now work at our hospital.

The hospital now has a capacity of thirty-five beds (ten were added), distributed among the three wards—one each for women, men, and children. There are also a few beds in an intensive care ward and private rooms for patients and infectious cases. These thirty-five beds are barely able to house the patients flooding the hospital on a daily basis.

Malaria is currently the cause of over forty percent of hospitalizations in Togo, and it is certainly the most common disease. Unfortunately, there is no vaccine for malaria, and resistance to the drugs currently available is a major problem throughout the world. Especially frustrating is the fact that young children are most often affected by malaria, which can be a lethal disease.

Above:
Bird's-eye view
of The Village of Light.

Left:
Landowners bargain
over the price of
the land.

Blind students with teachers and staff.

Kay in the hospital with broken bones stabilized with the fixator.

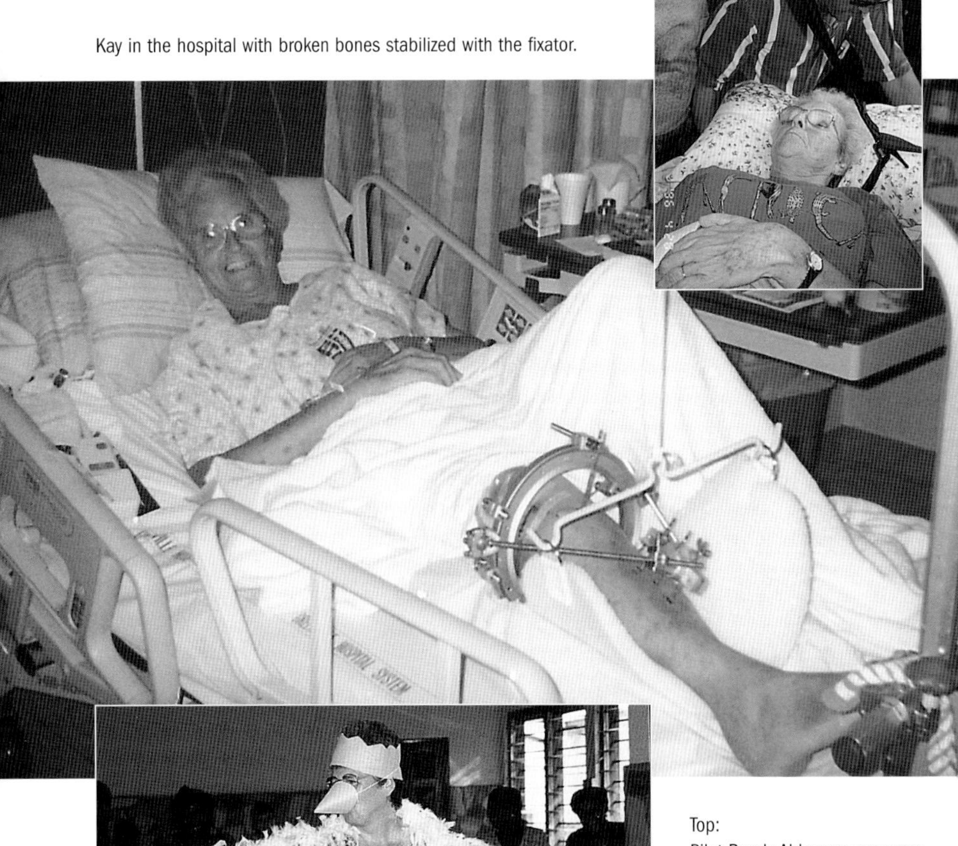

Top:
Pilot Randy Alderman prepares the Cessna 206 for Kay's evacuation to Ghana.

Left:
Jane, the new "Mother Hen."

Bottom:
New staff at The Village of Light.

Above:
The 25th Anniversary of The Village of Light.

Right:
The gravesites of Tim Matchett and Dal Washer.

Below:
Kay receives the civilian medal of honor.

REPUBLIQUE TOGOLAISE
TRAVAIL - LIBERTE - PATRIE

ORDRE
DU MONO

LE PRESIDENT DE LA REPUBLIQUE TOGOLAISE

Madame Katherine Washer

OFFICIER DE L'ORDRE DU MONO

02 - 12 - 99

Lomé, 02 Décembre 1999

68/99

The Order of Mono certificate and medal.

Left:
Missionaries and pastors in Togo.

Below:
Students and teachers at The Village of Light.

Above:
Thanking God for the family He is giving us. Kay's 80th birthday with her four children, fifteen grandchildren, and twenty-one great-grandchildren.

I have no greater joy than to hear that my children walk in truth. — III John 4

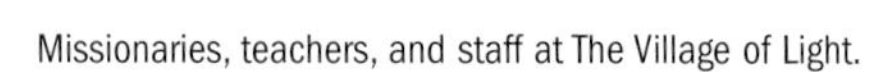

Missionaries, teachers, and staff at The Village of Light.

When I first went to Africa over fifty years ago, leprosy was the most feared disease. Both medically and spiritually, the missionaries of that earlier era showed great compassion, just as Jesus did, for those whose bodies had been eaten away by leprosy. Today it is AIDS that is the scourge of Africa, destroying the lives of millions. It is not a simple thing to tell a man that he has AIDS, nor is it easy to counsel him as he faces the distressing abbreviation of his life. What's worse, most of those who come to the hospital with AIDS do not know Christ. Undoubtedly, the problems posed by AIDS are enormous. But the same challenges brought on by AIDS and its effects are also opportunities to reach those dying from the disease with the gospel, as well as reaching children orphaned by the deaths of their parents.

Typhoid fever is also common in Togo, since it is caused by bacteria that can be transmitted easily through contaminated food or water. The disease can be fatal, though antibiotics are effective if administered early enough. Even missionaries at the hospital are not immune to typhoid. An outbreak could put medical workers in the hospital for days, or keep them limping along, trying to find time for rest among their many duties, while also hoping not to spread the disease to anyone else.

With all the challenges at the hospital, "The battle for life is a daily reality at our little thirty-five bed hospital," Dr. Bob Cropsey wrote. He and his wife laid aside a fine practice in America to help with the construction and work of our hospital. Dr. Cropsey described one government district hospital as having "fewer drugs in the pharmacy than most Americans have in their medicine cabinet!" In contrast, the Karolyn Kempton Memorial Hospital, though not as fully equipped as we would have liked, endures as a haven of real safety for hurting people.

God has continued to bless the efforts of our staff: in 2004 we learned that our small hospital had become the third busiest in the country. This number was due in part to the efficiency of our staff and our procedures, which allow us to have a quick turnover of patients. Furthermore, we have a remarkably low incidence of postoperative infections, and our quality nursing care allows patients to recover more quickly than is typical in a third-world country. Mostly, however, it is by resting in the joy that only Christ can give that our excellent doctors and nurses manage to keep going while they preserve the fine reputation that draws people to our hospital.

In the midst of all the rush and hurry, the hospital still insists on making time for evangelistic outreach. From the very beginning, it has been a place where spiritual healing is just as important as physical relief. It would be naive to think that every profession of faith was a genuine, lasting conversion. But, as Bea Ward, one of our missionaries, said, "It's a place to start. And it's an evidence of the hospital's commitment to evangelism. Our compassionate nursing staff and highly competent medical personnel go a long way to predisposing these hurting, needy people to listen to the story of a loving God who wants a relationship with them."

A typical day at the hospital (if there is such a thing as a "typical day") begins with a presentation of the gospel in the clinic waiting room, followed by evangelistic video tapes. Audio tapes in Ewé, Kabiyé, and French are distributed to patients who are interested. Some tapes have songs recorded by the church choir in Tsiko, while others have scripture passages read aloud. Many patients return to the clinic professing Christ as a result of these taped messages. Evangelistic services also are held each Sunday afternoon in the wards. And, recently, Bible training has begun at the hospital to train young Togolese men to be pastors and church leaders.

After twenty years of operation, our hospital was performing 850 surgeries yearly. Each year, over 9,000 patients were treated by approximately ten missionaries and eighty national personnel. In 2004, there were 748 salvation decisions at the hospital, more than two per day. These new Christians serve as the basis for Bible study groups all over Togo. Many churches have been started in faraway villages because a patient took the gospel back to their hometown.

As I watch the hospital ministry unfold, I wish I had another life to give to the Lord. Even now, I am still eager to help with this ever-expanding challenge, if only to pray that God would call young Christians, from Africa and elsewhere, to serve at our marvelous hospital in Togo.

ALL MY BABIES

The Lord hath done great things for us,
whereof we are glad.

— PSALM 126:3

While sweeping a classroom porch one morning, one of our blind students bumped his foot against a soft bundle. Reaching down, he found a tiny baby wrapped in an old cloth. He ran to our guard, Sammy, who found a note from the mother written in French and tucked in the baby's cloth.

> Bonjour,
>
> It is not joyful for me because I have come to leave my baby here. His father has refused that it is his. For me also, I do not see any possibility of knowing how I could support the baby. She was born 12.19.89. I do not want her also to suffer like I suffered. That is the reason I am looking for someone who will take her and support her. Whoever picks up this infant, do not complain against me or criticize me. Take this infant like your own. God bless you. Thank you.

Those of us who read the mother's letter were heartbroken by her evident hopelessness. We reported the incident to the local police and agreed to keep the baby until they could find the mother. They hoped that locating her would lead to other family members who might adopt the child. Word of the mystery baby quickly passed through our town.

Several days later, the mother came to us in the night, crying and hurting. She had many problems, both spiritually and mentally. She was unable to take care of her child, but the police had found some relatives who could. As we helped the mother work through her problems, we marveled at the grace of God, which brought her to a low point so she could find peace through Christ.

The baby left on our doorstep was neither the first nor the last baby that Dal and I cared for in Africa. Fortunately, I delight in African babies and it's easy for me to love them. Our American babies are beautiful, certainly, but God gave me a special love for African babies. When I go to church in Africa and see mothers with their babies, I can't keep my eyes off them. It's not that I want to hold them; I just enjoy admiring them and the way their mothers care for them. Though I do try, I don't seem to listen very well in church sometimes.

Unless the baby is a newborn, it will arrive at church snuggled on its mother's back, intimately close to her body, tied on with a new cloth. A mother will wait a few days until the baby's cord has dropped off, but once a baby can be carried on its mother's back, it stays there, like a baby kangaroo in its mother's pouch.

If a baby starts to fuss in the service, the mother will hold it in her arms or nurse it. As a matter of fact, all African mothers nurse their babies. The Togolese government, advised by the World Heath Organization, has made a law that women may not give bottles to their children. This is the best way to avoid contamination in a country where refrigeration is rare and sterilization is practically nonexistent. When a mother cannot produce milk, the government will teach her to make a porridge or gruel-like formula from different grains.

I've had many opportunities to care for unwanted or orphaned babies. As early as Yantala, Helen Bechtel and I cared for a baby whose skull bones had not grown together properly and whose mother had died in childbirth. Though that first experience was a sad one, as the little boy's deformity brought on an early death, I could never refuse to care for a little one in need. Whether the children God brought to us lived or died, we knew He had brought them to us for a reason. Now I think of these dear African children as all my babies.

One of my cherished stories is about a girl named Lydia. By a stream near Kpalimé was some tall grass that served as a garbage heap and a local bathroom. As a newborn baby, Lydia was abandoned on this garbage heap. The mother had put the baby and the afterbirth on a piece of cardboard and covered it with a bloody T-shirt. A farmer, passing by in the morning, had seen the bundle, but thought it was only trash. But when he passed by again in the evening, he saw the bundle move and drew near for a closer look. He quickly found someone to take it to the hospital in Kpalimé.

There they had named her Moisette, since she was found in the grasses near the stream. I heard about this all through Elise, the woman who cooked at the Blind Center. Elise and her husband, Kwadjo Paul, were Christians who attended our church. They were not able to have children. Elise asked me to go with her to see if they might be able to adopt the baby. The police and the social workers felt it might be possible but asked that the baby be kept in my care while they finished the search for the mother. I agreed.

My living room quickly became a nursery, with Elise and many other ladies helping me care for the baby and feed her night bottles of formula. The tiny girl soon grew nice and fat. She was a darling, beautiful baby, but she very rarely smiled. I thought perhaps she felt the sadness her birth mother went through when she had abandoned her on the garbage heap.

After ten days the police had still not found the mother. Even if they had, she would have had to go to prison, since that was the punishment in Togo at that time. The police eventually conjectured that the mother was a girl who came from Ghana in the night and delivered the baby on the porch of the school. We couldn't imagine why she would leave it to die; maybe she thought her baby was already dead.

Elise and Kwadjo Paul and I took many trips to the government offices in Lomé, where the legal adoption would be approved. The authorities had many questions for them. As an electrician and a builder, Paul had adequate finances to support a child. Both he and Elise were intelligent and capable and would make good parents. But even with their excellent qualifications, the social workers said it would be a year before Lydia could be officially adopted.

But God worked in the heart of the judge. The papers for Lydia's adoption were finished in the space of two months and the total cost of the adoption was only fourteen dollars. Elise and Kwadjo Paul were thrilled about getting a baby. They asked me to stand with them in church on the day Lydia was dedicated to the Lord. Up until the baby was adopted, we called her Moisette. But her new parents named her Lydia, from the Bible. When she grew to be a little girl, Lydia had a great interest in watching mothers nurse their babies. After a while she asked, in Ewé, "Mommy, did you nurse me like that?" And Elise replied, "No, I never did, but the white missionary lady at the Blind Center took care of you and bought milk for you and fixed bottles for you until you didn't drink milk anymore." It made my heart happy to be reminded that I had helped raise Lydia and put her into the arms of a good Christian family.

Another story begins in the Kpalimé hospital. I would often visit patients there, and if I found a woman who spoke Zerma, I would talk with her and help her feel more comfortable. One day, a baby girl was born whose mother died in childbirth due to the African medicine she took before coming to the hospital. Because the child's father had also died, the baby was called an *enfant malheur* or "cursed child." The mother's family was Muslim and they did not want anything to do with this *enfant malheur*. The hospital had no way to keep the child, so they asked me if I would take it.

I was happy to feed bottles to the little orphan, but I knew I would not be able to keep her permanently. It occurred to me that the missionary nurses taking Ewé lessons might care for the baby until the family could find someone to adopt her. I quickly found two sisters, Chris and Mary Ann Thompson, who said that they were willing to take care of her. The Thompsons had been praying for company during the holidays to ease their homesickness. This baby was an unmistakable answer to their prayers.

The *Affaire Sociale* of the hospital prepared legal papers, making the Thompsons legal guardians of the baby for seven months. Chris and Mary Ann named her Noélle because she was born so close to Christmas. It was beautiful to see the girls make such a fuss over this little baby whose family gave her up because they thought she was cursed.

Through Noélle, God gave the sisters an opening into the hearts of nearby village women who came often to see the new baby and give friendly advice. Attendance at their ladies' Bible/sewing class increased and at least two women made professions of faith. The Thompsons' favorite verse during that time was, *The Lord hath done great things for us, whereof we are glad* (Psalm 126:3).

About a year later, we still had not found a suitable family, so the Thompsons' legal guardianship was extended. About this time, Dr. Cropsey returned to America and happened to meet a lovely African-American couple in Michigan who wanted to have a baby but couldn't. Dr. Cropsey asked if they were interested in a baby from Africa. They were very interested.

When we presented Noélle's family with the prospect of her being adopted by an American family, they seemed quite willing to go along with the idea. After we explained the adoption procedure to them, the family signed all the paperwork without any trouble. I was amazed by how agreeable they were through the whole process.

Noélle flourished in Michigan with her new Christian family. She was gifted in sports and academics. However, after years of being in America, she fell ill with meningitis and died abruptly. It was hard for us to understand how Noélle, while in Michigan, could die of a disease so much more common in Africa than in America. The sudden, unusual nature of her death also made it difficult to tell Noélle's African family the news. Unfortunately, they made it harder on us by insisting that the body be brought back. When this could not be done, they demanded to have some of her hair and fingernails to prove that she was actually dead. When we said this was not possible, they said we were trying to hide the fact that we had sold Noélle into slavery. We tried to explain to them that Noélle's American family loved her dearly and was just as sad as her family in Togo that she had died.

I still enjoy looking at pictures of Noélle growing up in Africa and enjoying her new family in America. We'll never know why God chose to end her life so soon, or why her African family reacted to her death in a way we could never have predicted. But sometimes I think of those two women who accepted Christ as Savior as a result of coming to see Noélle at Chris and Mary Ann's Bible study. And I think God knew what He was doing.

Another story began early one morning when a group of villagers woke me up at 3:00 a.m. They said a pregnant woman was on the road halfway to the hospital. I jumped in the car and motioned for some family members to come with me. I was not expecting the entire group of people to squash in the car with me, relatives or not. They wanted to see the show, I assume. I didn't have time to argue, so I started up the road to find the woman. Because the law in Togo requires that a woman deliver in a hospital or be punished, this woman had started walking to the hospital from two miles away. I caught up with her about halfway there, just as the baby was being born. Right there on the road in front of the car headlights and under the light of the moon, the woman started to deliver, slumping to the ground. I reached out just in time to catch a slippery, pinkish-gray baby girl. I put the baby in the mother's cloth, but I needed to lay the baby down and help the mother get to the hospital. So I pointed to a banana tree nearby and directed a relative to get a big leaf for the baby to lie on, so she would be close to her mother for a few minutes.

Most of the family and friends stood back to give us some room, but one old man from the family hung around too close. He had been drinking and his palm wine breath was none too pleasant. In his drunkenness he seemed to think he should cut the umbilical cord with a razor blade, but I kept fighting him off and pushing him aside, telling him no, no, no! The cord had not been tied, and I knew we could have lost both the mother and child if the drunken razor blade man had his way. Somehow, in all this chaos, we got the woman and the baby into my little car along with about twelve relatives. I could hardly see to drive, and the poor woman moaned with every bump, but we finally made it. All's well that ends well, as they say. But oh, for a video of that night!

Then there was Daniel. I first heard of him by word of mouth. Friends told me that a young girl had died in childbirth and that her baby was still alive. When this girl had been about to give birth, her family refused to take her to the hospital because she was unmarried and they didn't know who the father was. They thought the hospital bill was the responsibility of the husband. The village midwives were women who had learned only from experience, so when complications arose and the baby's head became locked behind its mother's pelvic bone, the midwives tried to force the baby to come. They pushed frantically on the mother's abdomen in an attempt to get the baby out. Finally, as the girl was dying, the midwives extracted the child, but they broke the cord. The baby lived, but with no mother to nurse it.

When I heard about the ordeal, the Holy Spirit prompted me to respond. I couldn't stand back and allow the baby to die. I decided to go to the village and see what could be done. When I arrived, I expressed my sorrow to the family over the loss of their daughter. Then I asked about the baby. They brought out a little bundle and put it in my arms. At that moment, as I looked down into the face of the newborn child, I realized I was the only one who could keep him alive. The grandfather said to me, "You must name it, because there's no father." After a pause, I said, "His name will be Daniel, from the Bible." So, I became Daniel's grandmother.

For five months I kept a close watch over him, visiting him, bringing bottles I had prepared and clothes I had found in the market. I worked with helpers and neighbors to take care of him until he was big enough to eat solid food and drink from a cup, big enough for his family to care for him again.

As a result, almost all of Daniel's family began attending

church faithfully. His older brother joined the baptismal class. God may have saved many souls in that family because of their contact with the gospel through Daniel's birth.

One day, missionaries from Burkina Faso brought us a couple from an area of that country called the Haute Volta. The husband was completely blind and the wife had partial sight. The missionaries had told them that they could learn to read and write in Braille or learn a craft to support themselves.

The husband's name was Dialeni Lampo. He came from the royal family of the Gourma tribe in Burkina Faso. A close relative of his was chief of the Gourma tribe, and Dialeni was heir to the throne. But he would never be chief because he was blind. He and his wife were sweet, and their mutual blindness helped them understand each other. When they reached the Blind Center, they already had one baby and were expecting their second.

Dialeni and his wife came from a mission environment, so they knew about spiritual things. But they did not speak Ewé or any Togolese language, so it was difficult to communicate with them. Moreover, they came to us in a very primitive state. The wife, still a young girl, wore nothing but a loincloth, and she didn't feel the need to change her ways. We had a hard time helping her learn such things as going to the bathroom in a private place. I was thankful that Da Pauline helped care for her baby and teach her how to be modest and clean.

As for Dialeni, our instructors taught him a few crafts, and he and a friend began to make stick chairs together. His friend would cut down neem branches and Dialeni would lace them with rawhide to make chairs. Eventually, Dialeni accepted Christ and, as he grew in the Lord, he also learned to read a Braille Bible.

Sadly, when Dialeni's wife gave birth to her second child, the baby wasn't strong and had problems. To complicate matters, she did not keep it very clean. Within a few weeks, the baby became so sick that we feared for its life and took it to the hospital. By this time the baby had begun to turn yellow-orange and the doctor diagnosed it with hepatitis. Though the doctor tried everything he could think of, the baby died. It was only five weeks old.

Da Pauline and I brought the baby's body back to the Blind Center. We wanted it to have a proper funeral, so I asked our carpenter to make a little coffin out of teakwood. Our staff helped us plan a sweet funeral and invited neighbors, staff and students, and people from the Kpalimé church.

It was Dal's suggestion that we choose a spot on the Blind Center property for a small cemetery, starting with the grave of Dialeni's child. From the very beginning, Dal was especially fond of a corner of our land that had a lovely view of the blue, hazy hills. He always planned to make a beautiful garden where two palm trees shaded a smooth carpet of green grass. Now he suggested that the area should be reserved for burying missionaries and babies. This was a good idea, since a missionary or missionary child may die at any time in Africa. And it was undesirable to be buried in town since fetishers held ceremonies over their relatives' graves.

As funeral plans were under way, Da Pauline and I washed and dressed the baby. We had tried to make the parents understand that it was dead. But they had not touched the baby since it went to the hospital, and I sensed that they didn't realize what was going on. So before people arrived for the funeral, I wrapped the baby in a cloth and brought it over to them as they sat together in the Assembly Hall. I placed it in their arms and put their hands on the baby so they could feel it for the last time. It was painful to see the reality of the situation finally appear in their faces, like a tidal wave had swept suddenly over them. They sobbed and sobbed to realize their baby was dead. It made me so sad to watch. I saw that though their culture was so different than mine, their mother and father hearts were just the same.

Shortly before the funeral, one of our blind students said, "We have never touched a dead person. What do they feel like?" I thought for a moment and decided I was glad they wanted to know about death. Sighted people learn with their eyes but the blind learn by touch. Those who were interested touched the baby's body—its head, its arms—feeling how they had become rigid and cold. Death was a new concept for my blind children. But it was important for them to learn.

The coffin was left open during the service so the baby could be seen. Though its body had a tint of orange, it still looked like a little angel. During the funeral, the Blind School choir sang and a few men carried the coffin to the burial site. Before the coffin was lowered into the ground, it was closed and nailed shut. When they heard the hammering of the nails, the parents realized it was final and they wept.

Of the many people who came to the funeral, most were amazed that a baby would be buried in a coffin. In Africa, coffins are used only for adults who die, and sometimes not even then. Many were amazed that we were even having a funeral for a baby. Usually when a baby dies in Africa, the family has a small wake in their compound, then wraps the baby in a cloth or mat and buries the body in a grave with no coffin. Our neighbors, the priest and his wife, were impressed with the funeral. The priest said, "I have never seen a baby's body put in a coffin. You have done something very special."

Now, there are at least three babies buried in the little cemetery at the corner of the Blind Center property. Each grave is marked with a little cross and a marker with the baby's name, so that none of them will be forgotten.

Homegoing

It will be sunset for me here but dawn over there.

— DALLAS WASHER

One September day in Kpalimé, Dal and I received a long-distance call from South Carolina. Our daughter, Luann, and her husband, Joe, were sobbing and could hardly speak. "Someone has died," they said through tears. As they spoke, we learned that their son Jeffrey had been killed in a car accident. He was our oldest grandson and had just started college at Bob Jones University a few weeks earlier. He and two friends were going to a ballgame when a reckless driver plowed into them and sent their car over an embankment, where it crashed into some trees and overturned into a ravine. Two of the boys died, and the other was left with permanent brain injuries.

Luann asked if we would consider coming home for the funeral. She had never asked us to leave the field before, so we knew she needed us. But there was never any question in our minds about whether we should go. I wanted to put my arms around Luann and Joe. Our family needed to be together.

We called Ron and Ann to come over. It was difficult to tell them the news, as the realization of Jeffrey's death continued to settle in. We did not want to think of life without Jeffrey, who had resembled Dal in so many ways. As student body president of his high school, he would often give devotionals to the students, expressing his great concern for his classmates who pretended to be Christians but who were really unsaved. Echoing Paul's words, he would say that he was willing to do whatever it took to see them accept Christ as Savior.

Our furlough for that year had been scheduled for October, after the Blind School resumed classes under Ron and Ann's leadership. But Jeffrey's death changed our plans, and we decided to leave immediately. I had recently begun to experience severe headaches, fever, and weakness, all the more reason for our friends to advise us to take the next plane out of Togo.

Though we got home as soon as we could, we still missed the funeral, attended by over 500 people. Jeffrey had been a shining witness to his classmates and co-workers, and God used his testimony to soften many hearts. When Pastor Yearick gave an invitation after the funeral message, several of Jeffrey's classmates accepted Christ as their Savior. They wanted what Jeff had—a life centered on Christ, as expressed by a verse found underlined in his Bible: *I will praise thee; for thou hast heard me and art become my salvation* (Psalm 118:21).

Thankfully, Pastor Yearick had postponed the burial until our arrival. When we reached Greenville, we were rushed to the mortuary to see Jeffrey's body. I looked at my dear redheaded grandson lying in the casket and felt my heart burst with pain to see his handsome body now silent in death. *Why, God?* I thought. *Why was this beautiful young man taken from us? He was so dedicated to you, Lord. He offered to give his life for you.* It goes without saying that the death of a young person is especially painful. In times of such losses, we can only hide under God's wings and find comfort in Him.

The day after the funeral, I checked into the hospital. I was extremely weak and my skin had turned from yellow to a deep orange. After a few tests, the doctor diagnosed me with hepatitis A, explaining that the orange color was due to the extremely high level of bilirubin in my blood. I soon realized that I must have contracted hepatitis from the little baby who died, the baby whose parents were both blind. The doctor prescribed fluids to counteract my dehydration and bed rest to strengthen me. One week later, Dal also started to feel weak, and soon, he also began to turn yellow. He too had contracted hepatitis. We were allowed to recuperate at home, but isolated from visitors. Luann and Joe, even in their sorrow, took good care of us, and kept us in their home for awhile. Though we had returned from Africa to comfort them, they also comforted and cared for us.

With all the hard times we'd had in the previous months, it was especially sweet to have the family together for Christmas. But as soon as the holidays were over, we asked our doctor if we could travel to our supporting churches as we usually did on furlough. He gave us permission, but advised us to wait until we were no longer yellow, so people wouldn't mind being near us!

Besides visiting family and supporting churches, Dal and I attended some missionary conferences. Dal also had the privilege of preaching at our son Terry's ordination service. Terry and his wife, Sandy, had already spent one term in Kenya and planned to return for a second term. During our travels, we continued to lay our future plans before the Lord—not for ratification, as Dal would say, but for His divine guidance. The Lord's direction seemed clear as ever for us to return to Africa again.

We had heard from Togo that Ron and Ann were doing a wonderful job at the Blind Center. Ron said he would be willing to stay in his position for the rest of his term. Denny, about the same time, asked us to replace his family in Kara, in northern Togo, when they came home for their one-year furlough. As Dal and I prayed about this, the Lord gave us peace about going to Kara upon our return.

Since Denny's family planned to leave in May of 1989, Dal and I decided to return in April to ensure a smooth transition. In Kara, Dal would assume the role of church planter, helping to construct a church building and training Africans to serve in their home church. His goal was to work with the existing congregation in Kara to prepare them for independence by 1990. I hoped to continue to work with the blind as the need arose and to keep up a ministry for women and children. In a prayer letter from this time, Dal said that another one of my duties would be to "continue to be the sweet wife she has always been to me." I would like to state for the record that it was Dal who made it easy for me to be a sweet wife. I can't take any credit!

In the early months of 1989, after physical exams and medical tests, the doctor finally said we could return to Africa. We had already packed containers full of supplies, teaching materials, and evangelistic tools, so it was not long after receiving our clean bills of health that we were on a plane to Lomé.

We could barely contain our excitement about returning to Togo after such an unexpectedly long furlough. We felt it had been much too long since we had seen Ron and Denny and their growing families. We especially looked forward to our welcome at the Lomé airport. Our African family didn't disappoint us: it was thrilling to come through the gate and see so many African Christians waiting for us. Then when we drove into Kpalimé, we were greeted by a large group at our church shouting, *"Woezo!"* (We welcome you!)

Soon after we arrived, Dal conducted a wedding for Kwassiwa, the daughter of our old friend James. Kwassiwa and her new husband, Thomas, had postponed their marriage until our arrival. We hosted the wedding on the school property, with the lovely blue mountains in the background. We mowed our African grass with a tractor until it looked like an enormous green lawn, and the trees we had planted years earlier were lush and beautiful.

In the next few days, another big event took place: our field council meeting. Dal had been asked to bring the message. During his presentation, I remember wondering why he stumbled so much over his words. He kept forgetting terms or phrases, and I would have to fill them in for him. But his words were just as fervent as ever. He mentioned how thankful he was to be back in Africa, with words that suited him so well: "I have but one candle of life to burn, and would rather burn it out where people are dying in darkness than in a land which is flooded with light."

Before we could depart for Kara, we had a lot of packing to do. We had to decide what to take and what to leave at the Blind Center. Dal spent several days going in and out of the shipping containers, hand-picking his equipment for Kara. I worried about him because every time he came inside he looked hot and tired. I wished he wouldn't work so hard; it was as hot as an oven in the containers. But he would just laugh and tell me everything was fine.

On Wednesday, Dal supervised while the van we would take to Kara was packed. He also cleaned out our little cooler. But while doing so, he felt some chest pains. This was probably the first time Dal experienced angina attacks similar to those his mother used to have. He sat down until the pain dissipated and he could continue working.

That night, we went to prayer meeting at our church in Kpalimé. Dal introduced his message by saying, "This will be my last message to you." At the time, we didn't think much about these words, since he would be in Kara for some time. But when Dal repeated that "this will be my last time with you," I thought to myself, *Why are you saying that? Why can't you just say this is the last time until we come back from Kara?* Dal gave a wonderful message about joy on earth and anticipating joy in heaven.

After church, we prepared to leave early the next morning.

When Dal returned from taking out the garbage, he was breathless and sweating profusely, so he sat down to rest. I had looked in my nursing book earlier, so I read him the article describing the difference between angina and heart attacks. Angina attacks last only about three minutes. Although Dal's pain passed within three minutes, I still insisted on calling Ron, who lived next door. He came right over and listened to Dal describe his symptoms. Ron was as concerned as I was and made Dal promise to stop by the hospital on the way to Kara. Dal agreed, though he hated to be held back even an hour from his journey's goal.

When Dal woke me the next morning, I asked him if he was feeling well enough to travel. He said the pains had passed and he wanted to go ahead as planned. But when he tried to lift a package onto the van rack, he faltered and sat down on the ledge outside our kitchen door. He looked so discouraged. He wiped his forehead and said, "I don't know what's wrong with me. I just don't have any strength." Someone had to help him lift the box. I was concerned enough to call Ron again, and he said we should make sure to stop by the hospital.

We left Kpalimé around 8:00 a.m. with a huge van full of luggage and two grandchildren, Michael and Michelle, whom we were taking back to their parents in Kara after a visit in Kpalimé. The trip was uneventful, but thirteen-year-old Michael didn't remember ever going that fast before. He comforted himself that Grandpa had never been in a car accident.

When we reached the hospital about an hour later, Dal told me to go in and tell the doctor his symptoms, get some medicine, and bring it back. He did not like going to the hospital for himself, though he knew his friends would like to see him. But I said, "Honey, you need to come in. They need to see you and examine you. And you promised Ronnie that you would go in."

So Dal followed me into the hospital, and was immediately admitted to see the doctor. I sat in the waiting area and heard him joking with Dr. Bill TenHaaf and the nurses. While I waited, a man came up and asked, "Where is the *Alfaga* (teacher)?" I was surprised to hear him speak in Zerma, a language of Niger. I told him Dal was in the examination room. Then the man asked if I remembered him. Shortly after we arrived in Togo, sixteen years earlier, Dal had given blood for his little girl, helping to save her life. He saw me in the waiting room and wanted to express his appreciation again.

Inside the examination room, Dr. TenHaaf performed various tests on Dal. Unfortunately, the electrocardiogram wasn't working properly because the high humidity had corroded the wires, so the test results were discarded. But I wonder what they said. Nevertheless, Dr. TenHaaf realized that Dal's heart was unstable. He advised him to stay at the hospital one or two more days, to take medicine and to be more closely monitored. Dal was frustrated to postpone his trip and tried to talk his way out of staying. But Dr. TenHaaf was finally able to convince him that it would be best to spend the night with the Cropsey family, who lived on the hospital grounds.

The doctor told me there was no indication that Dal would have any serious problems. He asked me to drive back to Kpalimé and tell Ron and Ann so they wouldn't be worried. Dal also wanted Ron to radio Denny and Diane to let them know we wouldn't arrive until the next day. Dr. TenHaaf let me borrow his car so I wouldn't have to drive the huge van. But before I left, I went to get Dal a pillow since he was having trouble holding his head up to talk to the many people surrounding him. This was the last thing I did for him.

When I arrived in Kpalimé around 11:00 a.m., I went to talk with Ron and Ann. I stayed long enough to drink a Coke with them. They felt, as I did, that I should return to the hospital to take care of Dal. They would contact Denny and

Diane. So I left for the hospital right away.

Unfortunately, there were delays. May 25 is a Togolese holiday, and people were celebrating in grand style. Crowds filled the road to watch bicycle races. I begged the soldiers and police to let me through, but they said, "No, you'll have to wait. The bicycles are going to come by right now!" I had to stop the car and sit off to the side of the road while the race was going on. I wasn't worried at first, but I became increasingly frustrated. I wanted to get back to my husband as soon as possible.

Meanwhile, back at the hospital, the medical personnel had observed Dal for an hour, and they noticed no problems. They gave him nitroglycerin pills to control his angina attacks, and he was instructed to stop immediately if he suffered any discomfort with exertion. When he felt well enough, they let him walk over to the Cropsey home to stay until they could stabilize his symptoms.

Our grandson Michael was playing nearby with his friend Josh Cropsey when Dal emerged from the back door and started to walk up the hill. In a matter of moments, Dal experienced crushing chest pain and sat down on a stump to catch his breath. Michael and Josh looked up from their game just as Dal had a massive heart attack. The force threw him to the ground and flung his glasses into a nearby bush. To the boys, it looked like Dal had tripped and fallen, so they did not panic. They called to Steve Anderson, a missionary nurse walking past, and he immediately went into action. He sent Josh for medical equipment and called to some doctors and nurses coming out of the hospital. Within minutes, they had carried Dal into the emergency room.

This emergency room was not so much a room as an open space where everyone could see what was going on. Many people gathered around, and the air was filled with voices: the frantic voices of doctors and nurses working on Dal and the deep voices of male nurses crying out to God, "Oh, Lord, spare him!" The doctors and nurses did everything they could to revive Dal. They pumped his heart to get it to beat again. Steve Anderson gave him mouth-to-mouth resuscitation. But God wanted Dal with Him. After an hour and a half, the doctors and nurses realized there was nothing else they could do. Dal died on the emergency room table.

Soon after, missionaries Kelli Thayer and Karen TenHaaf drove down the road to meet me. They explained the situation to the police and were escorted through the crowds of bicyclists and onlookers. They found me sitting in the car, hot and frustrated. I asked if Dal was worse and they nodded their heads. They told me to return to the hospital immediately. While I went north, they continued south to Kpalimé to pick up Ron and Ann.

I drove as fast as I could, but after I broke through the bicyclists, everything became extremely quiet and still. I suddenly felt alone. So I cried out to the Lord, "Please spare Dal. Please don't take him!" But something told me Dal was gone. My heart sank within me. I felt weak and sick and began to cry, the tears blurring my vision so I could hardly steer the car.

When I arrived at the hospital, Dr. Cropsey came out to meet me. When I asked, "Is Dal worse?" he didn't answer me. So I asked, "Is he dead?" and he nodded. He put his arms around me and told me what had happened. I said, "Are you sure? Why did he die? I didn't get to talk to him! Are you sure? Why did I leave him?" He spoke to me with such gentleness and with great feeling. But I just couldn't believe that Dal was gone. It seemed only minutes before that I had left him on the examination table, talking and laughing and telling the doctors how he ran in place each morning. He said he used to count 1,000 steps, but since his chest pains he could only do about 300. Now he would never speak to me or smile again. Death was so sudden, and so final!

I cried a long time on Dr. Cropsey's shoulder. Afterwards, I was embarrassed at how I had wiped my wet nose all over his clean white uniform. Then he took me to the private room where they had placed Dal's body on a bed and covered him with a sheet. I had to remove the sheet to see my darling. Seeing Dal's dead body was the only thing that made me believe he was gone. He was blue, almost black, from the trauma he had experienced. I opened one of his eyes. It was fixed and didn't move.

The nurses gave me Dal's watch and billfold. They let me sit with him all afternoon while friends processed the paperwork that must be done when a foreigner dies in Africa. Later, missionary ladies brought me lunch and I realized I was hungry. I ate slowly as friends came by to comfort me and help me accept what had just happened.

The time with Dal's body that afternoon was almost like a pre-viewing. Ron and Ann arrived as soon as they could, with Melissa and Bradley. Just a few days before we had had so much fun with them. They would run down the hall and fly through the air with their arms out like Superman, landing with a big bounce on the bed. Grampa Dal tried it once and it almost knocked the wind out of him. Everyone laughed so hard while I stood by scolding, saying they would break the bed! Now Dal was gone forever—until we meet in heaven with the Lord. We all stood together, holding each other, crying hard.

Many others came by to pay their respects to Dal. I even saw the man who had thanked me earlier for Dal's help to his daughter. He was shocked and saddened by Dal's death, and I saw in his eyes that he wasn't saved. I hoped that Dal's testimony would cause him to reevaluate his life and turn to Christ.

I was numb for a good while. I felt like I wasn't alive, as if these things weren't really happening. I couldn't do much of anything except cry. The hardest part was facing the fact that I hadn't been with him in his last moments. *What were his thoughts as death came?* I wondered. I felt so sad that we hadn't said any kind of goodbye.

But when the doctors explained to me how they worked so hard on Dal, I knew it was God's will that I be absent in that last hour. I agreed that God had sent me to Ron and Ann, keeping me in transit long enough for Dal to die. It was better that I hadn't seen everything they had to do to Dal.

But there were so many reasons to praise the Lord as well. God had brought us to the hospital just in time for Dal's attack. He had even caused Dal to drive faster than normal so we would reach the hospital on time. It was miraculous that Dal even set foot inside the hospital. If we had not stopped, we would have been traveling over the mountains in the big van with Michael and Michelle and all our luggage when he had his heart attack. On that narrow mountain road there are no barriers. So many accidents have occurred on that road that a graveyard of broken trucks and cars lies in the valley below. If Dal had suffered a heart attack on the road to Kara, we would certainly have gone over the side of the mountain.

I sat in that little room holding Dal's hand for a long time. Eventually, Dr. Cropsey and Dr. TenHaaf came in to tell me the steps of preparing Dal's body for burial. In Africa, there are no funeral homes, and embalming is rare and expensive. Because of the heat, the doctors told me it would be best to freeze the body. Dal's body would be taken to the Agou hospital, where Ronnie would help prepare the body. The thought of Dal's body being frozen bothered me at first. But Dr. Cropsey assured me I wouldn't have to see him that way; the body would be taken out the night before the funeral, and it would look normal by morning.

Later that afternoon, I rode back to Kpalimé with Ann. I hardly remember the trip at all. When we arrived at the Blind Center, it seemed I had lived an eternity since leaving home that morning. I must have expressed discomfort about sleeping all alone, or perhaps Ann was especially sensitive to my needs, because she invited me to sleep at their house that night.

We had no plans yet for the funeral. When Ron returned he used the ham radio to call our other children and our mission. The mission called everyone we had a number for and told them Dal had passed away. It was still early enough in America to contact our home pastor, Pastor Yearick, before he left for work. He and his wife began preparing immediately to come to Togo.

Finally, it was too late to do anything else except go to bed. I spent that first night alone in Melissa's room. I lay in bed and cried—and wondered if I would ever sleep.

DAL'S FUNERAL

Death is just a swinging door. God is on both sides.

— DALLAS WASHER (From his Bible)

Dal had once told me, "If I die in Africa, I want to be buried here in Togo. I want to wait for the resurrection here with my African brothers and sisters." I always got upset when he talked about dying, and I would say, "Honey, you're not going to die here! Don't say that!" But he gave me instructions: "If I die here, you can just put some old boards together for a coffin—nothing fancy—and just bury me here at the Blind Center. It will be easy." I always tried to change the subject, but when the time came for Dal to die, it gave me sweet peace that I knew exactly where he wanted to be buried: in the little cemetery at the corner of the Blind Center property, where several little crosses already stood.

The day after Dal died we had to prepare for the wake, the viewing, and the funeral, all of which would be held at Kpalimé Baptist Church. During the four days between Dal's death and the funeral, friends and family traveled from other parts of Africa and America and all over the world. Terry came from Kenya. My brother Bob and his wife, Priscilla, came all the way from Georgia. Luann and her daughter Jennifer came from South Carolina with Pastor Yearick and his wife. David and Laya came from their church in Benin. David was a wonderful help because he knew how Africans carry out viewings and funerals. He also chose the theme for the funeral—being a good soldier of Christ.

After we announced Dal's death to the students, one of the young boys came up to me and asked me if he could have the kazoo that Dal had played at a recent party. I told him I'd have to think about it, because even though I knew it would have meant so much to him, I just couldn't seem to part with anything of Dal's yet.

In the swirl of all the preparations, Da Pauline was always at my right hand. She helped me choose what to wear for the funeral. In Africa, the grieving widow must wear black at the funeral. In some tribes, widows wear black for months or even years. But I didn't have any black clothes because I never enjoyed wearing black. There was no place to buy a black dress, nor was there time to have one made. So I hemmed and hawed until finally Da Pauline said, "You can wear whatever you want because you're a white lady." So I did. I wore a nice, gray-flowered dress that Mrs. Yearick brought me from America, and I felt much better than if I had worn black.

Many people stay up all night before a funeral to participate in the wake, a special event to honor the one who has passed away. It is different from a traditional wake because the body of the deceased is not present. So many people attended Dal's wake that many had to sit outside during the church program. All night people sang and gave testimonies of what Dal had meant in their lives. Our African friends advised us to provide something to eat for those at the wake so they would not fall asleep. Several lovely ladies from our church served cookies and fruit juice to refresh those who stayed up all night. I stayed only until midnight, but many others stayed all night. Some simply stretched out on the church benches and slept so they could be present when Dal's body was brought from the hospital.

At 2:00 in the morning, Ron, Denny, and Ted Allston brought Dal's body back to the church. They laid his body in a little room on a table draped with sheets. Dal looked distinguished in his suit and tie, and in his hands was his Bible. Early in the morning people started filing past to view him. Many had waited all night to see him for the last time.

In an African viewing, it is important that someone watch over the body. It is a high honor to be chosen for this job, so it was only natural that we would choose Da Pauline to care for Dal's body. She had been a part of our family for many years, almost since the beginning of the ministry.

One of the most precious moments that I remember during that time of grief was watching Da Pauline wipe the beads of moisture off Dal's hands and face. While she caressed him with a cloth, she sang and talked to him quietly. From the way she tended him with such grace and care, it was evident that she loved Dal very much. It made me cry just to look at her.

Many people came to mourn Dal's death at the funeral. It was not a small gathering by any means. Every ABWE missionary operating in Togo came, along with many other missionaries from the area. Africans who had known Dal came from all over West Africa: thousands had come to Christ through his ministry. Ron and Denny invited a group of Muslims from both Niger and Togo. They must have loved Dal and held him in high regard to come to a Christian funeral. They all sat in one area of the building, wearing their light-colored robes and turbans. They were quite conspicuous. Many government officials came as well, including two American embassy diplomats and the *Prefét* of our region. I was also glad to see our national pastors at the funeral—men who, starting as young boys, had grown spiritually through Dal's teaching.

Ted Allston, our missionary at the Bible Institute, introduced each speaker. First, Pastor Yearick, who had loved Dal like a brother, preached. Dal would have been pleased that he clearly explained salvation to the many unbelievers who had come. Then, Dennis and Ron, our two sons, got up to speak. Denny gave a message in Zerma and Ron translated his words from Zerma to French. They explained what motivated Dal to leave America so long ago and come to Africa as a missionary. Denny told the crowd that his father went to Niger simply because he wanted the people there to have the opportunity to hear the gospel. The messages at the funeral allowed Dal's passion for spreading the gospel to extend even after his death.

The funeral lasted for quite some time. There were several testimonies from Africans who had come to Christ under Dal's preaching. One of the missionary children, Becky Anderson, read a poem. David Allagbada gave a message in French. Eternity will tell of the impact of this service on the Ewé people of Togo and on Togo's Muslim community.

I know Dal would have enjoyed listening as friends and family sang his favorite songs. The congregation sang in French and Ewé. The hymns were joyful, praising God and encouraging people to be soldiers of Christ. We were accompanied by trumpets and trombones, which made our singing triumphant and strong. I was thankful for the music, because it helped take away some of the sadness, giving the funeral a joyous atmosphere.

After the funeral, people poured out of the church for the journey to the Blind Center, where Dal would be buried. The coffin was driven out to the beautiful burial site, and an AWANA group we had started in Kpalimé led the way, carrying flags and wearing their special uniforms. A number of other cars crept along after that, and many, many people walked. Many carried flowers. I was moved by the procession as I watched these people walk so far in the heat to go to Dal's burial.

Finally, everyone arrived, gathering around the place where the grave had been dug. Everyone stood. The landscape was wide and open with mountains rising in the distance. Dal's sons and close friends set his coffin down beside the freshly dug grave, which was in view of the road so that visitors could see his gravestone as they passed. The coffin was cut and carved by hand out of Togo's lovely red mahogany. Each layer of wood on the top became progressively smaller, forming a lovely tiered pattern. Ann and Luann had made the lining.

Pastor Yearick gave another short message. Then seven mango trees were planted around the grave to commemorate the seven churches Dal had started. I was honored to help plant the first tree. We later planted a frangipani tree so the flower petals would drift down and beautify the burial site.

I could tell it was difficult for the men to lower the coffin down. But they managed to get it into place. They then laid two-by-fours across the grave and corrugated aluminum sheets over the boards. They finished by pouring cement over the aluminum sheets. The metal and cement would protect the coffin from rain and from evil fetishers.

We did not yet have a gravestone, since it was being made from Togolese marble. We did have a forty-pound bronze plaque that Pastor Yearick brought from the States to affix to the gravestone. The inscription was simple:

Dallas Washer
"Beloved Husband and Father"
December 29, 1921–May 25, 1989
"Pasteur Tsi-tsi"

Pionnier de la Mission ABWE au Togo
"I have but one candle of life to burn
and would rather burn it out
where people are dying in darkness
than in a land which is flooded with lights."

I wonder now that I even noticed, but it was blisteringly hot that day. I don't know how the men stood in suits for so long. Late in the afternoon, the clouds started to roll in with the promise of rain. At first a rainstorm was a welcome thought. But then I thought of those who had not left. There was not room enough for all of them to stand out of the rain.

Soon it was raining heavily. Some said, "God is blessing you with the rain." But others said, "The rain is bad. It is unfortunate." People hid anywhere they could, and many had to wait before starting for home. All of a sudden a horrible thought struck me. I saw the hollow where Dal's grave was and I feared that his body was going to get wet. That was all I could think about. Finally, seeing I was so distraught, Ron promised to bring truckloads of sand to the site.

It was during this dark time that God reminded me of a particular verse, II Corinthians 5:1, which says, *For we know that if our earthly house of [this] tabernacle were dissolved, we have a building of God, an house not made with hands, eternal in the heavens.* Though Dal's grave was flooded with water and his earthly body had already begun to dissolve, I could still rejoice that he was now enjoying his new eternal body made with the hands of God.

After the funeral, we got out Dal's Bible, the binding of which was coming loose. The family all sat around the kitchen table to look at the notes Dal had written. The

Yearicks were still with us, and it was Mrs. Yearick who found the words Dal wrote in the space below II Corinthians 12. She read them aloud as we sat silently:

> Yes, Lord, I will be spent as a candle which is lit and gives out light, but in order to give out light it consumes itself in the interest of bringing light to others until there comes a time when it sputters for the last time and is consumed. I will gladly spend and be spent like this and SPUTTER OUT SOMEDAY IN TOGO—AFRICA.
>
> —Dal

After all that had happened, we were greatly moved by the passion that had inspired those words. Dal had even signed his name at the end of this promise to the Lord. It was amazing to us that the words had come true, that the Lord had answered his prayer by allowing him to sputter out in Togo.

In the Togolese culture, the bereaving wife must stay home for a month or more to receive visitors from faraway villages. During this time she may not shop in the market or even drive her car. So I stayed at my home on the school land so I could greet people as they came. At first I didn't know what to say. I much preferred to be alone. I'm sure everyone who has lost a husband or wife understands what I mean when I say I couldn't always talk about my feelings. Inside, my heart hurt so bad that it felt like my chest was about to break. I almost feared I, too, was having a heart attack. I tried to put my feelings down in prayer letters which I continued to write. But mostly I had conversations with God.

Finally, one sweet lady who sensed my sadness took my hand and said, "We've come to help you carry your sorrow." When I heard her kind words I realized this was a special time for my heart to heal from its loss. Da Pauline stayed with me the entire time as I received visitors. So many people came that we could not fit them in our house. So we arranged a receiving area outdoors in the shade of mango trees Dal had planted over the years.

From morning to night, there was a continual line of people waiting to speak to me. They would say, "Because your husband brought the Bible to our village . . ."—and then they would tell their testimonies. Many recalled Bible verses and messages Dal had preached. I was overwhelmed by those who said, "Pastor Tsi-tsi is my spiritual father" or "You are my spiritual mother," because *Tsi-tsi* means "the first"—we were the first to bring them the gospel. I couldn't help weeping out of thanksgiving that God had let Dal help to do all this. He had won so many people to Christ, too many to count—Frenchmen, government officials, and townspeople. At the same time that I cried over Dal's death, I rejoiced in my heart that God had privileged us to be the first to bring the gospel to these wonderful people. There, under the ripening mango trees that Dal had planted, God let us see the fruit that He had given Dal.

Especially in the days and months following Dal's death, I missed him most when I came home from a long day's work. No matter where I had been, I would step in the door and want to say, "Hey, honey, let me tell you what just happened" or "Dal, honey, what should I do about this or that?" I wanted to share what was happening in my life, but he wasn't there to talk to. This is the biggest loss for a widow: when her husband dies, there is no one to share her intimate thoughts and feelings with. However, the visits of those dear African people and the calls and letters from my friends and family in America helped me tremendously. I will always remember that summer as a comforting season that soothed my spirit as

I sat in the shade of mango trees. While the mangoes ripened, my soul grew healthy again from basking in the light of friendship and love.

It is comforting to remember that Dal is not gone forever. Even today I feel close to him. He is still himself, though he is in heaven now. Now he rejoices with the angels over every African that comes into the family by the blood of Christ. Dal was a pioneer missionary here on earth, and I know that in heaven he is still a "pioneer soul." I can imagine him exploring every corner of heaven and the universe and all the stars. He is even now exploring the presence of Christ.

In the Africans' mind, I should be buried next to Dal. They are sure to tell me this each time I visit Africa. But I do not prefer one burial place over another. If I die in America, we have a burial plot here. If I die in Africa, I will be buried next to Dal. But I will let God choose where I die. Whatever happens, I know I am going to heaven, and I think God will tell Dal I am coming. Perhaps Dal will meet me at the gate made of pearls or perhaps by the river, as the song says. Or maybe we will meet on Resurrection Day in the air.

UNDER HIS WINGS

He shall cover thee with his feathers,
and under his wings shalt thou trust.

— PSALM 91:4

Some people wonder why I stayed on the field after Dal died. It was clear to me that God would not want me to walk away from the wonderful work He had given us. And I knew in my heart that if I went back to America, I would immediately start counting the days until I could return to Africa.

I also knew Dal would be pleased for me to carry on the things we started together. I did, of course, have to adjust to his absence. I had to get used to sleeping, walking, eating, and praying alone. At this time in my life, I came to cherish the song "No, Never Alone," which described my relationship with God:

I've seen the lightning flashing,
And heard the thunder roll,
I've felt sin's breakers dashing,
Trying to conquer my soul;
I've heard the voice of my Savior,
Telling me still to fight on,
He promised never to leave me,
Never to leave me alone.

The world's fierce winds are blowing,
Temptation's sharp and keen,
I have a peace in knowing
My Savior stands between—

He stands to shield me from danger,
When earthly friends are gone,
He promised never to leave me,
Never to leave me alone.

He died for me on the mountain,
For me they pierced His side,
For me He opened the fountain,
The crimson, cleansing tide;
For me He's waiting in glory,
Seated upon His throne,
He promised never to leave me,
Never to leave me alone.

— Anonymous

I wasn't really by myself at the Blind Center. Ron and Ann stayed until 1990, and then a short-term couple, the Hewstons, came to help manage the school for awhile. Many friends visited me to make sure all was well. And Mama Pauline made the days pass easily, staying with me as often as she could.

God knew that keeping me busy was the best therapy as I grieved. Shortly after Dal's death, the majority of our freight finally arrived from America. As we tackled the huge job of unpacking the container, I was touched by the many things Dal had packed months before. There were Bible correspondence courses, a projector and generator for showing films, tracts, Bibles, and Christian books. Dal had also made dozens of notebooks for his Bible Institute students. I knew my job now was to encourage others to use these materials as Dal had desired.

God also filled my time by sending people who needed help. For instance, one of our Togolese pastors took me to a village where a baby named Kwassi was dying of *kwashiorkor*, or malnutrition. Kwassi's body was so swollen that his skin was breaking and peeling, and his little eyes were deeply sunken. His grandmother, a priestess, had cut slits in his skin to "let out" the sickness. The poor little two-year-old was obviously in unbelievable pain. With permission from his family, I took Kwassi to our hospital, where the doctor cared for him and bandaged up his wounds. He said the little boy could recover, but only if someone like me could oversee his care and make sure he received nutritious food. Without hesitation, I took little Kwassi back to the Blind Center, where Mama Pauline and I fed him good meat, eggs, fruits, and vegetables. In just three weeks he looked much better. Through this contact with Kwassi, his mother heard the gospel many times.

One of my new duties was writing regular prayer letters, a job Dal had done all our years on the mission field. At first I dreaded writing, not because I didn't want to share my life, but because Dal had always been the writer. It struck me that my name at the end of a letter looked small and alone. Instead of "In Him, Dal, Kay, Luann, Denny, Ronnie, and Terry," it was just "In Him, Kay." But there was still "Him." I was thankful for that.

In all these new changes and challenges, I was continually amazed at the physical strength God gave me. In doing the work Dal usually did I lost fifteen pounds, which was good for me. Even as the months and years lessened the pain and dulled the dread of being alone, I realized God had never ceased to shelter me under His wings. He continued to fill the empty place in my heart by giving me great happiness in my work.

Shortly after Dal's death, a Memorial Fund was started in his honor, and in a short time, the fund had reached $4,000.

The money was designated for the village ministry, which Dal would have been thrilled to see continue under the capable leadership of Ted Allston. Ted continued Dal's practice of visiting villages until a strong body of believers was formed. In fact, under Ted's ministry, the Christian population in the little village of Kpakopé grew to over 200. Dal's Memorial Fund helped them build a simple building of cement block with a metal roof.

Before I knew it, a year had passed since Dal's homegoing. On the anniversary of his death I received an unsigned note from someone at Woumé.

> Dear Maman Tsi-tsi,
>
> I praise the Lord very much that you are healthy for us to see and remember the great work the Lord has done through your husband. My Family and the Woumé church are some of his fruits.
>
> This is one year behind that our beloved Pastor Tsi-tsi had taken the lead before Us and you. I hope he is with the Lord and Savior Jesus now in Heaven the beautiful Home and a place of the real rest.

Eventually, though I enjoyed directing the Blind Center, I realized I needed another person to help me. And I knew Ron and Ann wanted to do church planting, not school administration. The search for the perfect match was like searching for a needle in a haystack. Not just anyone would do. We had plenty of people to teach Braille, but we needed a nurse because our children had many physical needs. This nurse would need a tender heart toward the visually handicapped. She would also need to improvise and make do with what we could offer. Most of all, she would need to love our Savior enough to labor among a very different people in a pagan land.

In 1990, God decided it was time. Jane Hankin, an LPN from New Jersey, had read an article about our work with the blind. She responded tenderly to God's leading and completed her French studies in May 1990, afterward traveling to Togo to help. We put her in charge of keeping the children healthy, well housed, and adequately clothed.

Having a new comrade at the Blind School was enough to keep me going for many more years. Jane took a lot of work upon herself and freed me to do the many things that had been piling up for a long time. Year after year, Jane took on a heavier burden for the school as God prepared her to take full responsibility.

In 1990, I took a quick trip home to be with my family. A week at the beach on Fripp Island, S.C., gave wonderful rest in a complete change of scenery. I also traveled to California to see my brothers and my mother, who was now 97.

When I returned to my beloved Blind Center, I discovered that the students had prepared a play and a special program to welcome me home. Our head teacher, Maître Kwassivi, gave thanks to God for the many years I had worked with the blind. The students then presented their play and sang beautiful songs. I was brought to tears as I heard the genuine love expressed by my African family. It was a sweet time of thankfulness, and a dream come true.

In 1992 we decided it was high time to revisit our goals for Togo and the Blind Center in the form of a long-term plan. We came up with about twenty-five particular goals, most of which we were already pursuing. Of course, none of this planning was done to impress people. We wanted our school to be the best possible institution of its kind so that God might be glorified and so that the name of Jesus might go forth into the land of Togo. But it was sweet to hear that others appreciated what we were doing. After a visit from Dr. Bob Jones III and his wife, Beneth, I received a letter from Dr. Bob that said,

> Our hearts are full to overflowing, as we have seen the fruits of the labors that you and Dal have been engaged in all these years in Togo. We knew it was a great work for God, but we didn't know the half of it. Your love for the blind children is a joy to behold. The evidence of your fruit-bearing lives is everywhere in the many churches all around Kpalimé. It is wonderful to see how much fruit can spring from two surrendered lives.

That was sweet praise coming from a couple I respected very much. But such kind words could never have prepared me for what happened a year later when Bob Jones University conferred upon me the honorary degree of Doctor of Humane Letters. As the citation was read, I was moved that so much recognition went to Dal's years of church planting and training pastors, as well as to our work with the blind. I was humbled by the award and thought, as I suspect many holders of honorary doctorates must think, *I really don't deserve such an honor* and *How am I going to live up to this?* But it helped me to remember that the degree was really recognizing the work that God did through Dal and me. We were just instruments for Him. All in all, the honorary doctorate was a great honor. But I don't make people call me "Dr. Washer." I still prefer "Kay."

My mother died on November 28, 1993. Though I had just been to the United States a few months before, I chose to fly to California for the funeral. It meant so much to me to honor my mother, a woman who loved God and had dedicated me to the Lord even before I was born. I stayed in the States over Christmas and was able to see ten of my grandchildren at the same time, a joy that brought tears to my eyes and a big lump in my throat. I thought of all that I would miss as the children grew up. But even as the holidays sped by, the Holy Spirit assured me that the work was not finished. I couldn't quit yet!

On the trip back to Africa I had to change planes in Amsterdam, so I stayed overnight before boarding the next morning. Although it was dangerous to carry cash, I knew that American dollars went a long way in Africa. Many supporting churches knew this also and had given me cash to help with our expenses at the Blind School. While I was eating breakfast in the hotel restaurant, I kept my purse close beside me on the floor with my foot inside the strap. Suddenly, a man snatched the purse out from under my foot and escaped out the door into the busy streets. Thankfully, my ticket and passport were in another bag so they were not lost, but $1,000 in cash for the next month's expenses was stolen. I notified the police immediately, but they were not able to catch the thief. It was a terrible experience for me, especially while traveling alone. I was so upset that I could hardly bear to tell my Togolese family, or my American family for that matter. But my home church in Greenville took up an "encouragement offering" and gave me $1,500 to replace the money I had lost. I was so grateful for their love.

That offering turned out to be crucial in 1994, the year that the U.S. Aid, which had helped feed our blind students, was denied for the first time. Thankfully, the offering kept us supplied for awhile, and we found several smaller groups that were willing to help us. But by summertime we were low on staples like rice, corn, and beans. We had to find more food before we could open the school again in October.

That year the rains did not come as usual and there was a great shortage of corn in Togo. To buy food for The Village of Light, we usually went to the markets when corn was sold at the lowest price. But not that year. Though we had to work hard to find food, the Lord helped us find just enough for the children if we used it sparingly. It was a lesson to all of us to depend on Him.

The food shortage in Togo came at a time when I was due to go back to the States for a short visit. My "mother hen heart" ached to think of abandoning my "chicks" to search for food. But Jane Hankin sweetly took over. I had to trust that God would meet the needs of my blind students. The flight out of Africa was long and tiring, but my mind raced, keeping me from sleep. Several hours into the flight we were served a lovely meal, even lovelier since I had been eating simple food for a long time. After the meal, I was amazed to see the flight attendants throwing away trays of untouched food. Because of our struggle at the Blind Center to find food, my feelings exploded and my eyes filled with tears. In Togo they would go through our garbage just to find a crust of bread, a bone—anything to eat. I stayed awake, talking to God.

When I returned to Togo toward the end of the year, I could sense a change. The famine had abated and the political situation was improving. After such a hard year, it was time for a celebration, and it just happened to be the twentieth anniversary of our Togo mission. During the first part of December, our national churches and missionaries came together for a conference in Lomé. Banners were put up around the city. A temporary palm shelter was built in an open field, and a PA system and 3,000 chairs were rented. Even our television station showed up. Togolese pastors and ABWE missionaries and board members, including Dr. William T. Maher and Dr. Will Davis, stirred our hearts to rejoice in all that God had done since Dal and I opened the field of Togo. My heart was full of joy as I looked at all the people who had heard of Christ through our ministry, those who had left their idols to be redeemed by the blood of Jesus.

May of 1995 marked six years since Dal's death. At last, the seven mango trees planted at his funeral had grown to maturity. May was mango season, and Dal's trees bore red, long fruit with sweet flesh like peaches. The churches these trees represented were also bearing good fruit, and some had even produced daughter churches.

That year I was also able to share in joy of a different kind as another generation of "Washer offspring" came into being. I became a great-grandmother for the first time when Laya's daughter Evodie gave birth to a little girl named Nancy Hope Fumike Hassouh. I especially liked the middle name Fumike, which means "God gave her to me to take care of."

My heart also rejoiced in the maturing of the Blind Center. It seemed like the students were continually gaining an interest in spiritual things. Now after almost twenty years, some students were married and had children. Some worked in their villages, and others went on for more schooling and became teachers. Many are staying faithful to the Lord, and some have led their families to Christ. Those we have taught over the years will always remain our "children."

We learned not to look for the fruit of our labors instantly in working with these children, but instead trusted the Lord to work in their lives as they learned to read and understand the Word. We prayed that as they grew, they would continue to follow the Lord. Our reward came from being in the place the Lord wanted us, and from finding joy in serving Him.

BUYING THE SCHOOL LAND

Though I walk in the midst of trouble,
thou wilt revive me; thou shalt stretch forth
thine hand against the wrath of mine enemies,
and thy right hand shall save me.
The Lord will perfect that which
concerneth me: thy mercy, O Lord,
endureth forever: forsake not the
works of thine own hands.

— PSALM 138:7,8

Over the years, several men had come to us, claiming that the land on which the school stood actually belonged to them. Like the rumors we had heard when we first acquired the land, these claims disturbed us, but the government continued to assure us that the land was theirs to give.

But these African landowners told a different story. They said the government had seized land all across Togo, promising to pay for it, but never following through. When the people protested, the government claimed the land was theirs and that the owners had disobeyed the law by not having their land surveyed and marked off. For years, these men said, the government tried to appease them by allowing them to farm the land if no one built on it, so many continued to farm parts of our land. But as the number of our buildings grew, less land was available for crops. Understandably, the people were not happy.

To those who came to dispute, we explained that the government had given us the land, saying it did not belong to anyone. We assured them that if they had a complaint, we would certainly be willing to discuss the issue with them and the local officials. Usually, the claimant would leave troubled and never return. We remained uneasy, wondering who was telling the truth—the government or the landowners.

The situation grew worse. The country fell into a state of ferment and political upheaval. General terror escalated and a civil war between two rival tribes began. We heard terrible stories of killing, strikes, and property destruction all over the country. Critics of the government who once confined themselves to seditious mutterings in the marketplace now openly hurled accusations. Foremost among these was the complaint that the government had seized land and had redistributed it for its own purposes. In some cases, men laying claim to property were willing to kill the current occupants in order to recover it.

More than once, men with machetes stalked our property, threatening to kill us because we were on their land. They never hurt anyone, but one time they cut down all the ripe bananas that we grew for students to eat. I would calm the terrified children, even though I was as frightened as they were. And each time I would go to the *chef de canton*, or district chief, and report the harassment. He would assure me that I had nothing to worry about, but I knew better. The issue of the land became a major topic in my prayers. I had long been uneasy about it. We desperately needed the Lord to show us what to do.

Then one morning I was awakened by an insistent sound outside.

Clap. Clap. Clap.

I cautiously peered out my window. It was barely dawn—the sun was just rising—but I could make out the forms of five Togolese men sitting on my front porch. They were clapping to summon me to the door. I dressed quickly and went outside.

"We are the representatives of the families that own this land," one of the men announced. "This is our land, and we have come to tell you we want our land back."

My mind whirling, I sent a message summoning Sammy, our big guard. I knew that although I spoke the language, I needed a native speaker to help me catch every innuendo in such a delicate situation. I also began to pray, thinking of all the buildings we had built, all the money we had invested. Surely God would not allow it to be taken from us now!

I tried to calm the men, but they became even more agitated. Over and over they demanded the land. They shouted accusations against the government. One of them, his eyes bulging with anger, shouted in my face, "This land over here down to the road, this is my land! Your husband's bones are buried on my land! I want you to dig up those bones and get them out of my land because it is mine!"

My mind went back over three decades to the Seltzer family in Algiers. My heart constricted in my chest as I remembered what had happened to Mr. Seltzer and his son when they refused to give up their house and plantation. I prayed that our situation would end more happily, though as I looked into the men's faces, I could sense my faith wavering.

Before they walked away, the angriest of the men turned to me one final time. "I am going back to my village," he warned. "I will return in several days. Then you must dig up your husband's bones and get them out of my land."

At Maître Kwassivi's direction, the teachers gathered all the children together in the Assembly Hall. He explained that some men had threatened Koklonaw and wanted to take away our school. Then he asked the children to kneel at their benches and pray. What followed was one of the sweetest experiences in all my time in Africa. Tears streaming down their cheeks, child after child lifted up his or her voice to the Lord for direction and protection. "Oh, God," they prayed, "don't let anything happen to Koklonaw! Don't let them take our school away!" Their simple faith reminded me that, while I might be their "Mother Hen," all of us were safe under the wings of an almighty God. After each child had prayed, Maître Kwassivi led us in songs of praise to God.

Bolstered by the prayers and singing of the children, I drove up the road to the *chef de canton*. As I walked through the large compound, I had to force myself out of my worries in order to greet the many wives and children. When I was announced to the chief, he greeted me warmly, his mustache scratching my cheek as he kissed me in the French custom. I laid the whole situation before him and asked what he could do. The chief notified the government officials, who again assured me that these men had no real claim to the land. They did, however, advise me to contact the American Embassy, which would provide the protection we needed. The situation was becoming too volatile for the Togolese government to guarantee our safety.

As I drove back to the Blind Center, I realized that we might actually have to leave our home. I looked around at the beautiful buildings the Lord had provided: the kitchen and dining area, the dormitories, the classroom building, the craft shed, the water towers, my own house, the Bible Institute buildings that were still under construction. Surely God would not ask us to abandon all of this. Surely He would not ask me to watch as Dal's grave was dug up. How could this situation be part of His plan?

At the Blind Center, we prayed and waited. The American Embassy had quickly sent a guard and we felt relatively safe, but we were anxious as we counted off the days until the threatening man was due to return. The day came, but no one arrived to desecrate Dal's grave.

That afternoon, Sammy and the teachers came to me in great agitation. Sammy had received a visit from the man's relatives. They said that when the man returned to his village, he had become very sick. He died from his illness, but not before he accused me of causing his death. His village was convinced that Madame had killed him from miles away.

We soon learned that the man had died in a cholera epidemic that swept through his village. But some of his family claimed that while he received treatment at the little bush clinic in his village, I had somehow, from afar, put poison in the injection he was given.

The teachers and I met for prayer. The Lord had prevented this man from carrying out his threats, but how could we combat such horrible rumors? As we prayed, the Lord showed us how He would have us respond: *Love your enemies, bless them that curse you, do good to them that hate you, and pray for them which despitefully use you and persecute you* (Matthew 5:44).

The body was brought to the village of Kpodzi, just a few miles away. I heard that the man had left behind a widow and several small children. So on the day of the funeral, many of us went, bringing blankets, clothing, and money for the children. We tried to express our sympathy for the bereaved family. Their reception was cool but not hostile. It was proper to bring gifts to a family in mourning, and the relatives approved of the gesture. Whether they believed I was innocent of murder we never knew.

Several weeks after the funeral, a delegation arrived at my house. The six men who gathered on my porch this time were some of the oldest I had ever seen. They were little and shriveled, some barely able to walk. However, I knew that these were the true heads of their respective families, not firebrands or hotheads.

I invited them inside the house. Without shouting or threats, they informed me that the land on which the school had been built belonged to their families. I replied that if the land had truly been taken from them, we were more than willing to make things right. As a mission we agreed that we did not want trouble among the people we worked with. We were sympathetic to their cause. We would pay for the land.

That promise began weeks of bargaining. Initially, Ron and I were told that the men expected a token payment for the land, perhaps as little as $2,000. We didn't think they were in it for serious money. But every few days, these little old men came demanding a new price for the land. After the first meeting, I began to hold negotiations in the Braille library with the *chef de canton* present. I made sure that the men saw the school, with our African students learning and growing. I wanted them to understand that the land was being used for the good of their own people. Each time they came, they would sit at the long table in the library to drink Coca Colas and eat the banana bread I provided while they negotiated with Ron. Food usually has a positive effect.

The first price the men named was astronomical. They claimed they would not take less than eight million francs, about $32,000. Apparently, they thought that since we were from America, we naturally had all sorts of money. Ron told them directly that we could not possibly pay that much. He then offered them three million francs. It was too little, they claimed.

Several sessions later, the old men arrived with a letter typed on onionskin. In it they outlined three options. First, Madame could pay a huge sum of money. Second, Madame could bring a factory from America so that everyone would have a way to earn lots of money. Third, Madame and the missionaries could pay for all of their young people to go to university.

Ron explained that the amount they were demanding was still more than we could pay. He explained how difficult it would be to convince an American company to build a factory in a village they had never heard of. When we came to option three, Ron tried to clarify the demand.

"How many young people do you mean?" he asked.

"All of them."

"Do you mean the ones who are ready for university now?"

"No, all of them. Whoever wants to go to university. Forever."

We all agreed that this would be a far greater burden than we could possibly bear. Ron told the men that we would discuss the price among ourselves and would meet with them again.

The talks went on, with more demands and different prices. The lawyer we had hired, Koffi Mensa, advised us to continue the talks until they offered us a price we could afford. So the talks continued.

One day the men arrived with what they claimed was their final offer. "The last price we will accept," they informed us solemnly, "is four million francs."

We excused ourselves to discuss the price. We agreed that four million francs, about $16,000, was still high, and far more than the land was worth. However, our lawyer advised us to accept because he believed the time was right for a bargain. We shouldn't draw out negotiations any longer. We returned to the library and Ron addressed the old men. "We accept your price. We will pay you four million francs for the land."

After the old men left, we sat around the library table. The $16,000 price was far more money than we had. Add to that the legal fees and surveying costs that would be included and the total came to about $20,000. The school was by no means a profit-making corporation. We did not have that kind of money sitting in our bank account.

Ron sighed. "Well, someone will just have to go back to the States to raise the money. There's no way that we can do that here in Togo."

We all agreed. "I'll go back," I said. "I would be willing to go raise the money to pay for the land."

I began making plans for a trip to the States. I really did not want to leave my students but, like Ron, I could see no other way of raising $20,000. One day as I was preparing for my trip, the telephone rang. It was a dear friend of mine from California who, along with her husband, supported one of the national evangelists in Togo. She had called to see how the evangelist's work was going. We chatted for awhile, and I mentioned the land negotiations and the price we had settled on.

"The price is $20,000?" the lady asked. "Well, I know that my husband and I would want to pay for that." I nearly dropped the phone.

As soon as I hung up, I ran to tell everyone. We had been praying about the money, but we had never expected the Lord to answer so quickly, and without anyone having to leave Togo!

My dear friends were as good as their word. Within a few days, a check for $20,000 arrived at our mission headquarters. Unfortunately, we had forgotten to tell the mission it was coming, and they were puzzled at first as to what to do with such a large sum. When we were finally able to explain the situation, the money was transferred to the Togo field account.

At last the day came for the exchange. None of us were comfortable about transporting the money, but Ron and Kurt Sager, an American builder who had come to help build the Bible Institute, volunteered for the job. They rode to the bank on motorcycles and returned with the four million francs in small 100 or 1,000 franc bills. The bills were heavy and cumbersome, but West African banks do not carry big bills in order to discourage thieves from robbing banks. We laid out the money in neat piles on my dining room table until it was covered with worn, dirty bills. The wizened old landowners waited outside to count the bills, and each of them came in separately, counting every bill to verify that the amount was correct. Then each one affixed his thumbprint to the contract. When they were satisfied that the money was there, the men took the money and renounced any claim to the property. At last, the land was ours, free and clear!

It was thrilling to see how the hand of God worked on our behalf, though in the midst of the trouble it was not always easy to see His presence. In one sense it seemed rather silly that we had to purchase land we had thought was "ours" for twenty years. But through it all, God intervened and showed us that the same God who opened the door to Togo was still working on our behalf.

OUT OF AFRICA

And we know that all things work together for good to them that love God, to them who are the called according to his purpose.

— ROMANS 8:28

In 1996, I visited my son Terry's family in Zambia, East Africa. Terry and Sandy's oldest children, Nathan and Kristy, had graduated from high school, so we concocted a graduation ceremony and a three-day safari for them, a gift few children could ever have.

We traveled a long distance to the wildlife park and rented a British-built lodge with a grass roof. It was like having our own private house in the middle of the African wilderness. Since big animals were common where we were, we did not have to travel far in our Land Rover to see elephants, lions, baboons, and monkeys. It was a treat to marvel at these stunning examples of God's creation.

When I returned to Togo, Jane picked me up for the two-hour drive back to Kpalimé. Zambia was two time zones away, so I suffered from jet lag, but I made it through dinner with nothing more than a light head. Afterwards, I volunteered to show Steve Carter, a visiting pastor, to the guest house. The front steps were obstructed by a mango tree so loaded with fruit that its branches were covering the steps and crawling with red ants. Instead of fighting with the ants, I led Steve to where we could step up onto the terrace. The step was a large one, and though I got one leg up on the terrace, my other leg was too weak to push off the ground. When I tried to give a little extra oomph, I torqued my leg and immediately heard two loud bangs, like gunshots, that signaled the breaking of my leg bones—my fibula and tibia. I lost my balance and fell sideways. I crash-landed onto a rock, and pain seared into my upper arm and shoulder. I knew I was in a bad situation. I half expected to look up into my mother's sorrowful face as she said, "Oh, Kay. Again?"

When I caught my breath, I looked down and saw my leg bending the wrong way. As I tried to reach it, I realized I couldn't move my arm. Steve called for help and almost everyone at the Blind Center came. As I lay in the mud, extreme pain already setting in, Jane and the others tried to find a way to transport me to the hospital. There was no 911 to call, or any ambulance service, so Jane splinted my broken leg in pillows, gave me Tylenol for the pain, and supervised as I was placed on a mattress. Just the move from the mud to the mattress was excruciating and I couldn't help but cry out. Ted Allston moved my Toyota station wagon close by and I was lifted on my mattress into the back.

The road to the hospital was land-mined with potholes, and although Ted drove as carefully as he could, I screamed in agony as my broken bones rubbed together. The Tylenol had done nothing to dull my pain, and every bump wounded me. In between cries of pain I prayed short, frantic prayers, like, *Lord, I can't do this. It's too far! Help!*

An hour later, at the mission hospital, I begged the doctors for pain medicine before they removed me from the car. Dr. Miriam Wheeler willingly complied and then took me in for X-rays, which showed that the humerus of my right arm and my shoulder were broken and the tibia and fibula in my lower right leg were shattered. Due to the complex fractures and lack of high-tech equipment, Dr. TenHaaf knew I would need to be evacuated to the United States.

He immobilized my bones in a huge, heavy cast, and I lay in a hospital bed while others searched for a flight. They searched for ten days. One airline wanted to charge us $15,000, since a stretcher would take up several first-class seats. Another canceled our reservation when they learned I was in a cast and had multiple fractures. Ron, in America, spent almost $600 in phone calls with us, trying to find me a flight. Finally, British Airways agreed to help, though they flew out of Accra, Ghana, an eight- or ten-hour drive away. They also required medical personnel to fly with me, so Ann Den Uyl, one of the nurses, volunteered. Together, our tickets cost a whopping $8,000.

In my condition, it would have been extremely difficult to go to Ghana by automobile. Providentially, a team from the States had just finished a hospital airstrip for medical evacuations. Up to that point, the rains had made the airstrip too muddy for takeoff. But we had no other choice but to try it again. Then there was the problem of how to fit three people and a stretcher into a small Cessna 206. Randy Alderman, the missionary pilot, quietly and capably took charge. "Gramma," he reassured me, "don't worry. We are going to get you out of here." After some measuring, he arranged it so my feet were in the tail and my head fit just behind the nurse's seat when it was pushed up to the instrument panel. Ann had to crawl through the window to get in.

The dirt runway was rough as the tiny white Cessna taxied out for takeoff. But God made the impossible possible and everyone cheered as the airplane lifted off the ground, flying victoriously like a white bird over the dark forest. My eyes brimmed with tears as I looked out the window and saw my African family waving goodbye.

The flight to Accra lasted almost two hours. Missionaries there in Ghana arranged for an ambulance to take us to the British Airways plane. In order for me to get into the plane, airport personnel had to lift my stretcher using the food elevator. Once inside, I had to lower my cast to the ground, stand up with the help of a gait belt, pivot on my good leg, and be lowered into the seat. This was the first of almost a dozen times during my trip that I went through this lifting and lowering. It was especially hard because I had broken my stronger arm, so my other arm, still weak from polio, was not much help.

After we settled into our seats, Ann and I watched the other passengers board. An African bishop from an ecumenical conference entered, wearing a flowing white satin robe with embroidered cutwork and a large bishop's hat. We noticed one of his feet was also in a cast and discovered he was going to London for surgery. Two other bishops boarded, and we began to feel that we were on a prestigious flight. Then, flight attendants announced that the king of Nigeria would be boarding our plane. Everyone else was asked to stand in honor of the king, who turned out to be a shriveled-up old man. We eyed him with interest as he strode down the aisle, robed in elaborate, flowing African clothes and a high turban. My pain was not severe enough to keep me from realizing our odd position in first class sitting side-by-side with a king and three bishops. We, as two saints, rounded out the little party.

Ann was prepared to knock me out if extreme pain set in. But even the medium-strength medicine took away my appetite, and I couldn't eat a single bite of the sumptuous steak dinner we were served. This was the only time I had ever flown first-class, and I couldn't even enjoy it!

A flight from England brought us to Atlanta, where Luann and Denny were waiting with a wheelchair. Denny also brought a van with a bed in it and we drove two more hours to Greenville. My family and Dr. Kendall, our family physician, met us at Joe and Luann's home to evaluate my condition. It was not difficult to see that I needed hospital care, so an ambulance was called for the trip to the hospital. When I finally lay down in my hospital bed I was relieved. God had preserved me through days of pain. Finally, my long trip out of Africa was finished.

Before anything else could be done, the doctors took care of a blood clot that had developed in my lungs from traveling. Then my leg bones were set and two metal rings were installed to hold my shattered bones in place while they grew back together. These fixator rings were secured with pins, wires, and screws. The doctors hoped my right arm would heal quickly so I could use crutches. Otherwise, my polio-affected left arm would not give enough support.

After the flurry of my surgeries had settled, I began to ask God, *Why did this happen?* I remembered what a faithful prayer warrior Dal had been. In comparison, I thought I had disappointed God by not spending much time in prayer. It took me awhile to realize that my accident was not "punishment" for any failure on my part. It was a blessing in disguise, because it confined me to my bed and gave me much more free time to spend in prayer.

Six weeks later, my tibia had not yet begun to heal, so the fixators had to stay in place. My prayer to God, one that would become familiar, was that He would cause my body to quickly form the calcium needed to knit my bones back together. Even though I was taking calcium, the knitting continued to go slowly. In those days of deep frustration, I took my strength from my newfound prayer life and from the words of many dear friends who sent cards and flowers.

Soon, the doctor decided against a bone graft and instead performed surgery to compress the two parts of my tibia together, overlapping them to encourage knitting. A few weeks later, an X-ray revealed a small amount of "callous" or calcium forming over the fracture. God had begun to answer our prayers! The doctor removed the unwieldy fixator rings and placed a padded metal brace on my leg instead. This contraption was still clumsy but made it possible to get around more easily in a wheelchair.

Therapy on my arm and shoulder was painful. I could barely lift my arm to comb my hair. I was also learning to hop on one foot with a walker since I was not yet allowed to put any weight on the broken leg.

By November, seven months after my fall, the fractures in my arm and shoulder had almost completely healed. But the tibia refused to knit together. A bone which does not form calcium as it should is called a "non-union." Although it would be difficult, my doctors decided to perform a bone transplant. A bone graft from my hip would be placed into the fracture site to "jump start" it and help the bones grow calcium.

During the surgery, I was awake, though I felt disconnected from my body. I could see a long leg going up in the air as the nurses scrubbed it with antiseptic, turning it yellow, but I didn't think of it as my leg. Next I felt the pressure of someone pushing, and then pounding. I was awake enough to ask, with typical interest in all things medical, how the surgeon obtained the bone graft. He told me he had made a window in the tissue of the hip and had simply scraped off some of the soft outer portion of the bone. I asked what it looked like, so he obligingly brought me a white dish with a pink substance in it. "It looks like pink ice cream!" I said.

After the difficult surgery, I stayed in the hospital for seven days. I was uncomfortable, but I kept telling myself, "If the bones knit by this method then I am willing to make it work." The hard part was when the bone specialist gruffly told me, "I don't want you to have any hope before five months!" His words made me cry, but afterwards I was thankful that he told the truth. I adjusted my emotions and planned for the long wait.

Luann and Joe were extremely gracious and opened their home to me again, since I could do little for myself. It was Christmastime, and I felt useless since I couldn't help Luann prepare for the holidays, much less think about returning to Africa. Though I was thankful for my children's hospitality, I became increasingly aware that, for all practical purposes, my independence was gone. I had lost my privacy and my decision-making ability. I could make no plans and had to depend on others. I was a child all over again.

After Dal's death, I had thrown my energy into the Blind School. I never allowed myself to think about retiring because I knew that would mean leaving the field. I joked, "I guess someday I need to retire, but I think God will tap me on the shoulder or even spank me a little and send me home." But I would never say the word "retirement" seriously. There were not enough workers at the school, so I couldn't leave.

But my fall moved Jane into the position of Mother Hen. She began running our small boutique, managing the accounts, supervising the teachers, supplying the classroom materials, teaching English and art, and spending time with visitors—all while caring for my dear little chicks and making sure they were provided for.

I was concerned that she was all alone leading the school. My hope wavered even more when I heard the children were praying faithfully for my healing. I wanted them to know that God answers prayer, but when each report came back negative, they began to ask difficult questions: "Where were Koklonaw's angels?" "Did someone put a curse on Koklonaw and an evil spirit throw her down?" "Can God not heal this kind of broken bone?" These questions challenged my faith as much as they did my children's. I didn't let them know, but I was emotionally crushed. I felt like I was serving a prison sentence.

Coming to thank God for my broken leg was just the beginning of my spiritual journey. The real reason that trials come our way, I learned, was to fulfill the chief end of man—to glorify God and enjoy Him forever. Glorifying God can assume a variety of different forms. I came to the conclusion that I should view my recuperation not as a "prison sentence" but as an "assignment." Since all things come from the hand of God, I knew I should accept this turn of events as the will of a Good Shepherd who wanted the best for me. But I still needed Him to hold my hand, because my trial was difficult. As I waited upon the Lord, He renewed my strength. And I believed that someday I would "run, and not be weary" and "walk, and not faint" (Isaiah 40:31).

One month after my bone graft, X-rays showed a beautiful "callous" of new cells covering much of the broken area. I imagined a battalion of calcium fairies, cousins of the tooth fairy. They climbed over my broken bones and poured calcium into the cracks to stick them together. Every time I drank my milk or ate my vegetables I liked to think about the good calcium fairies who would make my leg bone as strong and hard as cement.

Though I was healing inside, my leg was sore where the wires punctured it. I soon developed an infection, and the doctor prescribed a stronger antibiotic, advising me to keep my leg elevated. The pain was severe, but I knew the doctor would soon test my bone. If it was strong enough, he could remove the fixator. By now I joked that God had signed me up for Patience 101, but either I flunked it or else had moved on to Patience 102. My pastor said I should be careful—God might want me to go on to graduate school!

At last, the doctor removed the fixator and replaced it with a plastic cast. I felt liberated. Almost immediately the swelling and infection subsided and the X-rays showed that the fracture was covered over with new bone cells. I was able to start learning to walk with crutches so I could eventually walk alone again. You can imagine how I praised God!

At the same time God was healing my bones, he was also easing my mind about the future of the Blind School. Jane Hankin continued as general administrator, but God sent her Joan Schmitz to take my place as educational director. Joan was the answer to what I had prayed for so long. And then another family came, the Stadtmillers, who worked with the Neufelds to guide the school during its time of transition.

When I looked at the wonderful things God was doing, I saw He was answering my prayers for the Blind Center. Little by little, I also discovered He could still use me, even though I was far away from Togo. To my great joy, I helped raise $20,000 for a new kindergarten building. I also spoke on many occasions about the needs on the mission field. God was reassuring me that I could still be useful.

At last, my bone healed and the cast was removed. To me my leg was beautiful, even though it was scarred, bowed, one inch shorter, and had twenty-seven “dimples” from the wire and screw holes. The cost to rectify the damage done in moments was roughly $100,000. But my bone was whole again and it felt strong!

By December, I was walking, but with a few problems. My calcium cells had stopped “bridging” and the bone would move a little when I walked on it. The doctors tried electrical stimuli and the X-rays began to show growth. I could feel the "bridging" improve. I walked on my own (with a cane) and could even drive a little. I had pain only if I walked too much.

Finally, in March, the doctor said my bone had knit completely. When I heard those wonderful words, I asked the question that had been on my mind: When could I go back to Togo? "April," he said. "You can go back in April."

I lost no time preparing for my long-awaited trip back home. My doctor wrote to my mission, stating that my leg was healed. I was scheduled to leave on April 15, 1998, and began to pack with great excitement. Then one evening I had more pain in my leg than normal. By morning I could not put full weight on it. I had not fallen or hurt my leg, but the doctor ordered a special X-ray—a tomogram—and a CAT scan. Both of these showed that the bone had not formed a core and was missing the hard ridges that make the bone strong. My premature activity had bowed the leg and cracked the new callous on the fracture site. I was back to square one. Two years of healing were undone.

At the same time I began experiencing a strange pain which I blamed on arthritis until my headaches grew severe. An MRI revealed that three aneurysms had bled in my brain, leaving the right side of my face and my hand numb. I had to stay in the hospital in case surgery was necessary.

I couldn't avoid the truth: my trip would have to be delayed, for a long time, if not forever. But I had made a lot of progress since my accident and I knew with absolute certainty that God was a perfect Father who closed the door to Togo because He had other good plans for me.

My doctor felt these new developments warranted a bone trauma specialist with more experience in my type of fracture. Dr. Michael O'Boyle, who was from Florida, was called in. He came to see me in August. At our first meeting he said there were three options for my leg. One was to use a fixator (we quickly let him know our feelings about that!). Another was to use a rod, which increased the chances of infection in the bone canal. The third, which he favored, was to secure the fractures with a plate and screws. However, this choice might mean losing my leg if it became infected, if it didn't heal, or if the bone healed in the wrong position.

In the days after our meeting, his words bounced around in my mind. I would wake in the night, crying. I started to think that perhaps it would be better to keep my old, bent, broken leg than to take a chance on losing it. But I eventually consented to the third option, and my surgery was scheduled.

As I lay alone in my hospital bed, I reflected on the life of Amy Carmichael. The similarity between her situation and mine was striking. She had been sixty-four when she experienced her crippling accident; I was almost seventy. Our injuries were severe enough to incapacitate us, and hers left her an invalid for the remainder of her life. However, as I pondered the similarity, I admitted I didn't want to be like Amy Carmichael. I wanted to walk again. I knew that God would have to work on me a lot more before I could deal with being an invalid the rest of my life. But I also desperately wanted to accept whatever future He had prepared for me.

Even if my leg was preserved and I learned to walk again, I knew that the time had come for me to give up my life as a missionary in Togo. It would not be easy. I was still full of plans and projects. I would miss the excitement that came from working in the Blind Center. To give it all up would be difficult.

At this point, God used the words of Thomas Watson, a seventeenth-century theologian, to calm my heart. His book, *Romans 8:28, A Divine Cordial*, is an exposition of that famous verse, *And we know that all things work together for good to them that love God, to them who are the called according to His purpose.* Watson says that even the worst things in life can work for the good of a godly person. I knew I needed to trust that the results of my surgery would be what God knew was good for me, since He knows I love him. I prayed that God would be glorified in my life, no matter what.

As I went into surgery in August, I asked the doctor, "Do you know that thousands of people are praying for us right now—in Africa, South America, in the Pacific Islands, and all across America?" He responded, "That's really great, we need it." I didn't know his beliefs, but my heart had great peace to know so many were praying.

The surgery went well, though it lasted much longer than planned. After it was over, my leg had to be immobilized without bearing any weight for at least twelve weeks. Even touching my toes to the ground too early would spoil the meticulous work the surgeon had done.

After a month, my first X-rays showed a beautiful callous covering the rebuilt fracture site. The doctor was surprised and said, "Whatever you're doing—prayer, vitamins, calcium—keep on doing it!" I was ecstatic and imagined I would be walking on crutches by January or February. But the CAT scan revealed that the inside of the bone had not yet healed.

It frustrated me that I was unable to get around: I couldn't do housework on my tiptoes. But I felt good and kept as active as I could. Two of my grandchildren lived with me, and I enjoyed preparing meals for them. Luann and Joe took me to church every Sunday, and I volunteered for a local Christian service that provided food for people who were struggling. I sat in my wheelchair and prayed with each person who came. I especially liked to tell my African-American friends that I had lived for forty-three years in Africa. "Do I qualify to be called American-African," I would ask them. These people seemed eager to open their hearts to me, perhaps because I was an old lady in a wheelchair. They must have felt I was no threat to them! It was thrilling to lead several to Christ through this ministry. It helped me feel like a missionary again.

I am pleased to say that God used my fall for good. Through my accident, He answered the continual prayer of my heart, *That I may know Him* (Philippians 3:10). God drew me out of the busy life at the Blind Center and brought me close to Himself through a sick bed and a wheelchair, that I might know Him. Because of my broken bones I love the Lord more than ever before.

By the end of my journey I had to undergo four surgeries. As my doctors tried valiantly to put Humpty-Dumpty back together again, I learned that God has a plan He is working on at every moment of our lives. Even tribulations and afflictions teach us something. At last my heart no longer cried out to God for comfort but instead was full of peace, knowing that He was orchestrating my life according to His plan.

RETURN TO AFRICA

And thou shalt remember all the way
which the Lord thy God led thee
these forty years in the wilderness.

— DEUTERONOMY 8:2

Throughout my long recuperation, I never stopped hoping that I could return to Togo. Even while I learned to accept the fact of my retirement, I still longed to visit Africa once more. My mind and body weren't worn out just yet.

One reason I wanted to return was because my abrupt departure in 1996 had made it impossible for me to conclusively turn the work over. I was also unable to pack my possessions or move out of my house. My belongings waited in a container until the day I could return and decide what to do with them.

I also wanted to bring closure to my life of forty-three years in Africa. Because I was hurriedly medivaced out, I didn't have time to say goodbye to my friends and co-workers. According to custom, I felt I should officially turn the school over and say my goodbyes. The most painful goodbye would be at the grave of my husband. I was fully aware of the emotional difficulty in seeing Dal's grave once more and then leaving it all over again.

Part of me was fearful of the many things that could happen to my fragile bones while traveling. I would be in Africa during the hottest part of the year, so I was concerned that I could adjust to the heat. But I clung to a wonderful promise from God that I had claimed through my surgeries, the frightening MRIs, and the times when we wondered if my leg would ever heal: *Fear thou not; for I am with thee. Be not dismayed, for I am thy God. I will strengthen thee; yea, I will help thee; yea, I will uphold thee with the right hand of My righteousness* (Isaiah 41:10).

To my great joy, I was invited to return in October 1999 for the twenty-fifth anniversary of the Blind Center. My Togolese friends wanted to rejoice together in all that God had done in our students' lives, so they asked me to stay for two months. I was no longer an energetic missionary, but I was excited about going back at last. But I knew the trip would be possible only if God gave me a good leg to walk on—good enough to merit the well-wishes of my protective doctor.

As the trip drew closer, I found that God was answering my prayers. My doctor said I could walk on my leg without the brace, but that I was to use it anyway, like an insurance policy. He said if the weather was too hot to bear, I could go without it. I would also travel with a wheelchair, just in case.

Once I received the go-ahead, I began to pack with great anticipation. I included as many gifts as I could round up, including some musical instruments that I had collected for the churches. At the request of my Togolese friends, I also began preparing a speech on "Remembering What God has Done." It was not at all difficult for me to write about the graciousness of God to our Blind Center. The words came easily because God had blessed us in so many ways.

My return to Togo was three-and-one-half long years after my nasty fall. I had to be pushed in a wheelchair over the rough terrain, but often, I felt strong enough to use it like a walker. It was with glee that I walked my wheelchair along the paths of my beloved Blind School. I had come home at last.

My days were busy as I met with teachers and staff for flag raisings and prayer times, and I spent time making a video of all that went on at The Village of Light. I was thrilled to see forty-five blind children attending school that year. The elementary school had just started. The little kindergarteners were so sweet and precious, even with their blind eyes. Maître Kwassivi's wife treated them with great kindness.

When I wasn't visiting at the school, I worked on cleaning out my container. It was dirty, sweaty work—like cleaning out a hot attic in summertime—but my goal was to finish before new missionaries who were coming would need the storage space. I had help from many friends, and it was a pleasure to give my things to needy families in the churches.

The anniversary celebration was held on October 15 at the Blind Center. At least 1,000 visitors came from nearby villages, along with friends from the many churches associated with our mission. The festivities lasted all day with skits, singing, and a soccer game played by blind students with a beeper ball. There was also a special performance by the Blind School choir, preaching by the Togolese pastors, and many speeches by staff and visiting dignitaries. Part of the program was even broadcast on television.

When it came time for me to speak, I expressed how I rejoiced to be back in Togo. I told them the story of Joshua, who brought the Israelites to the banks of the Jordan River. God told Joshua that he would help them just as he had helped the Israelites cross the Red Sea. God made the river stop and stand up like a wall so that the children of Israel could cross over on dry land. Then they chose twelve men, one from each tribe, to pick up a big stone and carry it out of the river so they could make a monument to remind them of what God had done. When their children looked at the monument and asked what it meant, their parents would be able to tell them how God had helped them cross the river. I wanted my listeners to see that this anniversary celebration was like building a monument to glorify God for all He had done for the Blind Center over twenty-five years.

I explained how the Holy Spirit led me to start the school so blind people could learn Braille and read the Word of God. Then I described God's blessings to us over the years, from providing land and buildings, to sending the American Embassy to drill our well, to bringing teachers and students each year, to His miraculous protection from the snakes that roam our land. I thanked God for providing our school with food, for paying for our school property through the gift from our friend, and even for protecting the grave of my husband, Pastor Tsi-tsi, from those who threatened to dishonor it.

"Our God has been faithful in the past," I concluded, "but He will also be faithful in the future. If we obey Him, He will do us good and not evil. We never want to forget God's hand over us. *'These things your eyes have seen; teach them to your sons and your sons' sons.'*"

I went to bed that night worn out from all the festivities. But though I was exhausted, the good memories and images kept dancing through my mind. I was overwhelmed by the rich harvest that God had cultivated from the seeds Dal and I had helped to plant many years ago. It was one of the happiest days of my life.

In the days following, I visited many churches. It would have been impolite for me to leave without saying goodbye to the churches my husband started and to thank the many chiefs who received him into their villages. I also wanted to see for myself how God had prospered Dal's ministry. Through his work of witnessing and discipling, churches were created out of nothing. Now these same churches were increasing in numbers, and some even were planting their own churches nearby. I was relieved to see the churches growing so well.

The Togolese Christians gave me a wonderful welcome. I was smothered with affection—kisses on both cheeks, sometimes twice on both cheeks. They called me "Mama Tsi-tsi," after the name for Dal, which meant "the first or oldest person." African culture shows great respect to old people, which is a very enjoyable custom, especially when you are the old one!

One of the villages I visited was Woumé, the village that had been steeped in witchcraft before hearing the gospel. Through a series of miraculous events, this had become one of the strongest national churches in Togo. The church had outgrown its first two meeting places and now had a large building. I also visited Kpakopé, the church nestled in a vast valley. There were now not one but two churches in the valley—and many had been saved out of idol worship.

My visit was not without its sadness. A few weeks into my visit, we heard the shocking news that a fellow missionary in Lomé, Tim Matchett, had been shot and killed. This kind of horrible incident had never happened before in Togo. We were all stunned.

Later we learned that Tim had been visiting churches. To spare his wife and three children the long, hot drive across town and back, he had dropped them off at the American Embassy recreation center so they could swim in the pool.

As Tim approached the center that evening, the guard on

duty noticed two men on a motorcycle following Tim's truck. When Tim parked, the men went on both sides of his vehicle. One man had an automatic rifle and ordered Tim to hand over the keys. When Tim reached for them, the man must have thought he was reaching for a gun and shot into the truck three times. One of the bullets entered Tim's heart and killed him immediately.

Inside the center, Helen and her children heard the gunshots and huddled together, frightened. Outside, the gunmen threw their motorcycle into the bed of Tim's truck, flung Tim's body to the ground, and sped away, unaware that their gunshots had punctured the front tire of the truck. When they passed an army camp near the border with Ghana, soldiers gave chase to the suspicious, limping vehicle. The soldiers and thieves traded gunfire, resulting in the death of one thief and two soldiers. The other thief fled by foot across the border and died later of serious wounds in a clinic in Ghana.

We who knew Tim were aghast at the news of his sudden death. Our hearts ached for his wife, Helen, who had lost a husband; for his children, who had lost a father; and for the pastors he had trained, who had lost their beloved mentor. The question *Why?* was on everyone's mind. Our comfort was the knowledge that God is faithful and works all things together for good in the lives of those who love Him. We trusted that God would somehow use Tim's death.

Many people helped to arrange the traditional African wake and funeral at the Witi Church in Lomé. Tim had shared Dal's love for the Togolese, with the same joy in his ministry, the same obedience to God's call. During the years of political turmoil, Tim had expressed his desire to be buried in Togo should something happen to him. It seemed appropriate, then, that he was laid to rest beside the body of his dear friend Dal in the lovely green foothills of Kpalimé.

Thinking about Tim and Helen's life together brought back

so many memories of my own married life with Dal on the mission field. I remembered the joys and struggles we had shared, and I marveled at the care and protection God provided throughout our forty years together in Africa. Perhaps it was then, at Tim's burial service, that I first considered writing a book about my life with Dal in Africa, not only for my children, but also to honor all the missionaries in West Africa. The one most deserving of honor is not Dal or Tim or any other missionary, but the Lord Jesus Christ. It was for His sake we went.

Because I was leaving in early December, we celebrated Thanksgiving and Christmas very close together. The missionaries and their children gathered for a Thanksgiving dinner where they gave me an official farewell from the field. They attached a beautiful cloth banner to the wall that said, "I thank my God upon every remembrance of you." They also presented me with a small gold charm in the shape of Africa. I wear it now on a chain around my neck, as a reminder of my memories of life there.

Also in November, we celebrated an early Christmas. We asked local tailors to make special outfits as our gift to the blind students. This was a once-in-a-lifetime gift for them, and they were thrilled. I had also brought a load of other toys from America for them to enjoy. Playing "Santa Claus" took my mind off leaving my dear blind children.

During this last visit to Africa, I was contacted by our local government official. I had told this official earlier about the permissions I had secured from President Eyadema to start the Blind School. I told him I would visit the president every time I needed a new permission. This local official finally told me he had arranged a visit for me with the president on the day I planned to leave Togo. We would have a special visit in the morning at his palace. Then in the evening, I would leave for America.

The day I left Togo, December 2, 1999, many teachers and missionaries came to Lomé to bid me goodbye. In order to make our appointment with the president, we had to leave very early in the morning. I remember it was terribly humid in the Lomé seaport, and I'm sure I looked horrible as the humidity flattened my hair. When we arrived at the palace, the guards allowed only a few others to come in with me. They would not let me take my wheelchair in, so I walked into the palace on the arm of the *Chef de Protocol.* Finally, we were seated in the president's office on blue leather chairs surrounded by gold-leafed woodwork and a number of cameras. I was a little concerned that I would be on television with my limp hairstyle, but there was nothing I could do. The president, however, seemed quite comfortable. He made sure we were served the drink of our choice and chatted with us cordially. He didn't seem to be in any hurry.

During our visit, the *Chef de Protocol* asked me to stand. I did, and he led me to the center of the room, asking the others to stand as well. President Eyadema came forward with a red velvet box. I had no idea what was going on. President Eyadema approached me and announced that he was giving me the civilian medal of honor, the Order of Mono. Then he opened the red box and I saw there was indeed a medal inside. President Eyadema proceeded to read an official citation, and then he took the medal out to pin it on my shoulder. It was made to hook onto a man's lapel, so President Eyadema faced a bit of a challenge trying to get it to stick on my dress. If it had not been for the serious look on his face, I might have laughed as he tried not to show his confusion. He finally managed to hook it on the lace of my collar. Then he kissed me on both cheeks.

When I sat down the *Chef de Protocol* brought me other gifts, a beautiful filigree bracelet made of African gold and a large woven chief's blanket with the Togo flag and the American flag woven into the design. The whole incident reminded me that we had to thank God for President Eyadema's keeping the doors open to the gospel. In my personal interaction with him, he was always gracious.

Throughout the presentation, television cameras rolled. Later, friends sent me copies of the newspaper pictures. My face showed marked signs of bewilderment beneath my lifeless bangs. It was rare for a woman to receive a medal in Togo. I was overwhelmed. I had entered the president's palace to thank him for his support and left with a prestigious decoration. It was a great honor, but I did not feel like the honor belonged to me. The honor should go to Dal, who encouraged me in my work, and to the missionaries and Togolese teachers who worked with me in The Village of Light. And honor must go to the Lord Jesus Christ, who called me to Africa as His servant. He put compassion in my heart for the blind.

My prayer

One generation shall praise thy works to another,
and shall declare thy mighty acts.
They shall abundantly utter the memory
of thy great goodness, and shall sing
of thy righteousness.

— PSALM 145:4

As I come to the end of my book, these verses bring me great comfort. We are told to pass down to our children's generation, and to our grandchildren's generation, the mighty acts of God. It was a delight to find that "they shall abundantly utter the memory of thy great goodness." Actually, this book is really made up of my many memories of the goodness of God, even if they came in difficult times. Even though I am eighty years old, my long-term memory has helped me remember the mighty acts of God so I could write about them. "Sing of thy righteousness" reminds me of how God helped the churches to have a Ewé hymnal.

From the beginning of the work in Togo, one of the pleasant surprises we found was that the Ewé people loved to sing. In fact, they are quite skilled in music and harmony. During our years in Niger in a Muslim culture, we heard only chanting. But in Togo, wherever missionaries shared the Word of God, the people loved to sing to the Lord in their native tongue. Missionaries and national Christians in Lomé and Kpalimé translated and wrote hymns, and each group would share their songs with one another. But soon we all wanted our own hymnbook! This desire blossomed into a small hymnbook that was typed under the direction of Ann Washer, using stencils and an Ewé typewriter, and was mimeographed into 100 or 200 copies. This small stapled hymnbook fanned the fire for more translations and hymn writing. The Togolese love for singing eventually produced a larger hymnbook, including songs in Ewé and French. Sacred Literature Ministries in Greenville, S.C., printed 1,200 copies for us and 3,000 more in a later revision.

With more believers and churches, there was a great need for a larger, sturdier hymnbook. We also wanted to include Kabiyé songs from the north of Togo. Now that we were in the computer age, the unusual letters and accent markings of the language could be used. We secured permissions for songs that were not in the public domain and we paid royalties for those that were. Eventually, 6,000 copies of the hymnal were printed. And in 2006, 12,000 copies with a hard cover were produced. This hymnbook has truly been a wonderful tool in uniting many churches from the coastal border in Lomé all the way to the northern border in Dapaong and across the border into Ghana. It is thrilling to hear an African congregation joyfully singing of the righteousness of their God. It is a little like heaven will be, when people from every nation of the world will sing our great Redeemer's praise.

Since I am retired and cannot return to Togo, I have a great responsibility to pray for my own family but also for the work God put in our hands in Togo. It is not a burden but a pleasure to pray for every person and ministry that has a part in the great harvest of souls there. Of course, not a day goes by without my thoughts and prayers for the fruitful Blind Center ministry. I pray that the school will be academically excellent but most of all that it will be centered on the Word of God. I pray that Joan Schmitz and Cindy McFarland and the other workers will live pure lives that show the gracious love of

Christ. I pray that the Holy Spirit will give them tender, compassionate hearts, ready to respond to the needs of others. I pray that they will have a sweet concern for new students who have never been away from their families, and that God will send children who will be open to hearing His Word. I pray that students will continue to live for Christ when they return to their villages.

Like the Blind School, the summer camp ministry has also flourished, aided by summer teams from supporting churches, colleges, and other organizations. Youth from near and far come to the Blind Center facilities each summer to participate in Bible-centered programs that include basketball and soccer, a trampoline, big-ball games, and a waterslide. Campfires, Bible studies and chapel programs match athletic opportunities with spiritual ones.

The churches Dal helped to start in Lomé and Kpalimé continue to bear fruit as more people are saved and begin taking part in Bible studies and discipleship. But the gospel is still going to new villages. Beky Poteat, a young, energetic missionary, assembles small groups of young Togolese Christians, taking them in her jeep—"God's car," as she calls it—up into the mountains of northern Togo to evangelize the villages there. These are not easy trips: the young people load the jeep with camping equipment and evangelization materials and they rough it. I know Dal would be excited to see these young ones, especially the girls, doing the work he used to do.

The hospital also remains a fruitful ministry. They still need more full-time surgeons, but doctors continue to sacrifice their time and talent to work at the hospital for long shifts, while the nurse-training program teaches Togolese men and women both nursing and the Bible. Additional facilities are still being built to enlarge the hospital's capabilities, and a project has begun to expand into the Muslim territory of Togo with community healthcare and evangelism. Each of these developments serves to reach the ultimate goal of the hospital: winning souls for Christ. And, indeed, more people receive Christ by means of a hospital stay than through any other missionary endeavor in Togo. Many who come to Christ at the hospital return to their villages eager for their neighbors to hear the good news.

God works in amazing ways; the excitement of just one new believer can result in a nucleus of believers in a village. And, as God leads, this little group may begin studying Bible courses together. Perhaps one of the men may take the responsibility of leading his little group. And, sometimes, this man begins to wish that he had more Bible training so he could be of better help to his little flock. It is becoming common for men from all over Togo to begin attending our Bible Institutes in Kpalimé, Lomé, or Tsiko.

But it's not easy for them to leave their village, nor is it easy for them to find money to attend the Institute. Many times, our missionaries will find other young Christians to take a man's place in his village while he attends school. Gifts from villagers and even from supporting churches in America help to meet financial needs. And after a man has completed his coursework, he will return to his village to carry on the work of the Lord. This is one of the most important and most influential works of the ministry in Togo: the training of Togolese pastors in the Word of God.

As fledgling churches sprout left and right and as missionaries work hard to plant new churches, the Christian community in Togo is multiplying. From the seven seedling churches that Dal planted, a great forest has grown up. There are now at least sixty thriving Christ-centered churches in Togo. These churches and their pastors now make up the national organization called ASEBTO. Each church can trace its beginnings to Dal's dedication and faithfulness in Togo.

In the same way that the work in Togo grows bigger and even more beautiful each year, so does my family! My four children have given me fifteen grandchildren and eighteen great-grandchildren, and the numbers continue to increase. Recently, at my eightieth birthday party, my children and grandchildren and great-grandchildren lined up for pictures, and my heart was filled with thanksgiving to God for making me the richest grandmother in town.

The most important, most wonderful part to me is that in each family Christ is being honored. God has continued to bless each generation, calling many grandchildren to serve the Lord as missionaries, in Africa or elsewhere. They are carrying on the legacy that started many generations ago.

My family is getting too big to describe everyone's activities in great detail. But I would like to give you a snapshot, to show what God has been doing in their lives. Even though they are not technically family, David and Laya are still busy in Benin expanding their own church, building new churches, training would-be pastors in the Bible, and keeping up their bookstore ministry.

Kwami, James' son, is now an evangelist for the Source of Light mission in Togo. Along his traveling route he holds question-and-answer sessions for those who cannot attend a Bible Institute.

My daughter, Luann, and her husband, Joe Whitaker, teach at Hampton Park Christian School. Joe teaches sixth grade while Luann teaches first grade and serves as elementary school supervisor. Their son James teaches math and coaches sports at the same school. Jennifer, their daughter, is a paralegal. Luann and Joe have four grandchildren.

My first son, Denny, studied aviation at Moody Bible Institute and at flight school in North Carolina. He continued his studies at Bob Jones University and met Diane, who became his wife. In 1982 they moved to Togo, where they served in several ministries. In 1991 Denny trained at the University of Florida and he now works as a physician's assistant. Now that their six children are married and serving the Lord, Denny and Diane are preparing to return to Africa again. They have six grandchildren.

My second son, Ron, and his wife, Ann, moved to Togo in 1979 and helped by planting churches and by working with Dal in the construction of the Kpalimé Church. In 2000 ABWE asked Ron and Ann to work in the States with the Enlistment and Pre-field ministries. Ron is now the administrator of the ABWE fields in Africa. Their children Melissa and Bradley continue to serve Christ in their married lives. Ron and Ann have two grandchildren.

While Terry worked during his college summers at the Bill Rice Ranch in Murphreesboro, Tenn., he met Dave and Elwanda Fields and their daughter Sandy, who were on deputation to go to Togo. In 1975 Terry and Sandy were married in Togo and in 1983 they began serving in Kenya, later moving to Kitwe in Zambia. Two of their children, Kristy and Nathan, are now with them in Kitwe. Two other children live in South Carolina. Terry and Sandy have six grandchildren.

Each of these lives is precious to me, and I know they are even more precious in God's eyes. As I sat for the photographs at my eightieth birthday, I thought of Dal, sure that he too was rejoicing over the wonderful family God has given to us.

This story is really only the preface to a multitude of stories just waiting to be written. Each name in this book, each person I mentioned, has his or her own story that is just as interesting or even more interesting than mine.

I challenge those of you who read my book to live according to the Holy Spirit's calling and then to tell the story of how God has changed your lives, either by writing a book, or by your daily interaction with those who do not know Christ. May God's great work in all of our lives be glorified!

Dal Washer

1921–1989

ASSOCIATION OF BAPTISTS FOR WORLD EVANGELISM

The Association of Baptists for World Evangelism is an independent mission agency with headquarters in Harrisburg, Pennsylvania. ABWE exists to serve local churches in the task of sending missionaries around the world. Founded in 1927, ABWE now has 1,300 missionaries in over 75 countries and serves over 5,000 churches.

ABWE's goal is to plant churches, and many means are used to reach this goal. These include Bible clubs, Sunday schools, camps, kindergartens, primary schools, centers for the blind and deaf, literature production, literacy programs, hospitals and clinics, radio, Bible schools, student centers, campus work, and aviation. In each of these ministries, ABWE missionaries faithfully share Christ with men, women, and children.